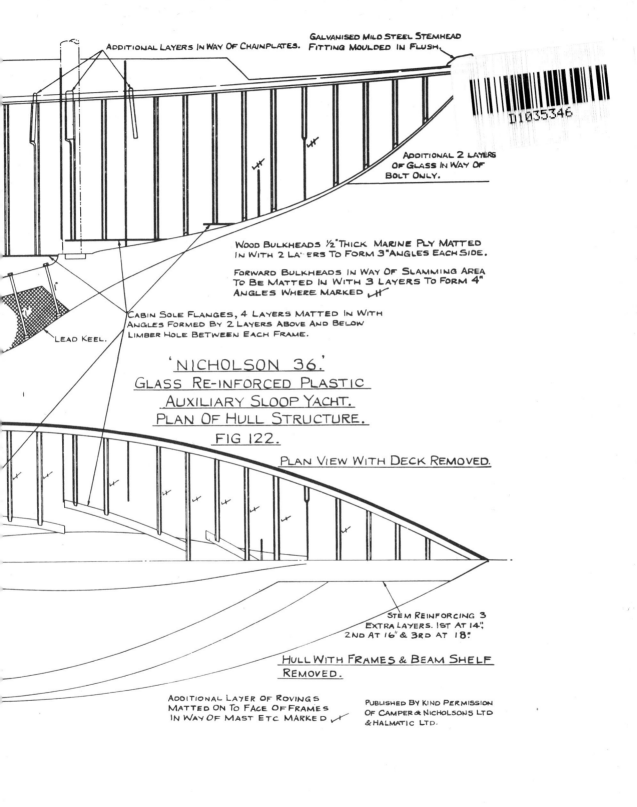

ADDITIONAL LAYERS IN WAY OF CHAINPLATES.

GALVANISED MILD STEEL STEMHEAD FITTING MOULDED IN FLUSH.

ADDITIONAL 2 LAYERS OF GLASS IN WAY OF BOLT ONLY.

WOOD BULKHEADS ½" THICK MARINE PLY MATTED IN WITH 2 LAYERS TO FORM 3" ANGLES EACH SIDE.

FORWARD BULKHEADS IN WAY OF SLAMMING AREA TO BE MATTED IN WITH 3 LAYERS TO FORM 4" ANGLES WHERE MARKED

CABIN SOLE FLANGES, 4 LAYERS MATTED IN WITH ANGLES FORMED BY 2 LAYERS ABOVE AND BELOW LIMBER HOLE BETWEEN EACH FRAME.

LEAD KEEL.

'NICHOLSON 36.'
GLASS RE-INFORCED PLASTIC
AUXILIARY SLOOP YACHT.
PLAN OF HULL STRUCTURE.
FIG 122.

PLAN VIEW WITH DECK REMOVED.

STEM REINFORCING 3 EXTRA LAYERS. 1ST AT 14", 2ND AT 16" & 3RD AT 18."

HULL WITH FRAMES & BEAM SHELF REMOVED.

ADDITIONAL LAYER OF ROVINGS MATTED ON TO FACE OF FRAMES IN WAY OF MAST ETC MARKED

PUBLISHED BY KIND PERMISSION OF CAMPER & NICHOLSONS LTD & HALMATIC LTD.

Yacht
Construction

Yacht Construction

K H C Jurd C Eng AMRINA

From the original
Practical Yacht Construction
by C J Watts MBE

Adlard Coles Limited

Granada Publishing Limited
First published in Great Britain by Adlard Coles Limited
Frogmore St Albans Hertfordshire AL2 2NF and
3 Upper James Street London W1R 4BP
First published 1947
as Practical Yacht Construction
Second edition 1952
Revised edition 1957
Revised edition 1963
Third edition 1970
Second impression 1971
Third impression 1974
This edition © 1970 Adlard Coles Limited and
K. H. C. Jurd
ISBN 0 229 97485 6
Filmset and printed in Great Britain by
BAS Printers Limited, Wallop, Hampshire

Contents

List of Illustrations

Foreword

WHEN I wrote the foreword for the first edition of this book I knew it contained a record of yacht building experience which could not be equalled. Since the death of the author, Charles Watts, the record of development in yacht construction has been ably continued by Ken Jurd, his successor, and present Chief Draughtsman of my firm.

Mr Jurd, who worked many years with Mr Watts, has not only recorded changes in practice by modernizing a great part of the text, but he has also added useful chapters on the use of light alloy and plastics, which are becoming common materials in yacht construction.

The fact that another edition of this work is wanted by so many means that those interested in yachts, their construction, rig and fittings, have found it a reference book of great value.

CHARLES NICHOLSON
Chairman, Camper & Nicholsons Ltd. 1963

Note Mr Jurd was appointed Technical Manager of Camper & Nicholsons Ltd in 1969

Preface

PRACTICAL Yacht Construction, by the late C J Watts, MBE, has, I believe, been a very informative work of reference within the full meaning of its title. Due, however, to changes covering the whole field of yacht construction, a revision became necessary. I have endeavoured to carry this out within the original framework without destroying its character. Some of the text has been re-written, the remainder amended in the light of these changes. The drawings have been treated in a similar manner.

Conventional hull construction covered in Chapters I and II has seen the acceptance of certain glues for main structural members and of plywood for decks. Changes in metal for fastenings and in combinations of dissimilar metals and certain timbers to avoid early deterioration have occurred. Lloyd's Rules have been revised with all the far-reaching consequences involved.

Chapter III has seen the auxiliary engine as a piece of equipment transformed from the status of something not even tolerated by most sailing men to that of an essential in all cruising boats at least.

Chapter IV has seen the change from gaff rig dominance to its virtual disappearance in the face of the more efficient Bermudan rig. It has seen the introduction of aluminium masts, stainless steel standing rigging, Terylene running rigging, and so on.

Chapter V has seen the introduction of lighter more efficient joinery, of better plumbing systems and plastic piping, of improved ventilation, of increased electrical equipment and of the diesel auxiliary engine.

Chapter VI has seen the acceptance of many of the old gadgets as essentials for competitive sailing; the increase in specialist firms manufacturing certain parts of the yacht or its equipment, such as the hull or masts or blocks.

Chapter VII has seen the emergence of the glass-reinforced plastic hull from its introductory stage to its acceptance, from dinghies to ocean racers and motor cruisers, as well as the special distinction of its own section of Lloyd's Rules.

Chapter VIII has seen the introduction of special ship-building aluminium alloys in place of those previously manufactured to aircraft specifications.

Since this book was first published there have, in fact, been changes in construction and technique to a greater extent than in any other period in the history of yacht building, and this is the reason for the revision.

K H C JURD

Chapter I

Lead Keel. Almost the first job taken in hand is the lead keel. This must be carefully laid off in the loft and faired from the lines, the top and ends being fixed in the drawing office. Full-size sections are traced from the floor and the weight and centre of gravity carefully checked by the drawing office. Meantime, the number, size and positions of lead keel bolts must be fixed, and Lloyd's approval obtained if necessary. A template of the profile, plan of top, and section moulds are given to the shipwrights from the loft, and they proceed to make a wooden pattern, and a stout wooden box in which to make the casting, see Fig. 1.

The completed pattern after being placed in the box has moulder's sand rammed tightly all round it, being first well blackleaded so that it will come away easily and cleanly from the sand. As indicated in Fig. 1, the batter each end of the lead which fays against the false keel may be formed by steel plates, which can be readily removed for withdrawal of the pattern without disturbing the sand. The keel is cast, if possible, on the actual keel blocks which will be used in building the yacht.

Their height being arranged so that the keel, which must be cast level, will only have to be 'tripped' to its declivity for building.

It is the practice of some builders to bore the holes for the lead keel after the casting has been made; others consider this too troublesome and prefer to cast the holes in the lead. In the latter case iron bars are placed in the mould before the lead is run. The diameter of these bars is made equal to that of the bolts, and this is convenient, as standard bar may be used for bolts and moulding bars without additional machining. The holes thus formed are tight and require slight reamering, which is stopped 3 in. to 4 in. below the top of the hole and the bolts are driven for this distance, to make a tight fit. These bars must be correctly positioned longitudinally and transversely, due consideration being given to squareness to the keel and shrinkage of the casting. Concerning shrinkage, the usual patternmaker's allowance does not hold good here, owing to the lead being one solid mass which is 'fed' at three or four points for several hours after the mould has been filled, thereby making the actual contraction much smaller. The contraction allowance is 3/32 in. per ft. An actual example is a keel 25 ft long × 21 in. wide × 21 in. deep, weight 15 tons, which showed $2\frac{1}{4}$ in. shrinkage when cold.

The bolt holes in shallow parts of the keel, such as in way of the scarphs shown in Fig. 1, are best bored after casting. The diameter of the lead keel bolts is fixed, by Lloyd's

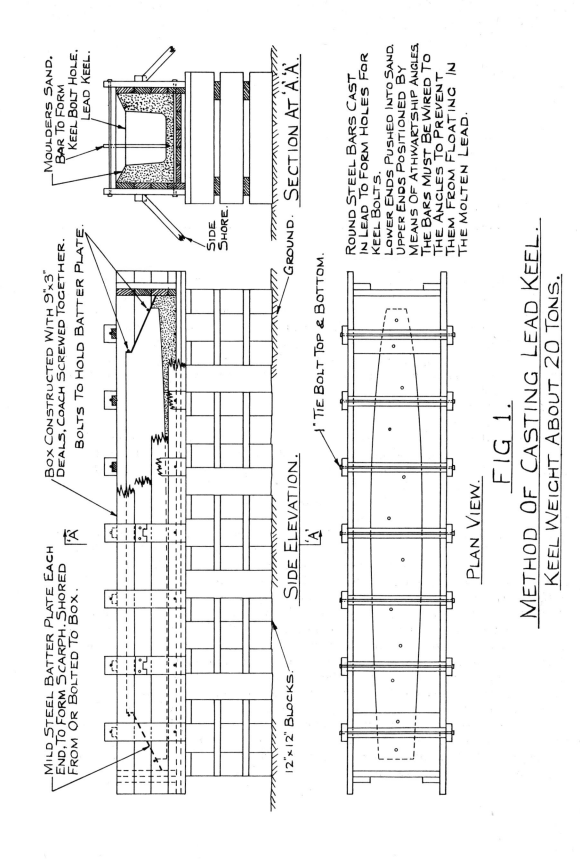

MOULDERS SAND.
BAR TO FORM
KEEL BOLT HOLE.
LEAD KEEL.

SECTION AT 'A.''A'.

SIDE SHORE.

GROUND.

BOX CONSTRUCTED WITH 9"×3"
DEALS, COACH SCREWED TOGETHER.

BOLTS TO HOLD BATTER PLATE.

MILD STEEL BATTER PLATE EACH
END, TO FORM SCARPH. SHORED
FROM OR BOLTED TO BOX.

12"× 12" BLOCKS.

SIDE ELEVATION.

'A'

ROUND STEEL BARS CAST
IN LEAD TO FORM HOLES FOR
KEEL BOLTS.
LOWER ENDS PUSHED INTO SAND.
UPPER ENDS POSITIONED BY
MEANS OF ATHWARTSHIP ANGLES.
THE BARS MUST BE WIRED TO
THE ANGLES TO PREVENT
THEM FROM FLOATING IN
THE MOLTEN LEAD.

1" TIE BOLT TOP & BOTTOM.

PLAN VIEW.

FIG. 1.

METHOD OF CASTING LEAD KEEL.
KEEL WEIGHT ABOUT 20 TONS.

Rules, based upon the sectional area of the keel in square feet, the spacing of the bolts in feet and the proportion depth to breadth at top. It is usual to space the bolts equal to the frame spacing and Lloyd's recommend that they are fitted alternately on opposite sides of the middle line, wing or side bolts being fitted when considered necessary on account of the weight or form of the lead.

A suitable material for the bolts is nickel-aluminium-bronze and to avoid forging, which is not always satisfactory with bronze, screwing the heads as well as the nuts makes a perfectly satisfactory job. A thick washer of the same material should be fitted under the nut, see Fig. 2. As in the case of other copper base fastenings passing through timber saturated with salt water, contact with iron and steel must be prevented to avoid electrolytic action which causes deterioration of fastenings and timber. See page 135. Bronze bolts are therefore best fitted in conjunction with wood floors. Galvanized mild steel bolts are sometimes used, in lead keels, in yachts of Lloyd's highest class when fitted in conjunction with galvanized mild steel floors and clips, the electrolytic action then being avoided. The threads should be well greased because of the absence of galvanizing on them. Sometimes keel bolts are cast in the lead, in which case they only extend for about half the depth of the lead and have nuts cast in. This method saves length on the bolts and leaves no holes to fill at the bottom, but makes the renewal of bolts very difficult. For further remarks and sketches relating to keel bolts see Fig. 2.

Keel and False Keel. Usually made of English elm, which has been proved reliable for this important part of the structure over many years. Teak is a first-class choice, although more expensive. Afrormosia is now being introduced in yachts of Lloyd's highest class. It is obtainable in long and wide pieces, is straight and clean grained, but should be properly seasoned before use, unlike English elm, which should be worked wet and not allowed to dry out. In racing yachts the whole of the centre line is often mahogany. If possible the main keel should be in one piece, and to Lloyd's Rules this must be so up to a length of 33 feet. A scarph should have a length of six times the moulding of the keel, see Fig. 3, its lower lip aft and be kept well clear of the ends of the ballast keel, stem and after deadwood. The keel moulding is fixed by Lloyd's Rules, the siding being determined by the lines of the yacht.

When everything is fair on the floor, the loftsman, having settled the rabbet and bearding lines, gives out, as information for making the main keel, a template showing top, bottom and maximum width, also moulds at various points along its length, usually taken at frames and showing the rabbet and bearding. In modern vessels the main keel is usually straight and the moulding parallel, so that no contour mould is required, but if the keel were rockered or curved then the loftsman would have to issue a contour mould. These moulds show the position of frames, floors, etc. The siding of the keel should be measured at the lower edge of rabbet and may be tapered at the ends to agree with the siding of stem and sternpost. A 'hook scarph' should be used in wood keels unless the moulding is small so as to make the hook interfere with stop waters, when a plain 'lip scarph' has to be used.

The method of marking out a hook scarph is as follows—Draw a straight line from the lips at the ends (Fig. 5), bisect, then according to size of hook, set off half each side of centre line. Then draw a line representing the face of scarph from the hook to lips at the ends. The hook should be square off the face, and when put together the scarph

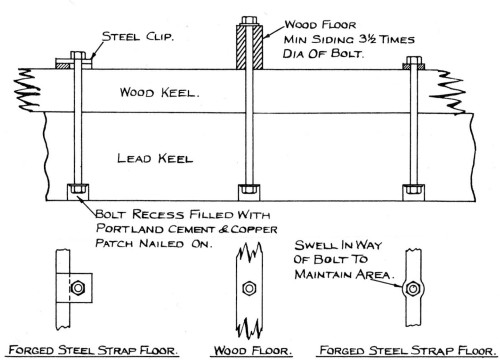

STEEL CLIP.

WOOD FLOOR
MIN SIDING 3½ TIMES
DIA OF BOLT.

WOOD KEEL.

LEAD KEEL

BOLT RECESS FILLED WITH
PORTLAND CEMENT & COPPER
PATCH NAILED ON.

SWELL IN WAY
OF BOLT TO
MAINTAIN AREA.

FORGED STEEL STRAP FLOOR.   WOOD FLOOR.   FORGED STEEL STRAP FLOOR.

FIG 2. BOLTING OF LEAD KEEL.
SHOWING ALTERNATIVE METHODS OF CONNECTING TO FLOORS.

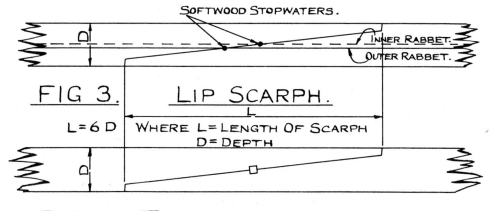

SOFTWOOD STOPWATERS.

INNER RABBET.
OUTER RABBET.

FIG 3. LIP SCARPH.

$L = 6D$

WHERE L = LENGTH OF SCARPH
D = DEPTH

FIG 4. TABLED LIP SCARPH.

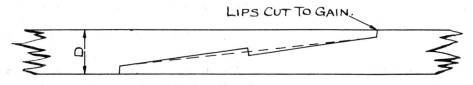

LIPS CUT TO GAIN.

FIG 5. HOOK SCARPH.
SHOWING METHOD OF MARKING OUT.

will draw close at the ends, as the ends are always cut to gain as the scarph comes together. Besides the 'lip scarph' and 'plain scarph' there is the 'tabled lip scarph', see Figs. 3, 4 and 5. An important point to remember is that the keel holding-down bolts for the floors must be put in before the wood keel is bedded down on the lead keel, as they cannot be put in afterwards. The nuts must be fitted on top of the floors. A water-way or 'limber' should be gouged along the centre line of the top of wood keel, clear of bolts, before the floors are fitted in place. The rabbet in the keel should be kept low enough from the top of keel to allow the heels of the frames to be efficiently housed and fastened. The plank land on the keel should be a minimum of twice the plank thickness.

The connection of the keel to stem and sternpost is dealt with under those headings. The false keel in the type of vessel here described may be likened to chocks fitted to complete the underwater form of the vessel in those parts not occupied by the lead keel. It is made of English elm, teak, afrormosia, mahogany, etc., shaped to the form required from templates and moulds supplied by the loft, and is bolted up to the floors and main keel in the same manner as the ballast keel, but with bolts of smaller diameter.

In order to prevent water finding its way up through the faces of the scarph and into the ship, stopwaters of soft wood are driven through from side to side in the positions shown in Fig. 3. As soon as possible after the keel has been laid and bolted together, it should be well oiled or varnished to prevent shrinking, assuming the vessel is being built under cover. To the same end, boards should be nailed over keel scarphs, especially where English elm is used.

Stem and Apron. Suitable materials for the stem are indicated in the following table:

| Material | | | |
Above scarph	Below scarph	Application	Method of working
English oak	English oak	Sturdy construction Weight saving unimportant	Straight grain sawn or grown (that is, curved grain)
Teak	Teak	Ditto	Straight grain sawn
Mahogany	Mahogany	Light construction	Ditto
Mahogany	English oak	Sturdy construction combined with weight saving above waterline	Ditto for full length. Or oak may be grown (if available)
Mahogany	Teak	Ditto	Straight grain sawn
Mahogany	No scarph	Light, strong construction with bolted scarphs avoided	Straight grain, bent and glued laminations

When a scarph is required it should be positioned above the waterline if possible, and an internal brass plate fitted under the nuts is an improvement when weight saving is not important.

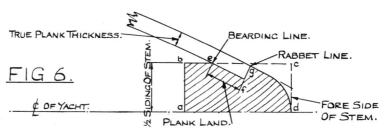

FIG 6.

SQUARE SECTION THROUGH STEM.

An apron is not required by Lloyd's Rules, and unless the form of stem is somewhat like Fig. 7, it is very unusual to fit one now, although its presence greatly improves the connection between stem and keel, and adds to the general stiffness of the fore end of the vessel.

An apron is usually adopted when the stem is not sufficiently wide to make a good landing for the plank ends, and it is fitted above a continuation of the stem, called a fore deadwood, which is a large knee connecting the keel and stem. When an apron is fitted it is much easier to replace the stem, should this ever be necessary, especially if the joint between the two members is at the rabbet.

The minimum siding and moulding of the stem is given in Lloyd's Rules, based on Lloyd's length, the siding being measured at the head and at the keel, but the moulding, of course, must be governed by the form of the vessel, being not less than is required to house efficiently the hood ends of the planking and at the lower end to make an efficient connexion with the keel and to allow for the fair line of the rabbet.

The information given out by the loftsman consists of profile moulds of the stem and apron, showing the rabbet, scarphs, frames, etc., and section moulds taken square to the profile, showing the rabbet and bearding, see Figs. 6 and 8. The stem should be bearded to suit the lines, the fore side being usually rounded, but below the water-line the bearding gradually blends into the siding and shape

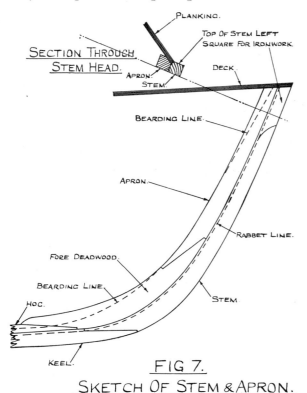

SECTION THROUGH STEM HEAD.

FIG 7.
SKETCH OF STEM & APRON.

of the keel, whilst it is advisable, at the stem head, to keep the stem rectangular for a short distance in order to simplify the ironwork of the fore stay and cable sheaves. Care should be taken that the scarphs of the stem and apron are kept clear of the bobstay plate, if fitted; also the scarph of the stem and keel should, if possible, be kept away from the vicinity of the heel of the mast.

The outside lip of scarphs should be aft in order to reduce the likelihood of the thin end of the wood tearing up when docking or slipping. The moulding of the stem increases towards the keel. This is not only correct for strength, but necessary because the stem is usually bluff at the head and fine at the heel, so that in order to keep the same amount of wood between plank ends, the rabbet must be farther from the fore side of stem at heel than at head.

Fig. 6 shows a section cut square to the fore side of a stem. These 'square sections' are used, in settling the rabbet and bearding lines, because they show the true thickness of plank, and the true amount of plank land. The position of the rabbet line is obtained by first settling off b c parallel to the centre line, a distance equal to the stem half-siding away. Then draw the inside of plank line, cutting b c at e. Now set off the amount of plank land required, e. f. From f g square to the plank surface; g is the rabbet line.

Laying Off. In order that a yacht may be properly designed, a lines plan has to be produced to scale, on paper. The scale is seldom greater than $\frac{3}{4}$ in. = 1 ft. or 1/16 in. = 1 in. so that the offsets taken from this plan are of necessity somewhat inaccurate when set off full size. The boat has therefore to be 'laid off' full size for two reasons, one being to 'fair' the lines and eliminate inaccuracies due to small-scale drawing, the other being to produce the full-size shape of the main members, such as the centre line, frames, ballast keel, transom, etc., so that templates may be made.

With steel vessels, the lines plan is drawn to the heel of frame line, from which the form may be judged quite well, an allowance of from 1 to $1\frac{1}{2}$ per cent of the moulded displacement being added to cover the shell plating. With wooden vessels however, the thickness of planking being correspondingly greater, this simple method cannot be applied. The lines plan has therefore to be drawn to outside of plank and at some stage the plank has to be 'taken off' in order that moulds may be made to inside of plank. The stage in laying off at which the plank is taken off is dependent upon the method of construction. For the smaller type of yacht with bent timber construction and a small number of grown or steel frames in way of mast, etc., the fairing is carried out complete to the outside of plank. Transverse sections are then lifted off in way of the building moulds and drawn on the screive board. The planking is then taken off each of these sections individually. With the larger type of yacht with closely spaced grown frames or steel frames, or these with one, two or three bent timbers between, the procedure is as follows—lay off the body plan to outside of plank to offsets from the lines plan, now 'take off' the plank, this being more accurately done from the full-size sections than from the lines plan. Then fair the fore and aft lines to inside of plank. The frames may now be lifted off and drawn on the screive board ready for making templates.

Whilst it is best to fair to the outside of plank when practicable, the second type of construction, mentioned above, requires so many frames on the screive board, drawn closely together, that to take off the plank at the screive board stage, would require a confusing number of lines superimposed on each other, making the method impracticable.

19

When taking off the plank, the actual plank thickness can only be used in the way of any parallel middle body, as away from this towards the ends of the vessel; a transverse section cuts the planking at angles other than 90° and so always shows an increased thickness, see Fig. 107. An exact method of taking off the plank is given in Attwood and Cooper's valuable *Text Book of Laying Off*, but for yachts up to 80 tons or more this method is unnecessarily accurate, so that the two approximate methods described as follows are quite suitable:

Refer to Fig. 107. Part of the waterline and body in the same vicinity are shown. Square to a point on the waterline, set off the plank thickness B C, to cut section line at C. Lift off the distance AC along the section and set off square to section in body plan, to cut waterline at C1. This is a point at the inside of plank. If this is repeated at regular intervals for each section in the body plan, the inside of plank body plan is obtained.

Another, and quicker loft method is by the use of bevel boards. In Fig. 108 three sections and three waterlines are shown. The method is similar for both views, so only the sections will be described. A universal bevel board is constructed in the ordinary manner by setting off a base line equal to the section spacing and erecting a perpendicular with inches marked upon it, see Fig. 17, and a line is scribed in representing the normal thickness of the planking. From the body plan measure the distance between A and B and B and C sections, normal to the shape, and take the mean. Set up this mean distance on the bevel board and measure across the bevel at this point (see Fig. 108) to the line representing the normal plank thickness. Then this last measurement represents the apparent plank thickness at that point along the square line X Y. Sufficient similar points are found to draw in and fair the complete section. The whole process is made quite clear by Fig. 108, where it is pointed out that although a similar method can be applied to level lines, it is quite sufficient to deal with one plane only.

Sternpost and Deadwood. These are usually made of English oak, teak or mahogany, the sternpost being in one piece, although sometimes an inner and an outer sternpost is fitted, whilst the deadwood is made up of one or a number of pieces. The number, size and disposition of the pieces depend upon the extent of the deadwood, and the requirements of the vessel; the presence or absence of a sterntube being an important feature.

The scantlings of the sternpost given in Lloyd's Rules, based upon the Lloyd's length, are given as a minimum siding and moulding. The moulding, of course, must be sufficient to house properly the hood ends of the planking and make a good connection to the keel; consequently it increases towards the keel, but in practice it is a good method to taper the back of sternpost siding, making it less at heel than at top, but maintaining the Lloyd's minimum at aft edge of rabbet.

If there is an aperture and a propeller on the middle line, a swell will probably be required in the sternpost to house the sterntube. Care must be taken to allow for this in selecting the wood, sufficient thickness being kept round the sterntube to take the hood ends, also the rebate line must be kept well clear of the aperture. A hollow is worked in the back of sternpost partially to house the leading edge of the rudder (see sketch, Fig. 9) and so save an opening or space between the sternpost and rudder which would be favourable to leeway and turbulence.

The sternpost is an important structural part because of the support it has to provide

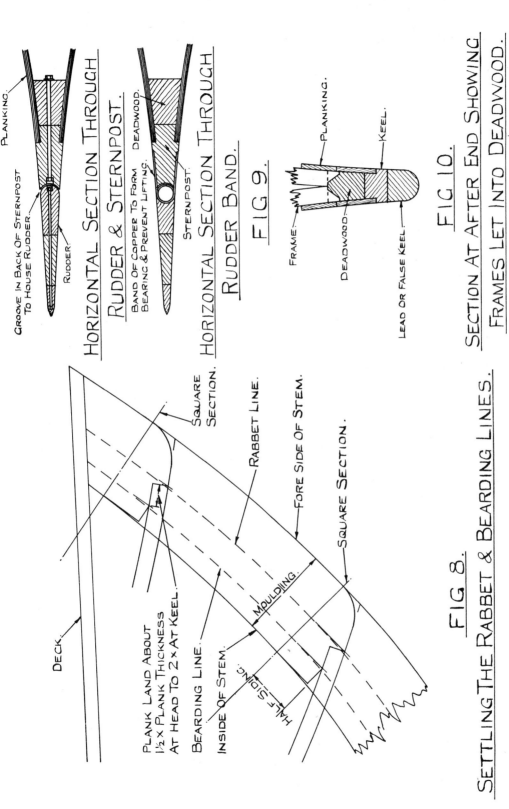

PLANKING.

GROOVE IN BACK OF STERNPOST TO HOUSE RUDDER

RUDDER.

HORIZONTAL SECTION THROUGH
RUDDER & STERNPOST.

BAND OF COPPER TO FORM BEARING & PREVENT LIFTING.

DEADWOOD.

STERNPOST.

HORIZONTAL SECTION THROUGH
RUDDER BAND.

FIG 9.

PLANKING.

KEEL.

FRAME.

DEADWOOD.

LEAD OR FALSE KEEL.

FIG 10.
SECTION AT AFTER END SHOWING
FRAMES LET INTO DEADWOOD.

SQUARE SECTION.

RABBET LINE.

FORE SIDE OF STEM.

SQUARE SECTION.

DECK.

PLANK LAND ABOUT 1½ × PLANK THICKNESS AT HEAD TO 2 × AT KEEL.

BEARDING LINE.

INSIDE OF STEM.

MOULDING.

HALF-SIDING.

FIG 8.
SETTLING THE RABBET & BEARDING LINES.

to the constantly stressed rudder; also it is the termination of the after end of the ship, carrying and uniting all the after ends of the planks, and possibly having to afford support to the working of a propeller. Consequently if the sternpost is not well connected to the deadwood it may work and so cause leakage.

Where possible the deadwood should be a large oak knee, but sometimes, if suitable oak is not available, teak is used, the deadwood being built up in several pieces of suitable shape and held together by bolts. The sternpost and deadwood are fastened together by long bolts, and in arranging these, care must be taken that none foul the sterntube; if necessary a certain number of 'blind' bolts must be used. The extent of the deadwood is important; in fine-lined vessels it should extend well forward and up, otherwise it will be found that there is not sufficient space for housing the lower ends of the frames, see sketch, Fig. 10. The bottom end of the sternpost (the seating or bed) is secured into its place on the wooden keel by a variation of the tenon and mortise joint, called 'tabling', this is to locate it in a horizontal direction, see sketch, Fig. 11. The tables consist of one or two rectangular pieces of hardwood let into the keel and up into the sternpost as shown in the sketch. It should be noted that the grain of the tables must be vertical in order to get the most strength. Often the sternpost is further secured by dovetailed metal plates, let into and screwed to keel and post.

The information from the loft consists of profile or contour moulds of the sternpost and deadwood, showing the rebate and bearding lines, frames, aperture, etc., with section moulds taken at frames and at square sections. The connection of the sternpost to the framing of counter is described on pp. 25 and 26. Where there is an aperture for the propeller it should be of ample size to give a good clearance for the tips of propeller blades (about 1/5 dia. is a good clearance) and clear of the sterntube flange, its perimeter should be faired away or streamlined, in order to permit an easy and unbroken flow of solid water to the propeller. This is a very important point today, because of the small diameter of modern propellers brought about by the very high revolutions of modern engines. Care must be taken to see that the deadwood length in way of the sterntube is sufficient to give enough width inside the plank to house properly the sterntube flange, and ensure that the gland studs are accessible. It is good practice to fit a floor at this point, the floor serving to tie up the high part of the deadwood to the adjacent framing, and preventing any movement, which would result in the shaft getting out of alignment, hot bearings, leaks and other evils.

Where a propeller is fitted to one side of the centre line an external bossing becomes necessary, and it may take the form of a gunmetal casting or 'sleeve piece', but more often it consists of a solid chock suitably shaped as a bossing, and made closely to fay the plank, to which it is well bedded and secured. Inside the ship a similar chock should be fitted, or a strong partial floor, in order that the sterntube flange may be tightly hove up by the nut at the outer end. A side drive also requires a propeller bracket, which should have good broad palms on the arms, well through-bolted to the sternpost and the outer planking, with a chock inside if necessary, spanning several frames. The length of the bearing should be four times the shaft diameter, and it might be noted here that plastic bushes have been tried with good results, also cutlass rubber bearings are very good, these materials being particularly suited for water lubrication.

A modern idea widely adopted in ocean racing vessels is to align the propeller shaft close to the centre line, just clearing the rudder stock, and to fit the propeller under the

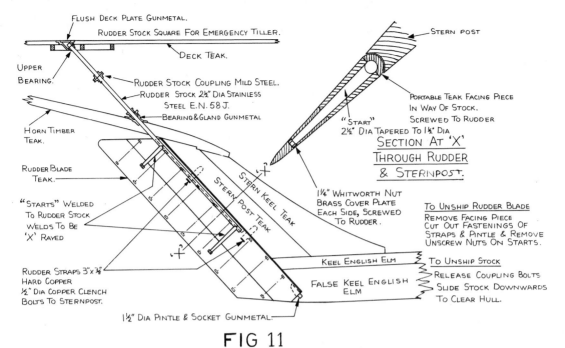

FLUSH DECK PLATE GUNMETAL.

RUDDER STOCK SQUARE FOR EMERGENCY TILLER.

DECK TEAK.

STERN POST

UPPER BEARING.

RUDDER STOCK COUPLING MILD STEEL.

RUDDER STOCK 2½" DIA STAINLESS STEEL E.N. 58 J.

BEARING & GLAND GUNMETAL

PORTABLE TEAK FACING PIECE IN WAY OF STOCK. SCREWED TO RUDDER

HORN TIMBER TEAK.

"START" 2½" DIA TAPERED TO 1½" DIA

RUDDER BLADE TEAK.

STERN POST TEAK

STERN KEEL TEAK

SECTION AT 'X' THROUGH RUDDER & STERNPOST.

"STARTS" WELDED TO RUDDER STOCK WELDS TO BE 'X' RAYED

1¼" WHITWORTH NUT BRASS COVER PLATE EACH SIDE, SCREWED TO RUDDER.

TO UNSHIP RUDDER BLADE
REMOVE FACING PIECE
CUT OUT FASTENINGS OF STRAPS & PINTLE & REMOVE
UNSCREW NUTS ON STARTS.

RUDDER STRAPS 3" x ⅜" HARD COPPER ½" DIA COPPER CLENCH BOLTS TO STERNPOST.

KEEL ENGLISH ELM

FALSE KEEL ENGLISH ELM

TO UNSHIP STOCK
RELEASE COUPLING BOLTS
SLIDE STOCK DOWNWARDS
TO CLEAR HULL.

1½" DIA PINTLE & SOCKET GUNMETAL.

FIG 11

DETAILS OF RUDDER & FITTINGS FOR A 48 TON KETCH. SEE ALSO FIG 12

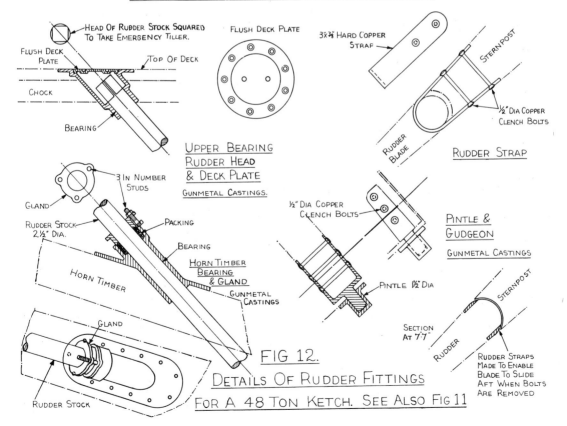

HEAD OF RUDDER STOCK SQUARED TO TAKE EMERGENCY TILLER.

FLUSH DECK PLATE

3 x ⅜" HARD COPPER STRAP

STERNPOST

FLUSH DECK PLATE

TOP OF DECK

CHOCK

BEARING

½" DIA COPPER CLENCH BOLTS

RUDDER BLADE

UPPER BEARING RUDDER HEAD & DECK PLATE

GUNMETAL CASTINGS.

RUDDER STRAP

GLAND

3 IN NUMBER STUDS

PACKING

½" DIA COPPER CLENCH BOLTS

PINTLE & GUDGEON

GUNMETAL CASTINGS

RUDDER STOCK 2½" DIA.

BEARING

HORN TIMBER BEARING & GLAND

GUNMETAL CASTINGS

HORN TIMBER

PINTLE 1½" DIA

SECTION AT "7.7"

RUDDER

STERNPOST

GLAND

FIG 12.

RUDDER STOCK

DETAILS OF RUDDER FITTINGS FOR A 48 TON KETCH. SEE ALSO FIG 11

RUDDER STRAPS MADE TO ENABLE BLADE TO SLIDE AFT WHEN BOLTS ARE REMOVED

SKETCH OF RUDDER WITH METAL MAIN PIECE

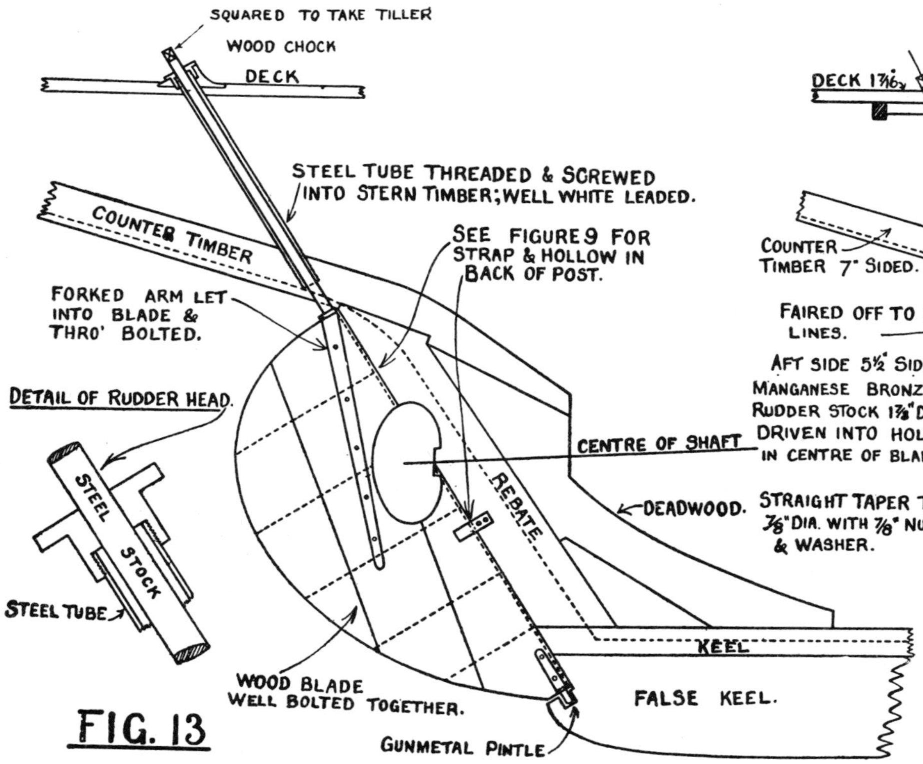

SQUARED TO TAKE TILLER

WOOD CHOCK

DECK

STEEL TUBE THREADED & SCREWED
INTO STERN TIMBER; WELL WHITE LEADED.

SEE FIGURE 9 FOR
STRAP & HOLLOW IN
BACK OF POST.

FORKED ARM LET
INTO BLADE &
THRO' BOLTED.

COUNTER TIMBER

REBATE

CENTRE OF SHAFT

DEADWOOD.

DETAIL OF RUDDER HEAD.

STEEL STOCK

STEEL TUBE

KEEL

FALSE KEEL.

WOOD BLADE
WELL BOLTED TOGETHER.

GUNMETAL PINTLE.

FIG. 13

RUDDER & STERNPOST IN YACHT WITH NO APERTURE

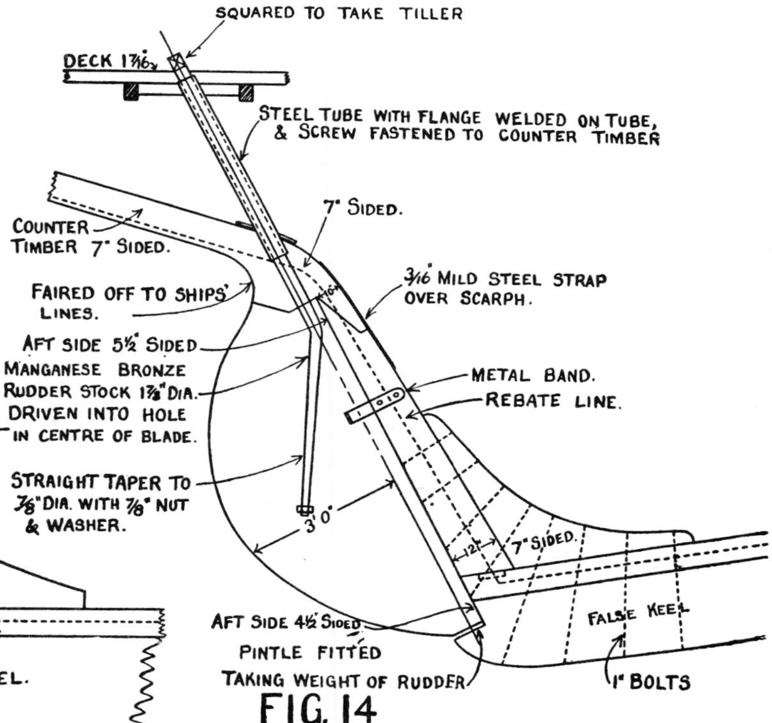

SQUARED TO TAKE TILLER

DECK 1⅞.

STEEL TUBE WITH FLANGE WELDED ON TUBE,
& SCREW FASTENED TO COUNTER TIMBER

7" SIDED.

³⁄₁₆ MILD STEEL STRAP
OVER SCARPH.

METAL BAND.

REBATE LINE.

7" SIDED.

FALSE KEEL.

1" BOLTS

12"

3' 0.

AFT SIDE 4½ SIDED
PINTLE FITTED
TAKING WEIGHT OF RUDDER.

COUNTER
TIMBER 7" SIDED.

FAIRED OFF TO SHIP'S
LINES.

AFT SIDE 5½ SIDED
MANGANESE BRONZE
RUDDER STOCK 1⅜" DIA.
DRIVEN INTO HOLE
IN CENTRE OF BLADE.

STRAIGHT TAPER TO
⅞" DIA. WITH ⅞" NUT
& WASHER.

FIG. 14

counter entirely abaft the rudder, just as much to one side as is necessary to clear the rudder stock and sternpost.

This does away with a propeller shaft bracket, makes a neat job, almost a centre-line installation, and the actual bossing can usually be incorporated in the horn timber. The whole idea is illustrated by Fig. 15. Notice that it requires careful loft work, and skilful boring when lining up the tailshaft.

Figure 15

Sketch of Stern, showing
Horn Timber & Shaft Swell in One Piece,
THUS KEEPING PROPELLER CLOSE IN TO MIDDLE LINE OF SHIP.

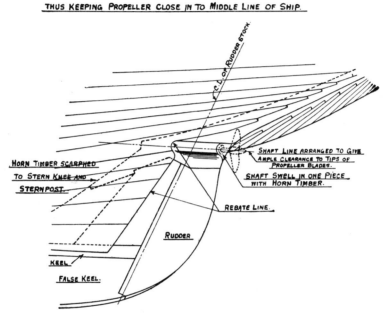

HORN TIMBER IS OF THE USUAL SHAPE, BUT WITH A SWELL ON ONE SIDE TO FORM A BOSSING TO HOUSE THE STERNTUBE. THIS SWELL MAY BE SOLID WITH THE HORN TIMBER, OR IT MAY BE PARTIALLY BUILT UP BY GLUEING & BOLTING, IN ORDER TO SUIT THE SIZE OF THE TIMBER AVAILABLE.

Counter Timber and Horn Timbers. These are made of English oak, teak or mahogany, and in the case of the older type of vessel with a wood mainpiece to the rudder are usually double, and called 'horn timbers', but if the rudder mainpiece is metal as is now usual, a single horn timber is sufficient. In effect it is a continuation of the keel along the counter, consequently it must be firmly attached at its forward end to the sternpost. In some cases it is carried over the head of the sternpost, the latter being scarphed to it and secured by long bolts, with the rudder stock passing through it into a metal tube. In other cases it is cut at the after side of the rudder trunk and side pieces are carried along one each side of the rudder trunk and securely bolted to the stern timber on the after side and to the sternpost on the fore side.

25

The moulds supplied from the loft are profile moulds showing the position of frames and section moulds square to the profile. Horn timbers for the older type of vessel may be described as the two main pieces of framing which fashion and support the counter or overhanging stern of a wooden vessel. They are fitted and bolted on the sides of the sternpost, the rudderhead passing between them, and the rudder trunk being built above them. The transverse frames of the counter or stern are all halved to the horn timbers and the outer or after ends of the horn timbers are scarphed into the stern chock or transom. Another piece of wood is fitted between the horn timbers, faying them; this houses the outer plank ends and is usually called the 'centre' or 'king' piece, as the snapes of the plank ends run into it; the horn timbers taking the fastenings of the plank ends. With the type of construction in use nowadays, as shown in Figs. 13 and 14, the single counter timber is used and Lloyd's Rules require that it is to be securely attached to the sternpost, and the sectional area at its forward end must not be less than the Rule sectional area of the sternpost, and it may be gradually reduced towards its after end, where the sectional area is not to be less than three-fourths of that required at the forward end.

The 'stern chock' or 'archboard' is described on p. 66, but in the small sailing yachts with short counters which are popular now, the stern is sufficiently deep to fit a transom, in which case, a stout oak knee, grown to form (transom knee) is fitted, through-bolted to the counter timber and to the transom. Where a single counter timber is fitted as shown in sketches (Figs. 11 to 14) it must, of course, be rabbeted to receive the outer planking, the ends of which generally run into it in the form of snape ends, see Fig. 15. Care must be taken that the rebate is wide enough, and has sufficient wood behind it to fasten efficiently these hood ends.

Rudder. Made with a steel or bronze stock and a teak or mahogany blade. The diameter of the rudder head, if of wood or steel is given in Lloyd's Rules under the Lloyd's length, but if it is to be of forged bronze, the diameter given in steel is to be multiplied by 1.05 or if of cast bronze is to be multiplied by 1.25. When the rudder is of wood, the fore edge of the blade is rounded off to fit into the hollow of the sternpost, about $\frac{1}{8}$ in. clearance being allowed, see p. 20 and sketch Fig. 9. The thickness is tapered away aft, leaving sufficient on the after edge to allow for a bolt to be housed properly. The diameter of the fore edge should not exceed the siding of the sternpost, remembering that the siding at the back of post may taper from head to heel as mentioned on p. 20.

The rudder head has to pass through some form of gland or tube in order to keep water out of the vessel. If a metal stock is fitted, with a tiller or quadrant above the deck, then the stock can be housed in a metal tube well screwed and bedded into the counter timber, as shown in Fig. 13. When the tiller and quadrant is below deck, a gland should be fitted on the counter timber. In small vessels the rudder is usually hung to the sternpost by copper straps, as shown in Fig. 11, to give some side support and to prevent lifting, but large vessels often have metal pintles. In this case a locking device is necessary to prevent the rudder from lifting. In both cases a bottom pintle is required to take the weight, as shown in the sketch. Figs. 12, 13 and 14.

Frames and Timbers. *Laminated frames* can be said to have taken the place of grown frames as a method of construction. They can be of smaller scantling than the old grown

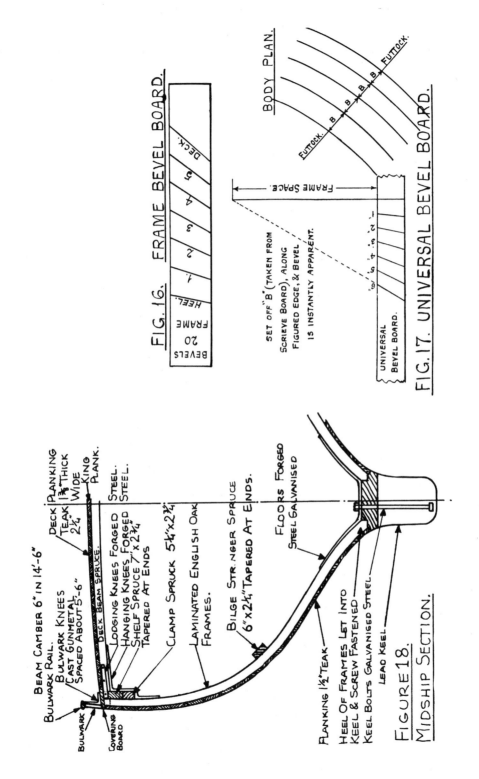

FIG. 16. FRAME BEVEL BOARD.

FRAME 20	BEVELS	HEEL	1	2	3	4	5	DECK

FIG. 17. UNIVERSAL BEVEL BOARD.

BODY PLAN.

Futlock. B B B B Futlock.

FRAME SPACE.

SET OFF "B" (TAKEN FROM SCRIEVE BOARD), ALONG FIGURED EDGE, & BEVEL IS INSTANTLY APPARENT.

UNIVERSAL BEVEL BOARD.

FIGURE 18. MIDSHIP SECTION.

BEAM CAMBER 6" IN 14'-6"
BULWARK RAIL.
DECK PLANKING TEAK 1⅜" THICK 2¼" WIDE
KING PLANK.
STEEL.
STEEL.
BULWARK KNEES CAST GUNMETAL SPACED ABOUT 5'-6"
LODGING KNEES FORGED
HANGING KNEES FORGED
SHELF SPRUCE 7"x2¾" TAPERED AT ENDS
DECK BEAM SPRUCE.
CLAMP SPRUCE 5¼"x2¾"
LAMINATED ENGLISH OAK FRAMES.
BILGE STRINGER SPRUCE 6"x2¼" TAPERED AT ENDS.
BULWARK
COVERING BOARD
FLOORS FORGED STEEL GALVANISED
PLANKING 1½" TEAK
HEEL OF FRAMES LET INTO KEEL & SCREW FASTENED
KEEL BOLTS GALVANISED STEEL
LEAD KEEL

27

frames, can use straight grained material in place of the grown or curved grained material and eliminate the weak frame butts. See Fig. 18. Lloyd's requirements for glues used for laminated members are that they should be of the resorcinal or phenolic types. It is claimed that these glues are completely weatherproof and will last a lifetime. The development of glues is a continuous process and it is advisable to keep up to date with makers' published literature and consult them on specific problems.

Aluminium alloy angle frames have high strength/weight characteristics, but special care must be taken in selecting the correct specification and in insulating it from contact with timber and other metals including fastenings. Suitable materials are the B.S.S. N.E.6 and N.E.8 for welded or riveted construction and H.E.30 for riveted construction only. See also Chapter 8.

Steel angle frames. These should be galvanized when used in conjunction with timber, and plank fastenings should be of galvanized steel.

Bent timbers of Canadian rock elm or English oak. The English oak should be cut from a young tree to give best assurance that the timbers will bend. These must be steamed and care must be taken that the steam is wet. If the steam is too hot it will dry the timber and cause it to be brittle instead of pliable. It is good practice to fit a few steel, aluminium alloy or laminated wood frames with this type of construction, especially at the mast, as stiffening and to hold the shape during construction.

Laminated frames, steel frames or aluminium alloy frames can be used with one, two or more bent timbers between and where this form of construction is adopted, or if bent frames only are used, the outer planking is secured to the bent timbers by clenched copper nails of square section, on copper rooves or, alternatively, silicon bronze wood screws which should enter the frames at a distance at least equal to the plank thickness.

Floors. The purpose of the floor is to bind the two sides of the frame together, stiffen the frame at its lowest point and provide additional connections to the keel. Various types of floors are in use.

Plate floors with heel bars and reverse bars or top flanges are best for use with steel angles frames, for the ease of their accurate assembly and efficiency of their connection to the frames. See Fig. 19.

With wooden frames, any of the following may be used:

Strap floors of galvanized iron, which take up a minimum of space and are therefore, most suitable where space is needed for tanks, cabin sole, etc. See Fig. 20.

Angle floors, of galvanized mild steel, provide an efficient connection at the outer edge of the frame, where it is needed, but owing to the relative thinness of the material, lose strength more quickly than strap floors if rusting takes place. See Fig. 21.

Wood floors of English oak are probably the most durable and if increased in width in way of the lead keel, may have the keel bolts passed through them, thus eliminating 'clips' to floors; the danger of dissimilar metals being in contact and setting up electrolytic action is avoided. See Fig. 22.

In order to comply with Lloyd's Rules, floors must be fitted to all laminated or steel

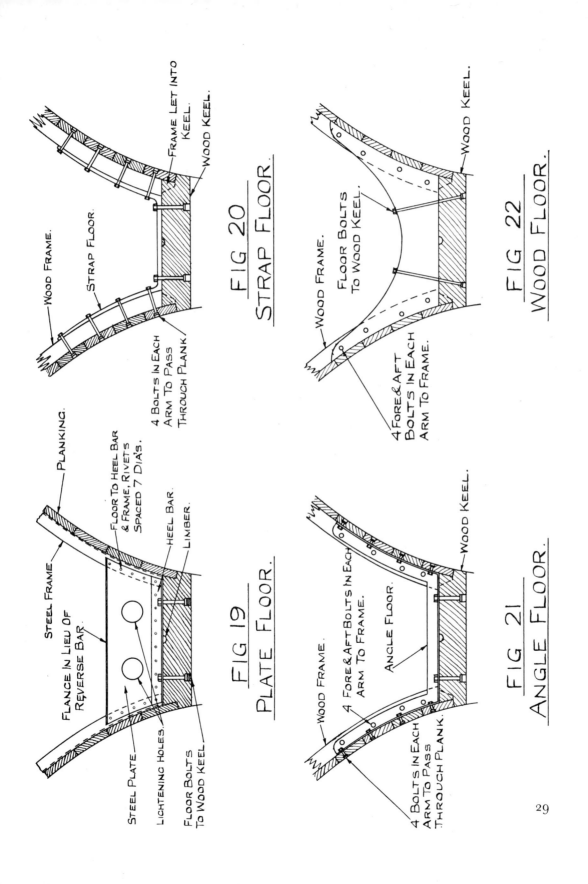

WOOD FRAME.

STRAP FLOOR.

FRAME LET INTO KEEL.

WOOD KEEL.

4 BOLTS IN EACH ARM TO PASS THROUGH PLANK.

FIG 20
STRAP FLOOR.

WOOD KEEL.

WOOD FRAME.

FLOOR BOLTS TO WOOD KEEL.

4 FORE & AFT BOLTS IN EACH ARM TO FRAME.

FIG 22
WOOD FLOOR.

PLANKING.

FLOOR TO HEEL BAR & FRAME, RIVETS SPACED 7 DIA'S.

HEEL BAR.

LIMBER.

STEEL FRAME.

FLANGE IN LIEU OF REVERSE BAR.

STEEL PLATE.

LIGHTENING HOLES.

FLOOR BOLTS TO WOOD KEEL.

FIG 19
PLATE FLOOR.

WOOD KEEL.

WOOD FRAME.

4 FORE & AFT BOLTS IN EACH ARM TO FRAME.

ANGLE FLOOR.

4 BOLTS IN EACH ARM TO PASS THROUGH PLANK.

FIG 21
ANGLE FLOOR.

29

frames. With bent timbers, if strap or angle floors are fitted, there must be one on every timber for the 3/5 L amidships and every third beyond this. Where the Lloyd's depth does not exceed 9 feet, they may be fitted on alternate timbers for 3/5 L amidships. Wood floors are sufficient on alternate timbers for 3/5 L amidships and every third beyond. When grown or steel frames are fitted with one, two or three bent timbers between, strap or angle floors are required on every bent timber for the 3/5 L amidships. Floors are not required on the bent timbers at ends, except when three bent timbers are fitted, when a floor is to be fitted to the middle timber.

The scantlings of floors are based on the Lloyd's depth D. Where the yacht is fine, such as in the vicinity of the after deadwood, plate or deep wood floors are required. Where frames are continuous from covering board to covering board at the ends of the yacht, no floors are required.

Floors are best made from templates taken from the ship, for although they are sometimes made from templates taken from the loft floor, the erection of a wooden vessel does not proceed with the same accuracy as that of a steel ship. The material for the floors may be ordered by the drawing office, the iron being ordered the correct size at the throat and drawn out for the ends. Iron and steel floors should be galvanized after being completely finished and drilled. Floors are through-fastened to the outer planking and to the keel, the latter fastenings being put in before the keel is bedded down, as pointed out on p. 17, see also p. 48. Where the practice of widely spaced steel frames with bent wood timbers between is adopted, it is very necessary to connect the two frame legs across the centre line, either by means of a plate floor, or by means of a heel bar, which is a steel angle bar of somewhat larger size than the frames, and fitted the reverse way, or back to back, with arms running well up the frames. In the larger vessels plate floors are best, but in small yachts they will be found to interfere badly with tank stowage, etc. Sketches relating to iron floors are given in Figs. 2 and 19, 20 and 21, and in Fig. 49 a general construction plan is given for a typical 48 tons auxiliary ketch yacht, which clearly indicates the layout of the iron floors.

Shelf and Clamp. These may be made of spruce, pitch pine, larch, etc. The shelf is an important longitudinal tie, securing the upper ends of all the timbers and providing a ledge upon which the ends of the deck beams rest. In classed vessels the size of shelf is given in the rules, the sectional area being determined by the Lloyd's length L. The shelf should extend all fore and aft, and the two sides be connected with a breasthook at the stem, and crutches or knees at the sternpost, transom or archboard of counter. Beyond the three-fifths length amidships the sectional area of the shelf may be gradually reduced to 25 per cent less than required amidships. The shelf area is given between beams and the scoring in way of beams should not impair the efficiency of the shelf. As a guide a reduction of not more than 10 per cent should be aimed at.

Where bent wood frames are fitted between grown frames of greater moulding, packing or filling pieces must be fitted between the bent frames and the shelf to take the fastenings of these two members. The shelf must be efficiently scarphed. Shelf scarphs should be kept well clear of chain plates. Clamps of not less than 75 per cent the sectional area of the shelf should be fitted in addition to the shelf in way of the rigging. (See midship section, Fig. 18 also Fig. 49 and 50. In yachts with alternate steel frames and bent timbers, this clamp is sometimes replaced by a steel plate. Steel frames should be connected to shelf and clamp by bolts through short angle reverse lugs riveted to the frames.

The shelf is the principal medium by which the ends of the beams are attached to the sides of the vessels and it is therefore highly important that a good connection be made between the two members. This is usually effected by dovetailing the ends of the beams into the shelf with a screw fastening, in the manner described on p. 32 and sketched in Fig. 23, and by the fitting on the principal beams of hanging and lodge knees as described on pp. 32, 34. It is a common practice to make one-sided dovetails looking away from amidships, the reason for this being, that the dovetail is somewhat stronger if cut on the shut bevel formed by the closing in curves of the ship's sides. In way of coachroof carlings, the dovetails will be on the side towards amidships, for the same reason (see Fig. 23).

It should be noticed here that there are various methods in vogue for fitting the shelf and beams. That just described, and sketched in Fig. 23 may be suitable for small vessels, but it has the great disadvantage of very much reducing the effective sectional area of the shelf, and furthermore, the full strength of the beam is not maintained across the width of the shelf. Therefore in larger vessels it is usual and better to fit the shelf beneath the beams, as shown in the midship section Fig. 18, thus eradicating both the objections stated above. Here the beams are scored into the shelf and through-bolted. A method is shown in Fig. 24 which represents quite good practice for vessels of about 20 tons. In semi-composite vessels, where steel beams are fitted as well as steel frames, it is good practice to make the shelf a steel angle also, in which case it corresponds to the stringer angle or gunwale bar of ordinary steel construction.

Bilge Stringer. May be of spruce, pitch pine, larch, etc. The bilge stringer size in Lloyd's Rules is fixed by the sectional area, based on the Lloyd's length L. Beyond the 3/5 L this may be gradually reduced to 25 per cent less than the midship area. A bilge stringer is to be fitted on all yachts having bent timbers only and those with grown frames and more than two bent timbers between. When grown frames only, or grown frames with one or two bent timbers between, are fitted, a bilge stringer is only required if the Lloyd's length exceeds 30 feet. Two or more side stringers may be fitted instead of the above arrangement. If two are fitted, the sectional area of each must be at least 60 per cent that of the Rule bilge stringer. It is the usual practice to fit bilge stringers with their greatest dimensions along the face of the frame, in order to facilitate bending and not to take up too much space in the cabins, and with this object in view, in vessels of moderate size, the bilge stringer should be run so as to come under the berth bottoms.

Bilge stringers are continuous, so that such items as web frames and bulkheads have to be worked over them; they must be efficiently scarphed if not in one length. There must be at least one through bolt in the bilge stringers up to 7 in. and two above 7 in. moulding at each frame and bolts driven through the plank. Bilge stringers should extend as far forward and aft as practicable (to stem and stern) and be tied with breasthooks and crutches. Where bent wood frames are fitted between grown frames of greater moulding, packing or filling pieces are to be fitted between the bent frames and the stringers, and are to take the fastenings of the latter through frame and plank.

Where steel frames are fitted, short reverse lugs are to be welded to them in way of the stringer to take the bolt fastenings. Where widely spaced steel frames are fitted with bent wood timbers between, it is much better practice to make the bilge stringers of two steel angle bars, fitted back to back; this results in a neater and stronger job, taking up much less space in the vessel, and not cutting into web frames and bulkheads to such a great extent. It may be remarked here that in vessels framed in this manner, plate floors are customary, and in vessels, say 15 tons and upwards, should the keel run up high at the fore end, i.e., a cut-away forefoot, which is quite common in yachts of the cruising type, it is good practice to work a partial centre keelson to strengthen and stiffen the yacht in the vicinity of this shallow part, particularly under the mast. This usually takes the form of an intercostal plate between the floors, flanged and coach-screwed to the keel, welded to the floors, with a continuous top plate welded to the centre keelson and floors. A welded prefabricated structure may be used. Lightening holes may be cut in the intercostal plate. The ordinary method of fitting bilge stringers is clearly indicated in the midship section Figs. 18 and 50 and the construction plan in Fig. 49.

Beams, Half Beams, Carlings. Usually made of English oak, teak, spruce, larch, etc. The scantlings and spacing of beams are given in Lloyd's Rules, based upon the length of midship beam, a reduction being allowed before and abaft the three-fifths length amidships. A point to notice is that the beams are spaced independently of the frames or timbers and are not directly connected to the latter except by an occasional hanging knee. The positions of the beams are governed mainly by the positions of the deck openings such as skylights, companions, masts, cockpit, coachroof, etc., the spacing of beams between these openings made to conform as nearly as possible to the rule requirements. Notice that certain beams, such as those at mast and deck openings where two or more beams are cut, are required to be of larger scantling than the ordinary beams. It is also advisable to give some increase in scantlings in way of sampson post, windlass, main sheet, etc.

In the type of vessel under notice, the amount of camber or crop given to the weather deck beams is about $\frac{3}{8}$ in. per foot of beam length, which is considerably more than the standard round up. The lower edges of beams are usually moulded throughout the owner's accommodation in one of the styles shown in Fig. 25, the 'ovolo' and 'cove', being traditional for the main cabins, with a plain rounded corner in other cases. Nowadays elaborate mouldings are unusual. Beams should be of parallel siding, but in order to save weight and conform to correct girder principles, the depth or moulding should be greatest at the middle line and reduced at ends. The relative depths of hatch end beams, carlings and half beams must be arranged as indicated in Fig. 26 to avoid the troublesome and expensive necessity of mitring the mouldings on the beam edges. Carlings must be at least the depth of moulding less than the hatch beams which they butt into and the half beams must be the same amount less than the carlings.

All beams should be dovetailed and halved into the shelf and screw fastened. The usual practice is to make a one-sided dovetail on the side away from amidships. Hanging knees are required by Lloyd's on beams in way of masts, at ends of deck openings, and elsewhere to complete the number required by the rules, the number and size being based on the length of midship beam; in way of these the beams must be close to frames as they have to pick up beam and frame. These are described on p. 34, where lodging knees are also dealt with.

Where widely spaced steel frames with bent timbers between are adopted, it is

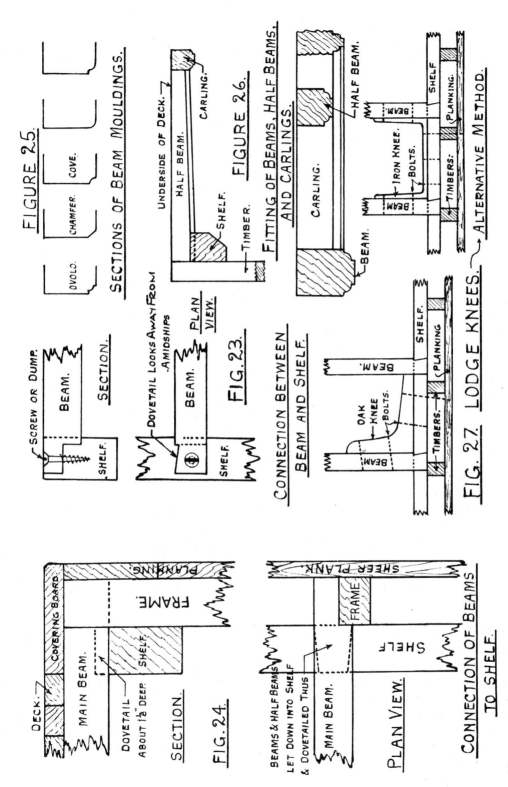

OVOLO. CHAMFER. COVE.

SECTIONS OF BEAM MOULDINGS.

FIGURE 25.

UNDERSIDE OF DECK.

HALF BEAM.

CARLING.

SHELF.

TIMBER.

PLAN VIEW.

FIGURE 26.

FITTING OF BEAMS, HALF BEAMS, AND CARLINGS.

CARLING.

HALF BEAM.

BEAM.

HALF BEAM.

SHELF.

PLANKING.

IRON KNEE.

BOLTS.

TIMBERS.

BEAM.

ALTERNATIVE METHOD.

SCREW OR DUMP.

BEAM.

SHELF.

SECTION.

DOVETAIL LOOKS AWAY FROM AMIDSHIPS.

BEAM.

SHELF.

FIG. 23.

CONNECTION BETWEEN BEAM AND SHELF.

SHELF.

BEAM.

PLANKING.

OAK KNEE.

BOLTS.

TIMBERS.

BEAM.

FIG. 27. LODGE KNEES.

DECK.

COVERING BOARD.

PLANKING.

FRAME.

MAIN BEAM.

SHELF.

DOVETAIL ABOUT 1½" DEEP.

SECTION.

FIG. 24.

SHEER PLANK.

FRAME.

BEAMS & HALF BEAMS LET DOWN INTO SHELF & DOVETAILED THUS.

SHELF.

MAIN BEAM.

PLAN VIEW.

CONNECTION OF BEAMS TO SHELF.

33

customary to fit the usual wood beams, spaced independently of the frames, and dovetailed into the shelf in the ordinary manner, but where the hanging knees occur on steel frames they are usually made of light steel plate brackets, welded to the frame, worked across the shelf to the best advantage, and attached thereto by flanges and wood screws, the upper edge of brackets being bolted to the side of beam. Those hanging knees which come on bent timbers are of the ordinary wrought-iron type as described in the subsequent article, and bolted through timber and plank, shelf and beam. A typical layout of the beams, carlings, chocks, etc., for a yacht of 48 tons is given in Fig. 49.

Hanging and Lodging Knees. Hanging knees are almost without exception made of galvanized wrought iron or steel, either forged or of angle bar mitred and welded. The length of arms and size of iron at throat and at point are laid down in Lloyd's Rules, based upon the length of beam, and the stipulation is that hanging knees are to be fitted to mast and hatch end beams, and to ordinary beams in number stated. These knees are fitted to the underside of the beam, and run down the inside face of the nearest frames, fitting closely over the shelf and clamp (see midship section, Fig. 18). They are fastened up through the beam and bolted through the frame and plank. They should be fitted at the same places as lodging knees and in any position where there is likely to be a considerable stress, such as in way of runners.

Lodging knees are generally of grown oak (although sometimes galvanized wrought-iron knees are used), and they are fitted between the beams which carry the mast partners, and any others, such as hatch end beams, where there is a great tendency to racking stresses. They are bolted through the beam and through shelf, timber and planking, see Fig. 27. Lodging knees can also be fitted with advantage to improve the connection between hatch end beams and long carlings. Sometimes in lieu of lodge knees, a steel plate is fitted along the beams and shelf in the form of a stringer plate. This is good practice and may be carried out with advantage in way of tall masts where the stresses set up by the rigging is severe. Plate should be galvanized and through-bolted to shelf and beams. In way of these plates the deck fastenings can be screwed from below. When plywood decks are used, lodging knees are not required. The same idea can be carried out in way of the masts and chain plates. In lieu of clamps, mild steel plates, of reasonable depth and thickness, are fitted in the form of sheer-strakes, which effectively tie together all the heads of the frames, and provide a good tie to the shelf, and a solid foundation to which to bolt the chain plates.

In the preceding article reference is made to hanging knees in relationship to steel frames and bent timber. In Fig. 49 a general construction plan is given for a yacht of 48 tons, which shows a typical arrangement of the hanging and lodging knees.

Pillars. Pillars should be fitted to the beams in way of the mast where halyards are fastened to the deck. Other places where pillars should be fitted are: wherever there is a special local weight or pull, such as under masts stepped on deck, under the windlass or capstan; under the sheet horses or buffers; under the forestay, or under large deck-houses and companions. Pillars are most commonly made of round iron or steel bars with solid forged heads and heels, but sometimes, for the sake of lightness, they are made of steel tubes, with forged steel ends, shrunk on hot, and pinned or welded. Of course, in small yachts, pillars cannot always be placed exactly where they would be most effective, and they often have to be arranged to come in the cabin bulkheads, in which case they are made of flat iron or steel bars, with a section equivalent in stiffness to the round section they supplant. Both heads and heels should be secured to the hull with two good bolts, and particular care should be taken to keep the centres of the heads and heels in line with the axis of the pillar, otherwise, instead of a direct thrust there will be a bending moment upon the strut. All pillars should be carefully fitted to serve as ties as well as struts, and should be secured accordingly.

Alignment is important, i.e., pillars under the various decks must be under one another if possible. 'Y' headed pillars are sometimes placed under the halyards at the mast and under sheet buffers or horses, in order to save space below. To take the pull of the halyards and tackles around the mast on deck it is often the practice to fit diagonal forged stays, with the heads under the deck made as palms large enough to take the halyard bolts, and the heel or foot secured to the mast. In the smaller yachts they are often simply screwed to the mast, but a better method is to fit a band round the mast with the stays secured to it. These stays transmit the upward pull of the halyards from the deck to the mast and, as the pull aloft is on the mast, the latter is placed in compression, and the deck is greatly relieved.

Chapter 2

Hull Planking. Teak is probably the best with iroko, a less expensive but good alternative. Honduras mahogany is a good choice for light boats with African mahogany as a less expensive alternative. With African mahogany special care must be taken in choosing the logs, as it can vary from very soft and light material which is not suitable for this purpose, to heavy and hard material. An average weight is about 33 pounds per cubic foot. This timber is likely to have 'lightning' or 'felling' shakes running across the grain making it useless for yachtbuilding so that the wastage is liable to be high. African mahogany is also susceptible to deterioration due to electrolytic action. It is widely used due to its low cost and ready availability and can be satisfactory, provided the necessary precautions are taken. Pitch pine is very suitable for under-water planking especially with teak or mahogany topsides. Its use is restricted in some areas due to its cost and the fact that it is not readily available. The thickness of outside planking is given in Lloyd's Rules based on the Lloyd's length. The width of plank varies, being usually from 5 in. to 7 in. wide from covering board down to turn of bilge, increasing to 9 in. or 10 in. wide at the garboard.

Single skin carvel construction is probably most suitable for the normal sailing yacht. Double skin construction means something approaching double work and cost for minimal advantage. There are exceptions such as clencher construction or cold mould-ing for round bilge dinghies and marine ply for chine boats.

The size of fastenings is governed by the thickness of the plank and the number of fastenings is governed by the width and thickness and the number can be single, double or treble. The length of planks is made to suit the timber available, say, 18 ft. to 20 ft.

Butts are square, with a seam on the outside for caulking. Butt straps are also required, unless they are positioned on grown frames, when straps may be dispensed with. For the smaller type of boat, however, with planking up to about $1\frac{1}{4}$ in. thick, scarphed butts are preferable and these should be feather edged inside and lipped outside to allow for planing off, positioned centrally on frames and be glued and screwed. Lipping may be dispensed with and feather edges adopted if suitable glues are used.

The shifts of butts is important and must be properly carried out, the requirements of Lloyd's Rules being that no butts of outside planking are to be nearer than 4 ft. to each other; no butts to be on the same timber unless there are three strakes between. A

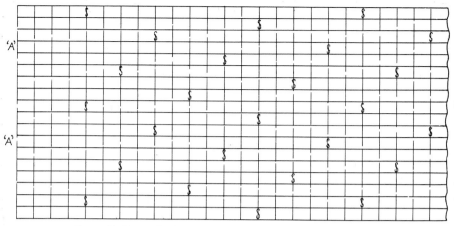

SHIFT OF BUTTS IN SHELL PLANKING
IN EXCESS OF LLOYDS REQUIREMENTS

SUITS 16'-0" PLANKING IF FRAMES ARE 1'-0" CENTRES.
OR 20'-0" PLANKING IF FRAMES ARE 1'-3" CENTRES.
NOTE THAT "A" STRAKES NEED TO BE 2 FRAME SPACES LONGER TO AVOID SHORT PIECES.

FIG 28

WITH DOUBLE FRAMES, BUTT CAN BE ON FRAMES.
OTHERWISE USE PLATE OR WOOD BUTT STRAPS.

DISADVANTAGE OF WIDE PLANKS
WHERE CURVATURE IS GREAT

FIGURE 29.

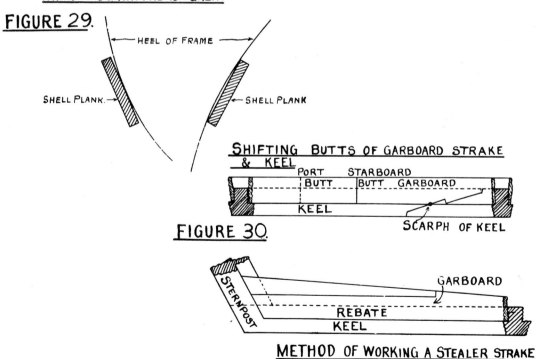

HEEL OF FRAME

SHELL PLANK.

SHELL PLANK

SHIFTING BUTTS OF GARBOARD STRAKE & KEEL

PORT   STARBOARD
BUTT   BUTT GARBOARD
KEEL
SCARPH OF KEEL

FIGURE 30.

STERNPOST

GARBOARD

REBATE
KEEL

METHOD OF WORKING A STEALER STRAKE

37

departure from this rule will be allowed at the ends of a yacht, to surveyor's satisfaction. One method, using 16 to 20 foot planks, is to start with any one butt and count to the right. The butt in the second strake is 10 spaces away, in the third 4 spaces, in the fourth 14 spaces, in the fifth 8 spaces, in the sixth 2 spaces, in the seventh 12 spaces, in the eighth 6 spaces. The butt in the ninth strake is in line with the first. There are thus seven strakes between each butt. The above gives sufficient information from which can be obtained the complete shift of butts (see Fig. 28). Certain end planks should be longer to avoid short pieces. The strakes of plank must be divided out on the frames to give fair lines.

Where there is excessive shape such as at turn of bilge and tuck, thicker planking must be used, to allow for hollowing. It is often advisable to fit wider planking at the heel when a raked keel is required, alternatively the extra width may be made up by fitting a stealer, see Fig. 30. The bottom plank adjacent to the keel is called the garboard strake, and care must be taken that the butts port and starboard are clear of each other and also clear of the keel scarphs (see Fig. 30).

At one time it was common to thicken up the garboard and one or two adjacent strakes, but modern shapes and methods of construction have made this idea obsolete.

To achieve some measure of economy in planking the sheer strake and adjacent strakes may be made parallel, until too much twist is encountered, when tapered planks must be resorted to. This is only done where the seams are hidden, with painted hulls, as the resulting run of planking is not particularly eye-sweet. When the appearance is important as with varnished hulls, the plank widths must be divided up on the scrieve boards or building moulds, to make every plank taper. A practice that is sometimes adopted is to spline the outer planking. The seams are caulked in the usual manner, but not payed or puttied. Instead, a small spline or strip of wood is tightly inserted into the open seam, and held with resin glue assisted by an occasional brad where the shipwright considers it to be necessary. This enables the outer surface of the planking to be planed and brought to a very fine finish, with no prominent seams showing. The garboard seams and plank end seams are best filled with painters' stopping for future caulking.

Deck Planking. Here again teak is the superior material, others being douglas fir and white seraya. These are lighter and cheaper, but are not so durable as teak. The thickness of deck is given in Lloyd's Rules under the Lloyd's length, and should be about $\frac{7}{8}$ in. for a 9 tonner, $1\frac{1}{8}$ in. for a 19 tonner, and 2 in. for a vessel of 80 tons. The width of the planks is more or less regulated by the class of the work, high-class finish with planks laid parallel to the ship's side requiring narrow strakes, whereas, in a low-grade job the planks may be fairly wide, if laid straight.

There are two main alternatives to a traditional laid deck. Firstly, for small craft marine-quality plywood, preferably canvas covered and secondly, for large craft plywood sheathed with a laid deck of teak. Both of these methods give a thinner deck, for the same strength, than the traditional laid deck, and eliminate the need for fitting lodging knees in sailing craft.

There are several systems in vogue for laying the deck, the best finish and appearance being obtained by laying the planks parallel to the deck margin or covering board, and of equal width throughout, in which case narrow planks must be used to obtain the best

TEAK SHEATHED DECK.
FIG 31
FOR THIN DECKS – UP TO SAY 1½" TOTAL THICKNESS

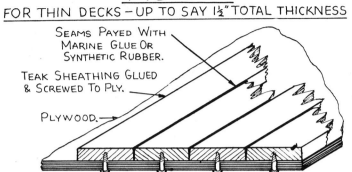

SEAMS PAYED WITH MARINE GLUE OR SYNTHETIC RUBBER.

TEAK SHEATHING GLUED & SCREWED TO PLY.

PLYWOOD.

results, say $1\frac{7}{8}$ in. for a 20 tonner and about $2\frac{1}{2}$ in. wide being correct for an 80 ton yacht. Another method, but somewhat expensive, is to lay the planks to the curve of the covering board, but considerably tapered at their ends, so that whilst the outboard strakes approximate to the curve of ship's side, the inboard strakes approach the straight line of centre. A beautiful effect can be obtained in this way, if carefully considered and executed, the width of the planks being about 3 to $3\frac{1}{2}$ in. amidships, tapering to 2 to $2\frac{1}{2}$ in. at ends for a 150 to 225 ton yacht and $2\frac{1}{2}$ in. to $1\frac{3}{4}$ in. for a 30 tonner. In that class of work where utility and cheapness are important considerations the deck planks are simply laid straight and parallel with the centre line of ship, the planks themselves being also of parallel section throughout, and fairly wide, 4 or 5 in. being common. The resulting appearance is not considered to be of yacht standard.

Sheathed decks up to about $1\frac{1}{2}$ in. total thickness should have the sheathing glued to the plywood and be fastened with round head screws from underside, see Fig. 31.

With decks of about 2 in. total thickness and over there are two main methods of constructing the deck. The recommended method is again sheathing on plywood, see Fig. 33. The second method is solid decking laid direct on the beams.

With the first method the deck planks are glued to the plywood and secret fastened with wood screws driven diagonally into the plywood and with side dowels when the planking is bent parallel to the ship's side, to hold the edges down. Synthetic rubber is used to fill the special rectangular seams, injected in liquid form.

With the second method the planking is secret fastened to wood beams by means of wood screws driven diagonally into the beams, or with steel beams by means of wood screws driven from below in the bosom of the beam. In this case a side dowel is fitted to each plank in each beam space and serves the additional purpose of making several planks work together when a heavy, concentrated, vertical load is applied. With this type of deck synthetic rubber filled seams alone are insufficient to guarantee lasting watertightness. Caulking with oakum or boat cotton first gives a more reliable deck.

The shift of butts for the deck planking should be the same as for the bottom planking. There are three types of butt in common use, viz., the square butt, the lip butt, and the scarph butt; the lip, or the scarph butt, being used when the beams are not wide

39

enough to allow a square one to be properly fastened (see Fig. 34). Plate butt straps may also be employed, but these should be avoided where weight saving is important. Lloyd's Rules state that deck planking should be quarter sawn, but also in a first-class job it is important that the dark grain, that is annual rings, should be laid vertically. The reason for this is that with the normal deck no coating is given to protect the wood, and under the severe alternating conditions of wet and dry, the annual rings tend to separate and if laid horizontally, will peel off in layers. If the annual rings are laid vertically as they should be, the compression due to caulking will tend to hold the wood together.

Where the underside of deck planks is exposed in the cabins, a bead is often cut along one edge to improve the appearance. In yachts where the decks are made of pine, it is the usual practice to make the covering board and king plank of teak or mahogany.

The covering board is the deck margin plank (see midship section, Fig. 18) and this usually runs out over the sheer plank and is fastened by bronze screws to the edge of sheer and to the shelf and beams. It is generally about three times the width of the deck planks. The king plank is a centre-line strake (Fig. 18) of about the same width as the covering board. It is screw-fastened to the beams and is necessary in those decks which are laid parallel to the covering board to receive the middle line ends of the deck planks, which are snaped into, and side fastened, to the king plank.

Bulwarks. Where the bulwark is fairly high it is usually made up in two pieces, consisting of the lower part, or washstrake and the upper part, or bulwark proper. Racing yachts, including ocean racers, usually have no bulwark at all, but a foot rail is fitted about 3 in. to 4 in. high. In cruising yachts of all sizes some form of bulwark is desirable, because not only does it give an added sense of security and safety, but it adds greatly to the dryness and comfort of the vessel when heeling over under sail. The actual height of the bulwark must be governed largely by the size and the appearance of the yacht, because it is obvious that a bulwark adds very much to the apparent freeboard of the vessel, and if overdone would spoil the outboard appearance. Three examples are: 30 ton yawl, 15 in. high, 50 ton ketch, 12 in. high, 78 ton ketch, 27 in. high, the latter being a high bulwark for the size of vessel.

A bulwark must not be allowed to trap water, as this added weight could impair safe stability. Large freeing ports must therefore be fitted to this end. Deck scuppers must also be fitted and their function is supplementary to freeing ports. Freeing ports are intended to dispose of a large volume of water quickly, after a sea has been shipped. They are usually fitted with horizontally hinged doors in yachts, which open easily when there is a pressure of water inside. In harbour they are fastened shut to prevent noise due to swinging.

Scuppers are intended to remove the small quantity of water which does not drain through the freeing ports, and to avoid showing streaks down the ship's side, they are piped to below the waterline.

In racing craft, however, where bulwarks and therefore freeing ports are not fitted, the scuppers are allowed to drain over the deck edge to save the weight of scupper pipes.

There are different methods of building up the bulwarks; some vessels have a hanging strake under the rail and a washstrake at the deck with a plain plank or board fitted between, called the bulwark; other vessels only have a plain board fitted between the rail and the covering board. The washstrake generally has a hollow or cove worked into it, from $\frac{3}{4}$ to 1 in. wide, which is gilded, and forms the gold line which yachts usually have, running in a fair line with the deck and rail, and ending in some suitable design on the bow and stern chocks. An old-fashioned method of ensuring that water clears from the deck, and a method which had much to recommend it, was to keep the bulwark up off the covering board (from $\frac{1}{2}$ to $1\frac{1}{2}$ in. clear), which formed a water course all fore and aft and prevented water lying on deck or round the bulwark stanchions, and in the event of shipping a sea, readily relieved the deck of water. This method is very rare in modern yachts, as it is not considered sightly. The ends of the bulwarks are housed in rabbets in the knighthead and stern chocks or archboard, as described, on pp. 44 and 66, secured by gunmetal screws. The bulwark is secured to the stanchions by bronze screws. In yachts of 20 tons and under it is quite common to have a low washrail with or without a capping, a safety element being provided by portable galvanized iron, stainless steel or brass stanchions with steel wire rope guard rails rove through, set up with lanyards. The height of this washrail or low bulwark is not by any means consistent, as the following list of actual instances will illustrate:

	13 ton sloop	*20 ton ketch*	*22 ton cutter*
Washrail	3 × 1 in.	10 × 1 in.	5 × $1\frac{1}{4}$ in.
Capping	2 × 1 in.	$3\frac{1}{2}$ × $1\frac{1}{4}$ in.	$2\frac{1}{2}$ × 1 in.
Material	Teak	Mahogany	Teak
Bulwark stanchion	None	$2\frac{1}{4}$ × 2 in.	None
Material	None	English oak	None

Where the washrail is of only moderate height it is fastened by long screws to the covering board and sheerstrake, but where the height is too much for this method and there are no bulwark stanchions, it is often the practice to fit gunmetal or galvanized-iron knees screwed to deck and washrail. With guardrail stanchions fitted on a low bulwark, a good practice is to provide a shoulder and thread at the foot to screw into brass sockets in the bulwark rail with a worked eye at the head, large enough to pass a shoe on the end of the flexible wire guardrails. Hook bars should be fitted at gangways.

Bulwark Stanchions. Teak is the best wood to use for these, although oak is sometimes employed. The latter is objectionable because it turns black at the deck, where it is let through the covering board, owing to the constant wet. Great care has to be exercised in placing bulwark stanchions, several of the more important considerations being as follows: A fairly equal and regular spacing is desirable on deck for the sake of appearance, whilst at the same time they should be kept entirely clear of all frames, beams and sidelights. There should be one on each side of the gangway, one near each side of the rigging to all masts, and one behind each davit and the catheads. The bulkwark stanchions behind davits and catheads should be of increased siding and moulding, being made particularly strong where they emerge from the deck because the stiffness of the whole davit depends upon the stiffness of the stanchion (see sketch, Fig. 57). Sometimes a small galvanized iron or gunmetal knee is also fitted to the deck on these stanchions.

Bulwark stanchions are carried down below the deck for a distance of at least two-thirds the height of the bulwarks and bolted through the shelf, clamp and planks. They are sometimes fitted square to the centre line, in which case the loft supplies section moulds at each stanchion, giving the height of rail, position of deck and bottom of stanchion, together with the necessary bevels; but more often the stanchions are fitted square to the side of the vessel, in which case section moulds only are given out, no bevels being required. Typical sizes of bulwark stanchions are as follows: 20 ton ketch, stanchions of oak, sided 2 in., moulded $2\frac{1}{2}$ in.; 78 ton ketch, stanchions of teak, sided $3\frac{3}{4}$ in., moulded $3\frac{1}{2}$ in. at deck to $2\frac{3}{4}$ in. at rail; 120 ton schooner, stanchions of teak, sided 3 in., moulded 4 in. at deck to 3 in. at rail, spaced about 39 in. apart. These are the ordinary stanchions—the ones at catheads, davits and gangways being about 25 per cent larger.

It is necessary to fix the position of the bulwark stanchions fairly early, because they are placed in position and secured before the deck is laid, the covering board being afterwards let down over them. The reason for this is because it is much easier, and makes a better job to cut the holes in the covering board on the 'stools', rather than in place, where, owing to the fact that the holes for the stanchions are behind the shelf and practically inaccessible, it would result in their lower edges being ragged and broken.

Main Rail. Should be of teak and kept bright and well varnished or bare and scrubbed. It should be of sufficient width properly to house the top of the largest bulwark stanchion, including the thickness of bulwark itself. The bulwark stanchions are tenoned into the rail and fastened by screws or dumps, dowelled down, and put through the rail into the stanchion on an angle; the reason being that they hold better thus than if inserted vertically into the end grain of post (see Fig. 35).

The greatest care must be exercised in getting the rail perfectly fair and 'eye-sweet', both in the direction of sheer and half-breadth. There are, of course, various different sections in use for rails, the most common being that shown at 'A' in Fig. 36, 'B' being a common variation with a rebate to take the bulwark plank. Typical sizes are $2\frac{1}{4}$ in. × 1 in. for a 20 ton yacht, $3\frac{1}{2} \times 1\frac{1}{2}$ in. for a 50 ton yacht and $5\frac{1}{2} \times 2\frac{1}{8}$ in. for a 78 ton yacht. The rail extends from the fore end right aft to meet the taffrail, where it becomes much wider, as the taffrail forms the stern part of the rail and has to cover the sharp angle made by the stern chock or archboard (see Fig. 67). A usual method of working the rail here is shown by Fig. 37. The various lengths of rail are scarphed together, generally by a hook scarph, through-bolted and dowelled. The forward part of the scarph is made outside, although in some cruiser stern yachts, this practice is reversed in the after body.

Knightheads. Are only seen on boats with a high wooden bulwark of between 1 ft. 6 in. and 3 ft. 0 in. and should be made of the same material as the bulwark stanchions, usually teak or oak. In sailing vessels of the cruising type, the knighthead may be considered as a very much enlarged bulwark stanchion, fitted immediately abaft the stem

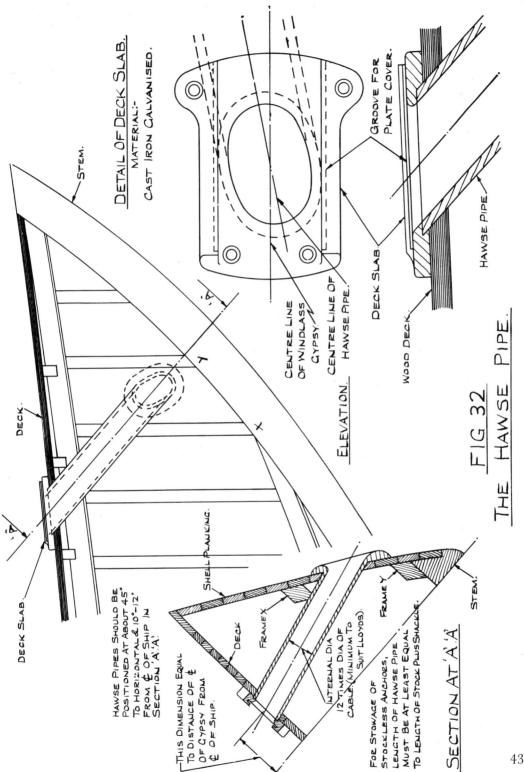

STEM.

DETAIL OF DECK SLAB.
MATERIAL:-
CAST IRON GALVANISED.

DECK.

DECK SLAB.

GROOVE FOR PLATE COVER.

CENTRE LINE OF WINDLASS GYPSY.

CENTRE LINE OF HAWSE PIPE.

DECK SLAB.

WOOD DECK.

HAWSE PIPE.

ELEVATION.

FIG 32
THE HAWSE PIPE.

HAWSE PIPES SHOULD BE POSITIONED AT ABOUT 45° TO HORIZONTAL & 10°-12° FROM ℄ OF SHIP IN SECTION 'A'A'.

THIS DIMENSION EQUAL TO DISTANCE OF ℄ OF GYPSY FROM ℄ OF SHIP.

SHELL PLANKING.

DECK.

FRAME X.

INTERNAL DIA. 12 TIMES DIA. OF CABLE (MINIMUM TO SUIT LLOYDS).

FRAME Y.

FOR STOWAGE OF STOCKLESS ANCHORS, LENGTH OF HAWSE PIPE MUST BE AT LEAST EQUAL TO LENGTH OF STOCK PLUS SHACKLE.

STEM.

SECTION AT 'A'A'

43

(see sketch, Fig. 38), for the purpose of reinforcing the bulwarks in way of the numerous fittings in that vicinity. The knightheads consist of large chocks (several pieces bolted together if necessary) of the same moulding as the bulwark stanchions, trimmed to the form of the vessel; fitted to fay against the back of the stem or apron on their fore edge and in the older type of vessel, kept far enough back to allow the bowsprit to pass without cutting into them much. The usual projecting ledge formed by the top of deck (mid-section, Fig. 18) is continued across the knighthead in a fair curve upwards. A rebate for the ends of the bulwark planking is worked at the aft end of the knighthead (see sketch, Fig. 38). The main rail is, of course, run along the top, and the knightheads are secured by means of blind bolts or banister bolts up through the deck, shelf, and breasthook, and by bolts driven endways through a bulwark stanchion fitted immediately abaft the chock. These large chocks serve the purpose of strengthening the bulwarks and stem head against the stresses caused by the bowsprit, mooring, anchoring, etc. Sometimes there is a hawse pipe or mooring ring fitted through them, usually there is a fairlead on the rail over, for mooring purposes, and often they carry other fittings such as eyebolts, cleats, etc. The name is derived from the old days of wooden ships, when they were in the form of vertical pieces fastened to the sides of the stem in line with the frame heads, forming side support for the bowsprit and an ending for the bulwark forward. See Fig. 39.

Hawse Pipes. Are usually of galvanized cast iron, or sometimes cast bronze, running from the deck, port and starboard, to the shell. They have a well-rounded flange at the outer end cast on, and the inner end is recessed into a separate cast deck slab. They form strong guides for the anchor cable and convenient stowages for anchors of the stockless type. They are used only in the cruising type of yacht of 40 to 50 tons and over and are discarded in favour of stemhead rollers on the small racing type of yacht, in the interests of weight saving.

Lloyd's Rules state that they should have an internal diameter of not less than twelve times the diameter of the cable. A sketch of a typical hawse pipe is given in Fig. 32.

Hawse pipes are most easily set off on the boat, rather than in the mould loft, by marking the centre at deck and shell and boring pilot holes. In order to mark the final holes in deck and shell, a rod may be lined up in the pilot holes and some form of compass arranged with the rod as centre. The final holes will be of a somewhat elliptical shape. See Fig. 40.

Fastenings. In post-war years rapid deterioration, of fastenings and timber around fastenings, has been experienced in some boats. This has been very noticeable with the combination of African mahogany planking on steel frames, with brass bolt fastenings. The wood discolours and deteriorates around the bolts, which in turn change structure and lose strength to such an extent that they will break off short if dropped. This has been put down to electrolytic action caused by the contact of dissimilar metals in the salt-water saturated timber. African mahogany and some other timbers have proved to be particularly susceptible to this danger, but teak and pitch pine are considered safe from it.

Brass wood screws have shown rapid deterioration also, even when not in contact with other metals, so that Lloyd's now require wood screws to be of gunmetal, bronze, etc.,

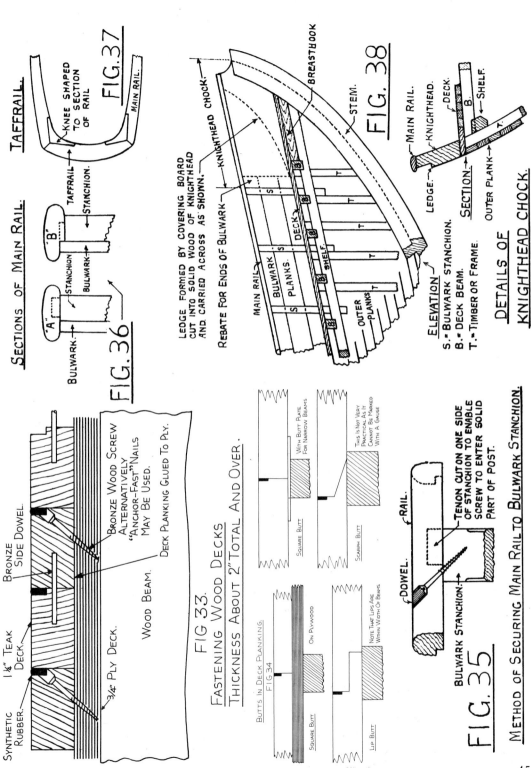

TAFFRAIL.

FIG.37

KNEE SHAPED TO SECTION OF RAIL.

MAIN RAIL.

SECTIONS OF MAIN RAIL.

"B"

TAFFRAIL.

STANCHION.

STANCHION.

BULWARK.

BULWARK.

"A"

STANCHION.

BULWARK.

FIG. 36

LEDGE FORMED BY COVERING BOARD CUT INTO SOLID WOOD OF KNIGHTHEAD AND CARRIED ACROSS AS SHOWN.

REBATE FOR ENDS OF BULWARK

KNIGHTHEAD CHOCK.

BREASTHOOK

STEM.

FIG. 38

MAIN RAIL.

BULWARK PLANKS.

DECK

SHELF.

OUTER PLANKS.

S.

B.

T.

MAIN RAIL.

KNIGHTHEAD.

DECK.

B.

SHELF.

OUTER PLANK.

LEDGE.

SECTION.

DETAILS OF KNIGHTHEAD CHOCK.

ELEVATION.

S. = BULWARK STANCHION.
B. = DECK BEAM.
T. = TIMBER OR FRAME.

SYNTHETIC RUBBER.

1¼" TEAK DECK.

BRONZE SIDE DOWEL.

BRONZE WOOD SCREW ALTERNATIVELY "ANCHOR-FAST" NAILS MAY BE USED.

DECK PLANKING GLUED TO PLY.

WOOD BEAM.

¾" PLY DECK.

FIG 33.

FASTENING WOOD DECKS.

THICKNESS ABOUT 2" TOTAL AND OVER.

WITH BUTT PLATE FOR NARROW BEAMS

SQUARE BUTT.

THIS IS NOT VERY PRACTICAL AS IT CANNOT BE MARKED WITH A GAUGE

SCARPH BUTT.

BUTTS IN DECK PLANKING. FIG 34

ON PLYWOOD

SQUARE BUTT.

NOTE THAT LIPS ARE WITHIN WIDTH OF BEAMS

LIP BUTT.

RAIL.

TENON CUT ON ONE SIDE OF STANCHION TO ENABLE SCREW TO ENTER SOLID PART OF POST.

DOWEL.

BULWARK STANCHION.

FIG. 35

METHOD OF SECURING MAIN RAIL TO BULWARK STANCHION.

45

when used as fastenings for main structural members. This has prompted manufacturers to produce silicon bronze wood screws as a stock item, specially for the boat-building trade. The sizes easily obtainable are, however, severely limited, so that in place of the larger screws, gunmetal dumps are sometimes resorted to. These, if properly bored for and driven, are very good, but must not be carelessly used or will result in splitting the planking. These occurrences have caused the disappearance of 'yellow metal' as a fastening material, which has always been of doubtful composition. They have caused the introduction in high-class yachts of galvanized mild steel fastenings through the outside planking, a practice hitherto reserved for the cheaper type of construction. They have also reaffirmed the value of teak as a material for planking, and there are examples of yachts with teak planking on steel frames, with naval brass fastenings, in first-class order after around thirty years of service.

In common with all other structures, the size and disposition of the fastenings play an all-important part in the strength of a vessel.

Lloyd's Rules state that fastenings may be of a suitable composition of the following materials:

Copper	Silicon bronze
Gunmetal	Aluminium bronze
Galvanized iron	Stainless steel
Galvanized steel	Monel

Through bolts are to be clenched on rings or washers or are to be fitted with nuts. Rings for washers are to be of the same material as the bolts. Short dump or nail fastenings are to be of the same sectional areas required for the bolt fastenings. Where bolt fastenings pass through the outside planking or centreline structure, suitable grommets are to be fitted under the heads.

Keel bolt and centreline fastening holes are to be treated with a suitable composition.

Copper through fastenings are to be clenched on rooves. When yachts are copper sheathed, no iron or steel fastenings are to be used in way.

The uses of the metals commonly met with may be roughly classified as follows:

Copper is used for through bolts which have to be clenched on rings.

Machining-quality bronze bolts are general when there is a nut each end or when the bolts are turned from solid.

Forging-quality bronze bolts are best kept to a minimum because of the danger of bad forging making the resultant bolts brittle, so this material should be used only when special heads are required, such as tee heads and bolts with bevelled heads which cannot conveniently be turned.

Galvanized iron and steel bolts are used as fastenings for steel frames, floors, knees, lead keels, etc.

Plank fastenings to frames may be either through or screw or a combination of these two. Care must be taken to ensure that each bolt is watertight around the head, so that it will not be a source of leakage, therefore a grommet of oakum and white lead must be placed under the head before driving in.

There are several types of head in common use, the type of bolt head being adapted for the purpose it is intended, and they may be roughly figured and described thus (see

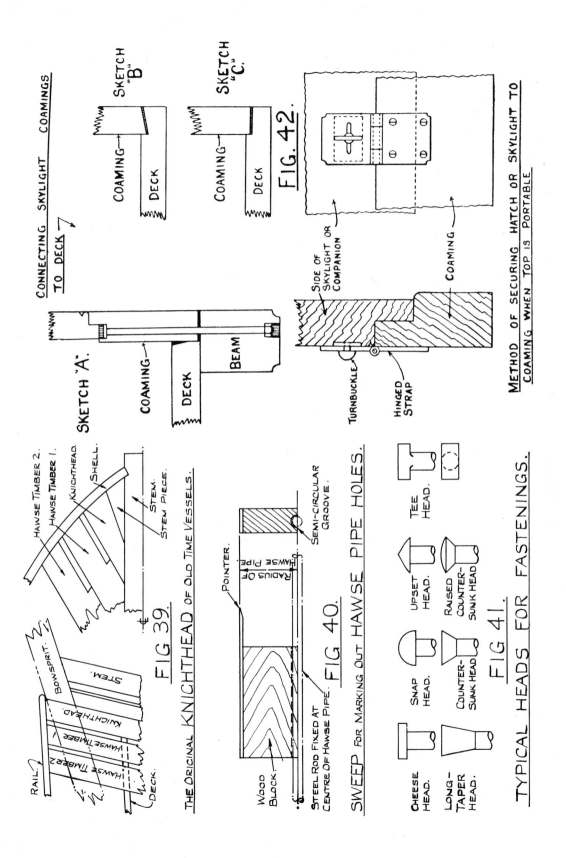

CONNECTING SKYLIGHT COAMINGS TO DECK

SKETCH "B"

COAMING

DECK

SKETCH "C"

COAMING

DECK

FIG. 42.

SKETCH "A".

COAMING

DECK

BEAM

SIDE OF SKYLIGHT OR COMPANION

COAMING

TURNBUCKLE

HINGED STRAP

METHOD OF SECURING HATCH OR SKYLIGHT TO COAMING WHEN TOP IS PORTABLE

HAWSE TIMBER 2.

HAWSE TIMBER 1.

KNIGHTHEAD.

SHELL.

STEM.

STEM PIECE.

RAIL.

BOWSPRIT.

STEM.

KNIGHTHEAD.

HAWSE TIMBER 1.

HAWSE TIMBER 2.

DECK.

FIG 39.

THE ORIGINAL KNIGHTHEAD OF OLD TIME VESSELS.

POINTER.

RADIUS OF HAWSE PIPE.

SEMI-CIRCULAR GROOVE.

WOOD BLOCK.

STEEL ROD FIXED AT CENTRE OF HAWSE PIPE.

FIG. 40.

SWEEP FOR MARKING OUT HAWSE PIPE HOLES.

TEE HEAD.

SNAP HEAD.

UPSET HEAD.

COUNTER-SUNK HEAD.

RAISED COUNTER-SUNK HEAD.

CHEESE HEAD.

LONG-TAPER HEAD.

FIG 41.

TYPICAL HEADS FOR FASTENINGS.

Fig. 41). 'Cheesehead' bolts are used for the outer planking and such bolts as are put through the vessel from outside. 'Tee head' bolts are used in narrow and confined parts, such as the front of the stem, where it is narrowed by the bearding.

Lead keel fastenings are best as screwed rod with a nut each end, as this avoids the necessity for forging. An upset head is used for blind bolts with a washer under heads and for bolts fastening deadwood, chocks inside the vessel, etc., whilst countersunk heads are generally used for fastening ironwork, knees, etc.

Four bolts are usually fitted in each arm of the floors, hanging knees, breasthooks and crutches. The bolts for these at the sides of a yacht must pass through the outside planking, and one should be near the throat, but not in it. There must be at least one through bolt in the shelves and the stringers at each frame up to 7 in. moulded and two over 7 in. moulded, and where steel frames are fitted the shelf and the stringers are to be attached to them by means of angle lugs or reverse bars.

The number of fastenings attaching the outside planking to the frames is laid down in a table based on the width and thickness of the planks.

Screw fastenings must enter the frames a distance equal to the thickness of plank as a minimum. Butt fastenings of outside planks must be not less than the diameter of the frame fastenings.

Skylights and Companions. Should be of teak throughout, in the robust type of cruising yacht, but in order to save weight in racing yachts mahogany or cedar is often used. They must be of strong construction, dovetailed at the corners and of substantial thickness. Shapes and sizes are innumerable and, of course, are regulated by the requirements of the vessel's accommodation, but the methods of constructing and fitting are more or less standardized and may be briefly described as follows. The foremost considerations are strength and watertightness, and with these points in view a stout coaming properly and efficiently fastened and bedded to the deck is most important. The best method, and that usually adopted in the best class of work, is to let the coamings down on to the beams and carlings and work the deck planking round them. This method is illustrated in sketch 'A' in Fig. 42, but an alternative method sometimes adopted in an indifferent class of work, or perhaps if a new skylight is to be fitted on an existing vessel, is to check the coaming into the deck planking as in sketch 'B', or to let it down into the deck about $\frac{3}{4}$ in., as in sketch 'C'.

An improved arrangement is to group the main deckhouse with as many hatches and skylights, etc. as practicable so that one nicely shaped structure takes the place of a number of small 'boxes' which appear to have been placed as an afterthought and tend to clutter the deck.

The coamings are fastened with bolts where possible (a common size is $\frac{3}{8}$ in. diameter and 15 in. pitch), but sometimes the fastenings are merely long wood screws up through the beams and carlings. Thickness of coaming should be about $\frac{1}{8}$ in. more than thickness of deck in small yachts. Before fastening the coamings care must be taken to see that they closely fit the deck or beams; thick white lead bedding is then applied to prevent any leakage and after being secured and fastened, and the deck margins fitted, they are lightly caulked and payed as the rest of the deck.

It is common practice to make the saloon skylight large enough to pass the fresh-water tanks, and the engine-room skylight to pass the engine, this greatly facilitates

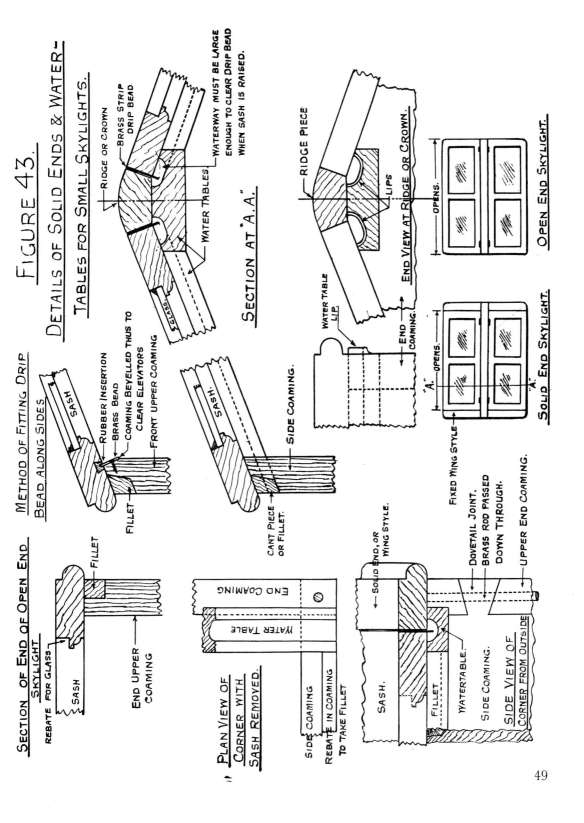

FIGURE 43.

DETAILS OF SOLID ENDS & WATER-
TABLES FOR SMALL SKYLIGHTS.

RIDGE OR CROWN
BRASS STRIP
DRIP BEAD
WATERWAY MUST BE LARGE
ENOUGH TO CLEAR DRIP BEAD
WHEN SASH IS RAISED.
WATER TABLES
GLASS.

SECTION AT "A.A."

RIDGE PIECE
LIPS
OPENS.
END VIEW AT RIDGE OR CROWN.
OPEN END SKYLIGHT.

WATER TABLE
LIP
END
COAMING.
"A"   OPENS.
"A"

METHOD OF FITTING DRIP
BEAD ALONG SIDES
SASH
RUBBER INSERTION
BRASS BEAD
COAMING BEVELLED THUS TO
CLEAR ELEVATORS
FRONT UPPER COAMING
FILLET

SASH.
SIDE COAMING.
CANT PIECE
OR FILLET.

FIXED WING STYLE
SOLID END SKYLIGHT.

SECTION OF END OF OPEN END
SKYLIGHT
REBATE FOR GLASS
SASH
FILLET
END UPPER
COAMING

PLAN VIEW OF
CORNER WITH
SASH REMOVED.
END COAMING
WATER TABLE
SIDE COAMING
REBATE IN COAMING
TO TAKE FILLET

SOLID END, OR
WING STYLE.
SASH.
FILLET
DOVETAIL JOINT,
BRASS ROD PASSED
DOWN THROUGH.
WATERTABLE.
SIDE COAMING.
UPPER END COAMING.
SIDE VIEW OF
CORNER FROM OUTSIDE

49

shipping. In this case the top must be made to lift off, and it is held down in the rebate of the coaming by a brass hasp and turn button (see sketch, Fig. 42).

In the larger cruising yachts and motor yachts there is nowadays a tendency to 'build in' engines under semi-portable hatches. This means that if an engine is required to be unshipped, there is a certain amount of work required to make the necessary deck openings. The advantage gained is that the deck over engines can be made flush and can therefore be used in the accommodation, or to provide a usable space on the weather deck. The choice can be stated clearly as on the one hand a hatch coaming of the type shown in Fig. 42 which permanently restricts deck space while providing an easily portable hatch. On the other hand the 'flush semi-portable' hatch provides a deck space which is available for constant use. The cost of removing engines with the latter type is reduced if carlings are built into the deck structure and piping and wiring are kept clear.

The watertightness of a skylight depends very largely upon the way in which the water-tables or gutters under the top sashes are worked. In this connection it should be mentioned that there are two methods in common use for fitting these sashes or flaps. One method is to make the hinged flaps project beyond the ends of the upper coaming, but the other, and better method, is to make fixed wing styles across the tops of the gable ends, making the flaps close between them, as shown by the sketch in Fig. 43. This makes a stiffer job of the skylight top and enables water-tables to be fitted on three sides of the flap.

The corners of both lower and upper coamings are dovetailed and they are generally secured by driving brass rod down through the dovetailed joint. The crown or ridge piece is a stout lengthwise member (see sketch, Fig. 43), which is shaped to show a presentable ridge, and carries the skylight sash hinges, and underneath the water-tables for the hinging edges of the sashes or flaps. These water-tables are carried through the end coamings, and terminate in small lips projecting beyond each end as shown in the sketch, Fig. 43. A point to notice here is that these gutters must be wide enough to clear the drip bead when the sash is raised, for, as will be observed from the sketch, the lower edge of the drip bead then describes a fairly large arc. Similar water-tables are fitted under the joints of sashes, and also under the ends of sashes when the solid end type of skylight is adopted. The drip beads consist of thin brass strips, well screwed to the edges of the sash flaps.

Along the fronts and across the ends of the sashes, where the open-end type is adopted, a wood fillet is secured which fits snugly into a rebate in the upper coaming when the sash is closed. In the best class of work this is further improved by fitting a brass bead to the coaming, which bites into a rubber insertion in the sash rail when the flap is closed. All these details are very clearly shown in the sketches given in Fig. 43.

Ordinary brass butts are generally employed for hinging small skylight sashes, but if the sash is very large and heavy, such as the engine-room skylights of large motor yachts, strap hinges should always be used, running right across the ridge piece and well down the styles of the sashes.

Skylight glazing may be carried out in a number of ways. For small boats Perspex is very suitable provided it is supported with sufficient wooden stiffeners on the underside and that the fact that it becomes semi-transparent can be accepted. Where ordinary plate glass is used it should be protected by round brass guard rods, brazed on to a flat

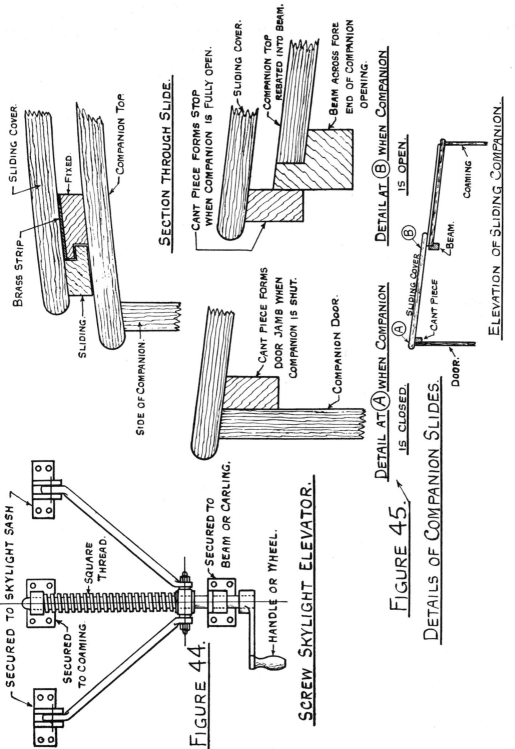

SECTION THROUGH SLIDE.

SLIDING COVER.

FIXED.

BRASS STRIP.

SLIDING.

COMPANION TOP.

SIDE OF COMPANION.

CANT PIECE FORMS STOP WHEN COMPANION IS FULLY OPEN.

SLIDING COVER.

COMPANION TOP REBATED INTO BEAM.

BEAM ACROSS FORE END OF COMPANION OPENING.

CANT PIECE FORMS DOOR JAMB WHEN COMPANION IS SHUT.

COMPANION DOOR.

DETAIL AT (A) WHEN COMPANION IS CLOSED.

DETAIL AT (B) WHEN COMPANION IS OPEN.

SLIDING COVER

CANT PIECE

(A)

(B)

BEAM.

COAMING.

DOOR.

ELEVATION OF SLIDING COMPANION.

FIGURE 45.

DETAILS OF COMPANION SLIDES.

SECURED TO SKYLIGHT SASH

SQUARE THREAD.

SECURED TO COAMING.

SECURED TO BEAM OR CARLING.

HANDLE OR WHEEL.

FIGURE 44.

SCREW SKYLIGHT ELEVATOR.

brass frame and secured in a readily portable fashion, to the wood sash. A better alternative is the use of armoured glass which avoids the necessity of fitting the brass guards. In order that the skylights may be operated from below, and to hold the sashes open when required, some form of skylight sash elevator is necessary. This may be simple and cheap, or elaborate and expensive; there is a multitude on the market to choose from. The shipyard is seldom called upon to make them for small yachts, but the keynotes of the choice made should be simplicity, strength and effectiveness, remembering that they have to hold down, as well as hold up. It is important that when the ordinary single-arm type of elevator is used one should be fitted at each end of each flap to avoid rocking if any weight is brought upon the open flap. For large yachts, where the skylights are large and the headroom great, a type of screw elevator is used which is very strong and effective. A sketch is given in Fig. 44. They are made of brass, and polished, or chromium plated to match the fittings of the room in which they are located.

The construction of companions and hatches is generally similar to skylights, except that a top and doors have to be provided in lieu of the sashes. The fixed, or standing part of a companion top is generally made with a good camber or round-up across its breadth, its length being straight and sloping down from the sliding opening. A sketch of the sliding cover is given in Fig. 45. It will be seen that rebated slides are fitted with a brass strip on top of the fixed slide for the cover to run on. Across the front of the sliding cover a cant piece is secured below, which forms a jamb for the doors when the cover is closed and a stop when it is open. When the companion is of reasonable height, hinged doors are fitted, usually double and rebating into each other, but very low companions often have only a shutter board fitting into grooves. Small hatches, such as those to forecastle or to sail room, have a flat, lift-off top, fitting in a rebate and secured by a locking bar and padlock. It is good practice to provide canvas covers and battening down arrangements for all skylights and companions.

Chocks under Deck. These are pieces of wood and in some cases flanged plates inserted between the beams under the deck planking to take holding down bolts and spread the load under the windlass, capstan, bollards, winches, cleats, dead-eyes and lead blocks, sheet tracks and blocks, rudder bearing, deck-mounted pumps, etc.

Having fitted the shelf, all the beams should be made, faired, and fixed in position, and then it is most important to set off all carlings for skylights and companionways, etc., and chocks required for the deck fittings and running gear, as mentioned above. If the beams are not buried flush in the shelf as in sketch 'A', Fig. 46, but only partially let in as sketch 'B', then chocks or eking pieces should be placed between to take runner blocks, bolts, eye bolts, or any other fastening through the shelf. In the case of chocks for capstan, bollards, or other fittings with an upward pull, the chock should be housed into the side of the beam and cut to gain from bottom, as shown in sketch 'C', Fig. 47, so that it will not pull up. Pump chocks, etc., may be fitted as shown in sketch 'D' in Fig. 47.

All carlings should be dovetailed into beams, usually on one side, and housed with shoulders square horizontally and plumb. See sketch 'E'. Good chocks should be provided under sheet winches, because these fittings often have a central spindle which heaves up with a nut under the deck in addition to their baseplate holding-down bolts and the pull on them is of a severe nature. A typical arrangement of deck is shown in Fig. 49, indicating the beams, half-beams and carlings, and chocks under various deck

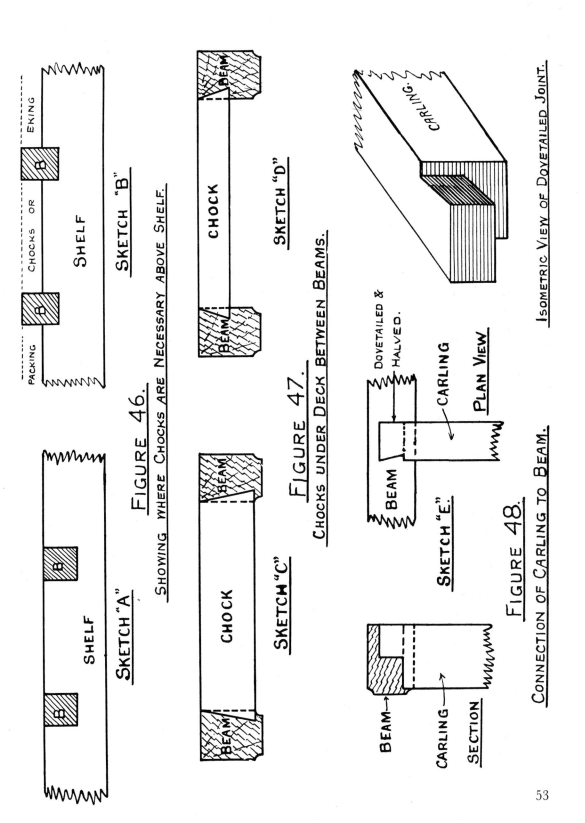

SHELF

B

B

SKETCH "A"

SHELF

PACKING

B

CHOCKS OR

B

EKING

SKETCH "B"

FIGURE 46.

SHOWING WHERE CHOCKS ARE NECESSARY ABOVE SHELF.

BEAM

CHOCK

BEAM

SKETCH "C"

BEAM

CHOCK

BEAM

SKETCH "D"

FIGURE 47.

CHOCKS UNDER DECK BETWEEN BEAMS.

DOVETAILED & HALVED.

BEAM

CARLING

PLAN VIEW

SKETCH "E".

BEAM

CARLING

SECTION

FIGURE 48.

CONNECTION OF CARLING TO BEAM.

CARLING.

ISOMETRIC VIEW OF DOVETAILED JOINT.

53

fittings, including those chocks along the middle line for taking the king plank and deck end fastenings, which are a necessity when the deck planks are laid parallel to the covering board.

Cabin Sole and Cabin Beams. The lower deck or cabin sole is a wood non-watertight flat, laid on wood beams of rectangular section, these cabin sole beams having no camber or round up. Cabin sole flat and beams are usually of red pine, Douglas fir, etc. According to Lloyd's Rules beams may be 60 per cent of the strength required for U.D. beams of same length, although in practice this cannot be taken advantage of fully with regard to size, as the fact that they are flat and not cambered also reduces their strength. The beams are spaced from 14 to 20 in. apart, dependent upon frame spacing and the thickness of the cabin flat itself, which, in small wooden yachts, varies from $\frac{3}{4}$ to $1\frac{1}{8}$ in., nearly always tongued and grooved. Struts under beams may be used to increase stiffness.

The actual size of beam should be commensurate with its length, a rough and ready rule being that the moulding or depth of beam should be $\frac{3}{8}$ in. for every foot of length for beams up to 10 ft. long, and that the siding should be two-thirds of the moulding. The ends of the beams are attached to the hull by being checked across, or butted against the frames, and screw-fastened. In the case of a vessel with steel frames and bent timbers between, the ends of the cabin sole beams should be bolted to the standing flange of the steel frames, and those beams which come in between may be checked over, and screw-fastened to a cant piece worked across the bent timbers. The cabin sole planks are screw-fastened to the beams from above, but where steel beams are fitted the screws are inserted from below.

Hatches in the cabin flat are very necessary, and should be ample in number to provide easy access to all parts of the space below the flat. In the type of vessel under notice the hatches are usually small, and simply rest in a rebate formed by the projecting edges of the adjacent end beams. In good-class work these hatches have a hard wood edge piece worked all round the opening as a safeguard against damage when getting gear up and down, but all yachts do not possess this refinement, and in some yachts the whole flat is in portable sections; but this practice, although it may be very convenient, is somewhat detrimental to the general strength and stiffness of the flooring. In the larger yachts there are sometimes long and wide hatches over the fresh-water tanks, etc., which require the cutting of several beams. These hatches should be properly framed out with carlings, and a rebate provided all round, and the hatch cover should be made in two or more parts if the size requires it. At one time it was usual to make the small hatch covers in grating form for ventilation purposes.

In every yacht there are a number of wooden bulkheads, partitions and fitments of different sorts which need attachment to the cabin sole. The most important of these is naturally the transverse division between the cabins, etc. There are several methods of connecting these, one being to fit a cant piece screwed to floor and to the bulkhead. Another method is to run the bulkhead down to the bottom of beam and screw it to the side thereof. This is obviously the thing to do when there is a difference in the floor level occurring at the bulkhead. Another method is to run the cabin bulkhead down on to the beam and connect it by screws 'steeved' or inserted in a slanting direction. The cabin flat is worked on each side of the bulkhead, requiring in some places, cants on the beams to support it.

54

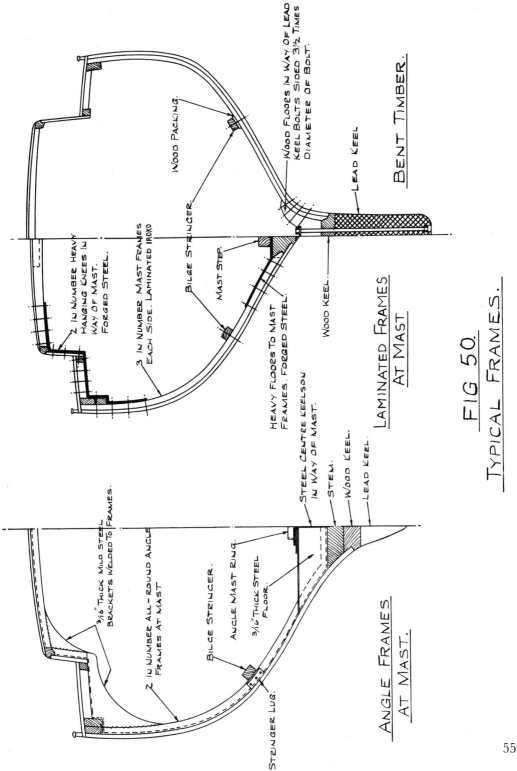

WOOD PACKING.

WOOD FLOORS IN WAY OF LEAD KEEL BOLTS SIDED 3½ TIMES DIAMETER OF BOLT.

LEAD KEEL.

BENT TIMBER.

2 IN NUMBER HEAVY HANGING KNEES IN WAY OF MAST. FORGED STEEL.

3 IN NUMBER MAST FRAMES EACH SIDE. LAMINATED IROKO

BILGE STRINGER.

MAST STEP.

HEAVY FLOORS TO MAST FRAMES. FORGED STEEL.

STEEL CENTRE KEELSON IN WAY OF MAST.

STEM.

WOOD KEEL.

LEAD KEEL.

WOOD KEEL.

LAMINATED FRAMES AT MAST

3/16" THICK MILD STEEL BRACKETS WELDED TO FRAMES.

2 IN NUMBER ALL-ROUND ANGLE FRAMES AT MAST.

BILGE STRINGER.

ANGLE MAST RING.

3/16" THICK STEEL FLOOR.

STRINGER LUG.

ANGLE FRAMES AT MAST.

FIG 50.

TYPICAL FRAMES.

55

Athwartship Stiffening. With the traditional type of construction, structural bulk-heads are not normally fitted for the size of vessel under notice, in fact they are not called for by Lloyd's until the length exceeds 50 ft. on the waterline and even then only definitely for full power yachts. The cabin bulkheads are not taken into account when assessing strength and it may be rightly argued that in some circumstances, such as the fibreglass construction mentioned later, it is a pity to have bulky wooden members and not use them for strength purposes. With the traditional type of construction, the bulk-heads although looking substantial are of necessity very poorly connected to the hull and are, of course, often required to be cut about, or moved completely, when a yacht is taken over by a new owner, with his own different ideas on accommodation. So it is safest to ignore them completely from the strength point of view, except for the specialized ultra-lightly built hulls.

Web frames are no longer called for by Lloyd's, in the wood yacht rules. Nevertheless athwartship stiffening must be provided in way of the pull of rigging and ballast keel. This may take the form of at least three special wood frames of increased dimensions each side, in way of the mast, with strong hanging knees attached to the mast beams at head and floors of increased size at heel. Similar special frames, etc., are fitted at each end of large deck openings such as in way of the raised coachroof. See Fig. 50. Alter-natively all-round angle frames of steel with plate floors and plate brackets at gunwale, galvanized after riveting or welding, results in a good job. See Fig. 50. There are dis-advantages with angle frames, however, and these are mainly that the bending and bevelling of angle frames and riveting or welding cannot be carried out by the average boatbuilding yard, also plate brackets intrude into the accommodation. With laminated wood frames and strap knees, the work may be carried out by boatbuilders and black-smiths and both of these trades are, of course, available at any boatyard. These frames usually provide stiffening in way of the ballast keel also, otherwise additional ones should be fitted.

In racing yachts where weight saving is made, which has a tendency to impair strength, one method used to reduce racking, due to the pull of rigging, is to carry the shrouds through the deck and attach the lower ends to the mast step or some convenient part of the structure adjacent to the heel of mast. This reduces racking, but the penalty is increased compression in the mast.

In yachts of fibreglass construction and plywood bulkheads, the bulkheads may be positively bonded to the hull to give transverse strength with great economy of weight.

Great care must be taken in stiffening the coachroof coaming, when the mast goes through the coachroof. The first sign of weakness here would be a 'working' between the coaming and deck with resulting leaks at sides of coachroof and this could only be remedied permanently by fitting the necessary stiffening as indicated in Fig. 50.

56

Chapter 3

Engine Seating   ·   Anchor Arrangements
Mast Partners and Steps   ·   Chain Plates
Davits   .   Cavils and Pin Rails
Stern Chocks or Archboards

Engine Seating. Small sailing yachts of the cruising type are usually auxiliary, being fitted with a petrol or Diesel engine. The engine is usually fitted well aft in a single-screw yacht, just forward of the sternpost. Various other arrangements have been tried, especially in the 30 to 100 ton range; when positioned well forward clear of the best part of the accommodation amidships, the length and run of shafting is so impractical that it is hardly worth consideration unless there are special accommodation requirements.

The actual arrangement of the seating depends upon the requirements of the engine, with regard to such features as width of bedplate, diameter of flywheel, depth of bolting face below centre of shaft, depth of crankcase or sump, etc., but generally speaking the principal points to observe are:

(1) The seating must be perfectly rigid in every direction; to ensure this in the vertical direction the seating must have a reasonable depth and be properly stiffened. The seating must be properly supported transversely by means of suitable floors if it is of steel, or by transverse bearers and iron knees if of wood. The seating should extend well forward and aft beyond the ends of the engine in order to distribute the weight and stresses set up by the thrust and the working of the engine itself. Above all, the engine seating must be properly secured to the adjacent framing and shell.

(2) Clearances and heights must be properly provided for. For instance, in some engines the flywheel projects beyond the bedplate and requires clearance in the fore and aft members. In other engines there might be a particularly deep crankcase, in which case the transverse members between the fore and afters require to be kept low enough to clear it: or perhaps the reverse gear bearing face is at a higher or lower level than the bearing face of the engine proper, and a step is required in the seating: or there may be projecting pipes or pumps, and so forth *ad nauseam*.

(3) Accessibility to all parts is extremely desirable although not always perfectly attainable. A save-all tray should be fitted under the engine to keep waste oil out of the bilges. If a steel seating is employed with transverse floors bolted against oak frames, a strip of teak or painted felt should be worked between, because oak contains gallic acid, which corrodes steel or iron. If the engine seating is to be constructed of wood, then oak or teak are, of course, the best materials, but with low-powered motors of the short compact type, a pine seating is quite good practice, provided the scantlings used are sufficient and the fastenings good.

Anchor Arrangements. The number and weight of anchors together with the size and quantity of cable, hawsers and warps are laid down in Lloyd's Rules based on the Equipment Numeral which is derived from the dimensions of the yacht with additions for erections such as deckhouses.

The chain locker is generally located under the cabin sole and consists of a boarded off space of sufficient capacity to take the cable. If there are two anchors, and two lengths of cable are used, there should be a division in the locker between the two lengths, and each length should be secured to a stout eyeplate strongly secured in the locker to which the inboard end of the cable is shackled.

There are two main methods in use for handling anchors and cables on cruising yachts.

(a) By hand direct or using a hand operated windlass, with the chain running over a roller at the stemhead. This method is limited to anchors light enough to lift on to the deck by hand for stowing.

(b) With heavier anchors using a power operated windlass with either a hydraulic or an electric motor to haul the anchors into the hawsepipes for stowing. See Fig. 32. This limits the choice of anchor to stockless of which there are several types including some of high holding power requiring to be less heavy than the traditional stockless pattern.

A third method superseded in new construction by (b) is using a 'cathead'. It is still seen on some sailing yachts of the thirties and as many of these are in excellent condition, the method may be worth recording. Briefly it consists of a fixed davit which overhangs the ship's side. See Fig. 60. The anchor is raised clear of the water by hand or mechanical means and the hooked cat block is attached to the anchors 'gravity band'. The anchor is then raised to the 'cathead' using a tackle, ready for quick releasing. The anchor is stowed on the deck and may be handled using the jib halliards.

In the event of stockless anchors being used, stowed in hawse pipes, it is usual to fit some form of cable compressor, a screw stopper, or a devil's claw, to hold the anchor up in the pipe. A compressor is also useful as an auxiliary means of holding the cable when riding at anchor, but owing to its small baseplate, it is obviously inferior to the windlass for this purpose. The cable compressor, or 'bow stopper', as it is often called, is fitted between the windlass and the hawse pipe, with the cable passing over it and operates by having a movable top block shaped to the form of the links, which can be raised or lowered by means of a handle. When lowered the shoulders of the block catch the end of one of the links, and so stop the cable. The dead nip so caused must not, of course, be applied when the cable is running out. Screw stoppers consist of a stout eyeplate, with a short length of chain, with a screw and slip attached. The slip can be fitted round a link of the cable, and the anchor boused home with the screw. A devil's claw consists of a screw generally attached to an eyebolt through the windlass bedplate, with two claws which grip round the shoulders of one of the cable links.

Mast Partners and Steps. Masts require to be well supported, both in the vertical and transverse direction. Vertically, in addition to the weight of the mast itself, there is the enormous thrust caused by the setting up of the rigging by means of screws, winches and tackles. Laterally there is the stress caused by the action of the wind upon the sails; stresses set up by the movements of the vessel, particularly when rolling, and the pulls

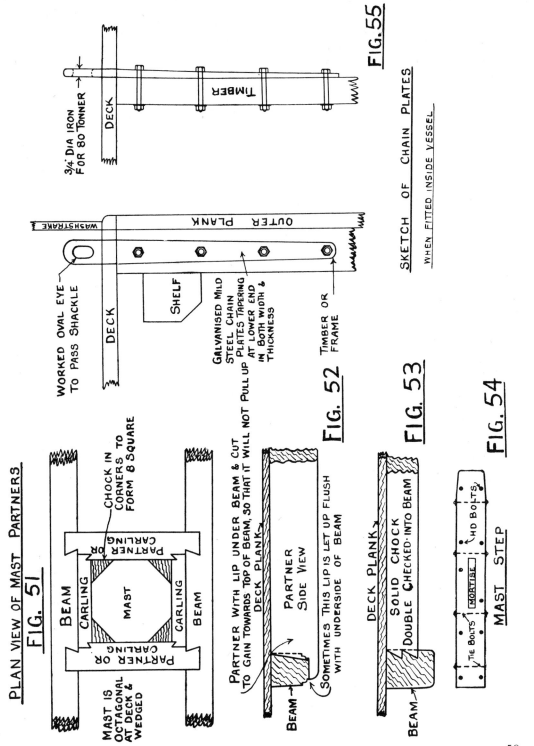

PLAN VIEW OF MAST PARTNERS

FIG. 51

BEAM

CHOCK IN CORNERS TO FORM 8 SQUARE

PARTNER OR CARLING

CARLING

MAST

CARLING

BEAM

PARTNER OR CARLING

BEAM

BEAM

MAST IS OCTAGONAL AT DECK & WEDGED

PARTNER WITH LIP UNDER BEAM & CUT TO GAIN TOWARDS TOP OF BEAM, SO THAT IT WILL NOT PULL UP

DECK PLANK

PARTNER SIDE VIEW

BEAM

SOMETIMES THIS LIP IS LET UP FLUSH WITH UNDERSIDE OF BEAM

FIG. 52

DECK PLANK

SOLID CHOCK DOUBLE CHECKED INTO BEAM

BEAM

FIG. 53

TIE BOLTS

MORTISE

HD BOLTS

MAST STEP

FIG. 54

WORKED OVAL EYE TO PASS SHACKLE

WASHSTRAKE

DECK

OUTER PLANK

SHELF

GALVANISED MILD STEEL CHAIN PLATES TAPERING AT LOWER END IN BOTH WIDTH & THICKNESS

TIMBER OR FRAME

3/4" DIA IRON FOR 80 TONNER

DECK

TIMBER

FIG. 55

SKETCH OF CHAIN PLATES

WHEN FITTED INSIDE VESSEL

59

of various tackles and winches around the mast used in working the sails. Usually, before and abaft the mast, a particularly stout beam is worked called the 'mast beam'; the mast partners are fitted in the form of carlings or fore and afters between the beams on either side of the mast. This frames out a space of same shape as the mast, but larger (sketch, Fig. 51), which is filled in solid in a suitable manner, leaving a space for the mast and its wedging. The whole assemblage is usually made of oak or teak, and there are several different methods of construction (Figs. 51, 52 and 53), but the purpose of all is to support the mast against the great lateral stresses caused when sailing; to provide a good foundation for the various eyebolts, hooks, mast bitts, and other gear at the base of the mast and a bearing surface for the wedges around the mast, which are caulked and sometimes canvas coated to make the hole watertight. Rubber is sometimes fitted here, in place of the wedges together with a watertight mast coat.

In the type of vessel under notice a mast step is placed in the keel, or on a platform built for the purpose, or on the deck on which the mast is stepped. In small sailing vessels the mast usually steps on the keel; the step consists of a large solid piece of oak or teak, well bolted down to the keel and tie bolted across to keep it firm and prevent it from splitting (see Fig. 54). The step should be a fair length so as to spread out the weight of the mast, and if it is near a keel scarph, it should overrun the scarph by a foot or so. A tenon is formed on the heel of the mast which fits into a mortise cut in the step (see sketch Fig. 54). It should be noted that the mortise in the step should be an inch or two longer than the tenon to allow adjustment in the rake of the mast. The tenon is to prevent turning and when the rake is adjusted the mast is wedged into the mortise to prevent further movement. See Fig. 49 for a typical steel mast step.

Chain Plates. These are made of galvanized steel, or sometimes, in racing yachts, for the sake of lightness, of high tensile steel as smaller scantlings may then be used. A typical method is to fit the chain plates inside the ship, bolted to the timbers or frames, with the oval eye just projecting above the covering board in the manner shown by the typical sketch in Fig. 55. Galvanized steel bolts may be used for fastening these chain plates. In order to suit the spacing of the shrouds, backstays, etc., it is sometimes necessary to fit a special short length of timber to accommodate the chain plate.

Davits. These must be galvanized if made of wrought iron or forged steel. Forged steel makes a lighter davit, because the safe stress on material may be taken at 6 tons per sq. in. of section, whereas for wrought iron it is only 4 tons. Davits of N.E. 6 or N.E. 8 aluminium extrusions can show a weight saving. These are best combined with Tufnol or nylon bearings and gavanized steel sockets. See Fig. 56. The span, or distance between davits, the outreach or overhang, height and diameter of the davits are, of course, directly dependent upon the size and weight of the boat to be handled, but the type in general use are the old-fashioned, round, turning davits, as practically all the later and improved types of davit are unsuitable for sailing yachts, being too heavy and bulky, occupying much more space than can be spared.

Davits are generally placed outboard (see sketch in Fig. 57) but sometimes they may be seen inside the rail, or even through the rail, but note here that outboard is the best position for the following reasons: (1) It keeps the deck and rail clear. (2) They are more easily and efficiently supported. (3) They throw the boat further off the vessel's side for a

BOAT DAVITS & SOCKETS

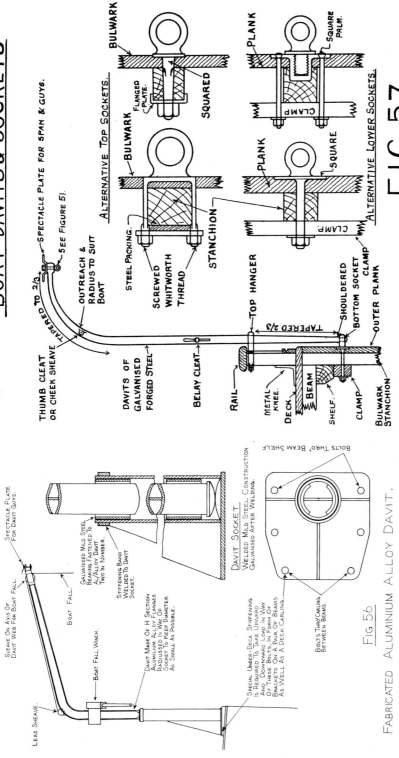

FIG.57

ALTERNATIVE TOP SOCKETS.

- BULWARK
- BULWARK
- FLANGED PLATE.
- SQUARED
- STEEL PACKING.
- SCREWED WHITWORTH THREAD
- STANCHION

ALTERNATIVE LOWER SOCKETS.

- PLANK
- SQUARE PALM.
- PLANK
- CLAMP
- SQUARE
- CLAMP

- SPECTACLE PLATE FOR SPAN & GUYS.
- SEE FIGURE 51.
- OUTREACH & RADIUS TO SUIT BOAT
- TAPERED TO 2/3
- THUMB CLEAT OR CHEEK SHEAVE
- DAVITS OF GALVANISED FORGED STEEL
- BELAY CLEAT.
- TOP HANGER
- TAPERED 2/3
- SHOULDERED
- BOTTOM SOCKET
- CLAMP
- OUTER PLANK
- RAIL.
- METAL KNEE.
- DECK
- BEAM
- SHELF.
- CLAMP
- BULWARK STANCHION

- SPECTACLE PLATE FOR DAVIT GUYS.
- SLEEVE ON AXIS OF DAVIT WEB FOR BOAT FALL.
- BOAT FALL.
- BOAT FALL WINCH.
- GALVANISED MILD STEEL BEARING FASTENED TO AL/ALLOY DAVIT TWO IN NUMBER.
- STIFFENING BAND WELDED TO DAVIT SOCKET.
- DAVIT MADE OF H SECTION ALUMINIUM ALLOY FLANGES RADIUSSED IN WAY OF SOCKET TO KEEP DIAMETER AS SMALL AS POSSIBLE.
- LEAD SHEAVE.
- SPECIAL UNDER-DECK STIFFENING IS REQUIRED TO TAKE UPWARD AND DOWNWARD LOAD IN WAY OF THESE BOLTS. IN FORM OF BRACKETS ON A PAIR OF BEAMS AS WELL AS A DECK CARLING.

DAVIT SOCKET
WELDED MILD STEEL CONSTRUCTION GALVANISED AFTER WELDING.

- BOLTS THRO' BEAM SHELF.
- BOLTS THRO' CARLING BETWEEN BEAMS.

FIG 56

FABRICATED ALUMINIUM ALLOY DAVIT.

61

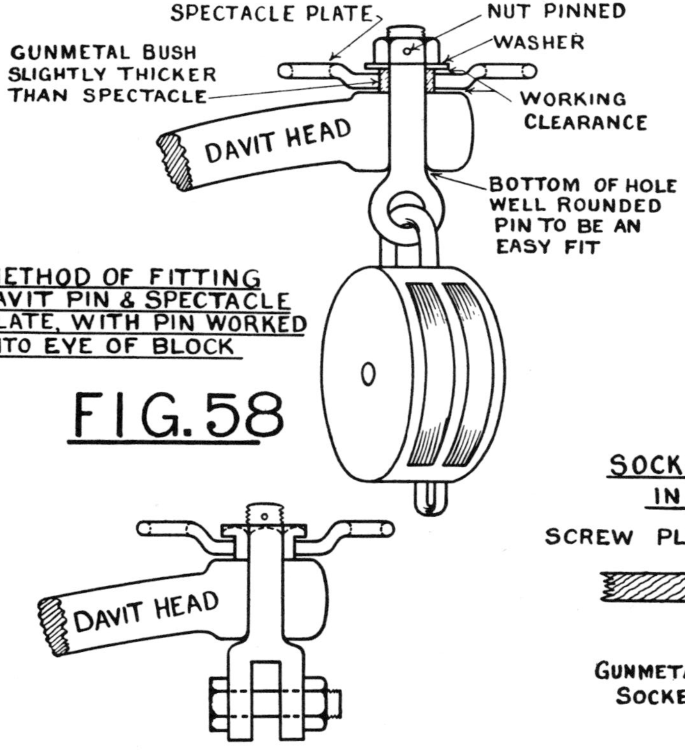

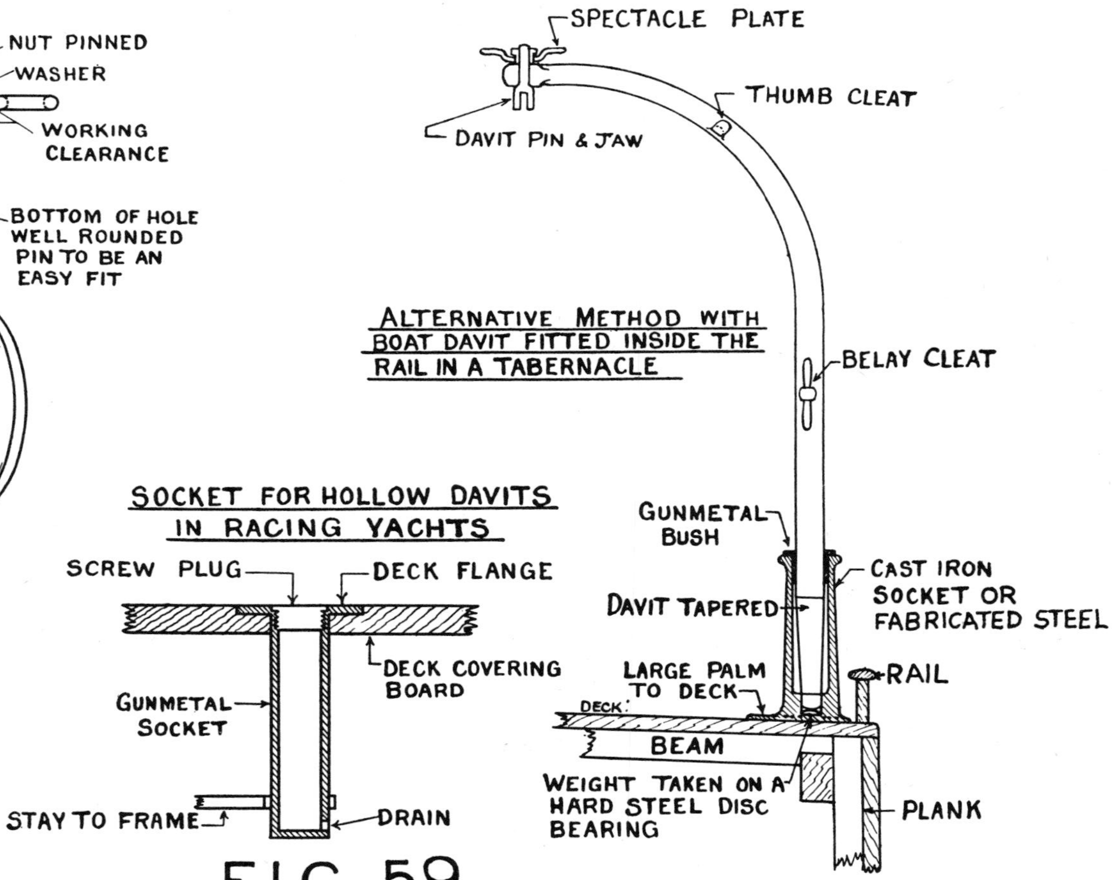

SPECTACLE PLATE

THUMB CLEAT

SPECTACLE PIN & JAW

BELAY CLEAT

CAST IRON SOCKET OR FABRICATED STEEL

RAIL

PLANK

GUNMETAL BUSH

DAVIT TAPERED

LARGE PALM TO DECK

DECK

BEAM

WEIGHT TAKEN ON A HARD STEEL DISC BEARING

ALTERNATIVE METHOD WITH BOAT DAVIT FITTED INSIDE THE RAIL IN A TABERNACLE

SOCKET FOR HOLLOW DAVITS IN RACING YACHTS

DECK FLANGE

DECK COVERING BOARD

SCREW PLUG

DRAIN

GUNMETAL SOCKET

STAY TO FRAME

FIG.59

NUT PINNED

WASHER

WORKING CLEARANCE

BOTTOM OF HOLE WELL ROUNDED PIN TO BE AN EASY FIT

SPECTACLE PLATE

GUNMETAL BUSH SLIGHTLY THICKER THAN SPECTACLE

DAVIT HEAD

METHOD OF FITTING DAVIT PIN & SPECTACLE PLATE WITH PIN WORKED INTO EYE OF BLOCK

FIG.58

DAVIT HEAD

ALTERNATIVE METHOD WITH DAVIT JAW & SHAPED NUT TO TAKE SPECTACLE PLATE

given outreach. (4) They keep the boat, when lowered on deck, snugger to the rail for a given outreach, and so encumber the deck less. (5) They are more easily kept clear of rigging and tackles. A sketch of a typical davit and its supports is given in Fig. 57. Notice that the principal stress caused by the load comes on the davit at the top hanger; in order to support this properly the davit must be fitted on a bulwark stanchion of enlarged dimensions (see p. 41). The bottom socket which takes the weight should have a large flat palm let into the outer planking. Sometimes these sockets are made to unscrew, in which case a large circular palm is provided, let into the outer plank with a boss of suitable depth behind, with a tapped hole to take the portable lower socket. The whole is secured with four bolts through plank and shelf, and a screw plug provided for insertion in the hole when the lower socket is not shipped. The davit pin, spectacle plate and upper fall block should be fitted in the manner shown in the sketch (Fig. 58), a style which gives every satisfaction in service, the worked eyes giving much more working latitude than the more usual davit pin jaws. The pin should be of generous diameter and the blocks large to prevent wet ropes binding in the score.

Davits for racing yachts are often made hollow in order to save weight. In this case they are made of galvanized steel steam tube, of a diameter sufficient to withstand the bending moment, with solid forged steel ends; there is no taper. The sockets are metal castings in the form of a tube with the lower end closed (see sketch Fig. 59) into which the davit ships, bearing on the bottom. A broad deck flange is provided and a screw deck plug for closing the top when the davits are removed. These sockets are fitted down through the covering board and are arranged to come behind the lining or in cupboards, if possible. The bottom of socket should be stayed to an adjacent frame, and a drain plug be provided. A method with a deck socket or tabernacle is also shown in Fig. 59.

An absolutely amazing fact is the number of small yachts with davits entirely unsuitable in arrangement and size for the boats carried under them. Common faults are insufficient diameter or too much height, resulting in very springy davits, not enough outreach or span (i.e., davits too close together), causing the boat's gunwale to scrape round the davit and making the handling of the boat hard and difficult work. These faults are due to insufficient attention to the task of setting out the boats and davits to scale, on paper, to determine the dimensions and to strength calculations being neglected.

Cavils and Pin Rails. This type of fitting is not now needed to such an extent as it used to be, due to the use of individual halyard winches with integral stowage reels. Where used they are commonly made of teak, well varnished, but sometimes the pin rails are of galvanized iron, whilst greenheart often finds favour for cavils and cleats. Cavils, pin rails, cleats, fife rails and mast bitts are all fitted for the purpose of belaying the various ropes necessary for working the sails and the ship, and may be roughly classified thus:

Cavils are long pieces of wood of rectangular section, with the ends worked into suitable rounded shapes for belaying (see Fig. 61), and with a suitable number of belaying pins fitted in conveniently spaced holes along their length. The cavils are fitted on the inside of the bulwark stanchions, to which they are bolted, and are placed wherever there is much belaying to be done, such as aft in way of the main or mizzen sheets and warps where it is quite common to extend the margin planks of a low poop to form cavils. They are also fitted at the sides of and slightly abaft masts, and forward near the catheads.

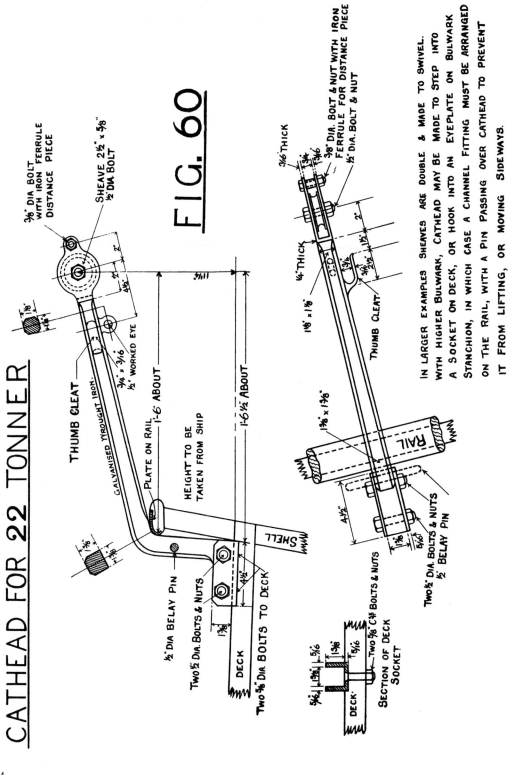

CATHEAD FOR 22 TONNER

FIG. 60

³⁄₈" DIA BOLT WITH IRON FERRULE DISTANCE PIECE

SHEAVE 2½" x ⅝"
½" DIA. BOLT

THUMB CLEAT

GALVANISED WROUGHT IRON.

¾" x ³⁄₁₆"
½" WORKED EYE

PLATE ON RAIL

HEIGHT TO BE TAKEN FROM SHIP

1-6" ABOUT

1-6½" ABOUT

2"
2"
4½"

⅞"
1½"

1⅛"
1⅜"

½" DIA BELAY PIN

TWO ½" DIA. BOLTS & NUTS

TWO ⅝" DIA BOLTS TO DECK

SHELL

DECK

4½"
1⅜"

SECTION OF DECK SOCKET.

⅝"
1⅜"
1⅜" 1¾"
⅝"

DECK

TWO ⅝" C# BOLTS & NUTS

³⁄₁₆" THICK

³⁄₈" DIA. BOLT & NUT WITH IRON FERRULE FOR DISTANCE PIECE
½" DIA. BOLT & NUT

1¾"
¾"

2"
1½"

¼" THICK

1⅜" x 1¾"

1¾" x 1⅜"

THUMB CLEAT

RAIL

4½"

1⅜"
⅝"

TWO ½" DIA. BOLTS & NUTS
½" BELAY PIN

IN LARGER EXAMPLES SHEAVES ARE DOUBLE & MADE TO SWIVEL.
WITH HIGHER BULWARK, CATHEAD MAY BE MADE TO STEP INTO
A SOCKET ON DECK, OR HOOK INTO AN EYEPLATE ON BULWARK
STANCHION, IN WHICH CASE A CHANNEL FITTING MUST BE ARRANGED
ON THE RAIL, WITH A PIN PASSING OVER CATHEAD TO PREVENT
IT FROM LIFTING, OR MOVING SIDEWAYS.

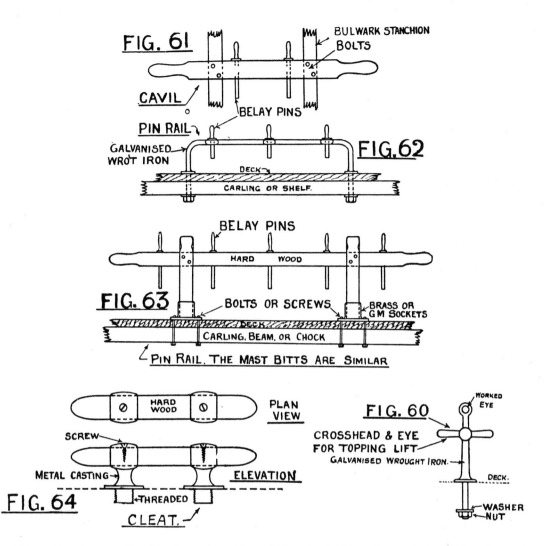

FIG. 61

BULWARK STANCHION
BOLTS

CAVIL

BELAY PINS

PIN RAIL

GALVANISED
WRO'T IRON

DECK

CARLING OR SHELF.

FIG. 62

BELAY PINS

HARD WOOD

FIG. 63

BOLTS OR SCREWS

BRASS OR
G M SOCKETS

DECK

CARLING. BEAM. OR CHOCK

PIN RAIL. THE MAST BITTS ARE SIMILAR

HARD
WOOD

PLAN
VIEW

SCREW

METAL CASTING

ELEVATION

FIG. 64

THREADED

CLEAT.

WORKED
EYE

FIG. 60

CROSSHEAD & EYE
FOR TOPPING LIFT
GALVANISED WROUGHT IRON.

DECK.

WASHER
NUT

Pin rails are usually fitted at the sides of the deck, just clear of the bulwarks and abreast of the masts, for the purpose of belaying the halyards, etc., of light sails carried aloft, consequently, with the bermudian rig, pin rails are not required. They are made in a variety of ways, sometimes of galvanized forged iron, with palms to the deck, and a suitable number of balls forged in the horizontal member to take the belaying pins (see sketch, Fig. 62). Vertical supports should be stayed if necessary. Sometimes it is preferred to make pin rails of teak or greenheart, in which case they are constructed in a manner similar to the sketch in Fig. 63, and fitted into metal sockets well bolted to the deck. It is usual to fit an eye in the after end to take the standing part of the topping lift purchase.

Cleats are fitted at various positions about the deck for special belaying purposes, such as for the main, fore and mizzen sheets, the headsail sheets, runner and preventer tackles, etc. Cleats may be made of wood, galvanized iron, or gunmetal, and they are sometimes made so that they may be readily taken away if desired in order to leave the deck clear of obstruction. Two threaded metal sockets are let into the deck, flush, and well fastened down, with screwcaps to fit. These caps may be taken out, and two metal castings screwed in (see sketch, Fig. 64), through which is passed a well-rounded oval rod of teak or greenheart, held in by two screws, so forming the cleat. These cleats should stand in line with the deck planking.

Belaying pins, consisting of straight G.M. rods are fitted horizontally through the bulwark stanchions clear of the cavils and pin rails for odd belaying. Fife rails are not usually met with in small vessels. They are massive pin rails fitted on deck round the foot of mast, and are mainly required in square-rigged vessels, for belaying the multitude of lifts, halyards, tyes, leech, clew, and bunt lines peculiar to this rig. A fitting often met with in the class of vessel here described is a topping lift crosshead (sketch in Fig. 65), which comprises an eye for the standing part of the lift, and a cleat for belaying the running part. Where pin rails are fitted, this is sometimes embodied at the after end of the rails.

Stern Chocks or Archboards. In a wood vessel of the type with a long fine counter, see Fig. 49, the stern chock is the solid piece of wood at the extreme after end of the counter and is a very intricate and necessary piece of work. It is usually made of teak, and in external form, of course, it has to conform to the lines of the yacht. Its purpose is to provide a solid attachment for the terminations of the deck planking, outside planking, bulwarks and rail, where the vessel becomes too small and fine to admit any other method but a solid chock being used. It is generally built up of two or three pieces of clean-grained teak, well glued and bolted together and securely fastened to the stern timber. It is rabbeted below to receive the hood ends of the bottom planking and above to take the deck plank ends, and on the sides to take the ends of the bulwark planking. Its top surface is hollowed, to fair out the deck up to the taffrail if necessary.

The stern chock is generally extended forward to the last bulwark stanchion and has the same moulding as the stanchion. This extension may be solid with the chock, or it may be an extension piece, tenoned or halved into the main chock as shown in the sketch, Fig. 67. The usual projecting ledge formed by the covering board is continued across the chock in a fair curve upwards, and if necessary, combined with the rebate for the bulwark plank ends. The main rail and taffrail is run along the top, of course, and the stern timber and shelves are let into the chock, which is secured, apart from deck and outer plank fastenings, by being bolted to the stern timber, and the two shelves with their crutch knees, and by bolts driven endways through the bulwark stanchion immediately forward of the chock. This stern chock is often referred to as the 'archboard', and it makes a neat, strong and practical way of finishing the long fine counter often embodied in the design of small wooden yachts.

Amongst the fittings which sometimes come on the stern chock may be mentioned fairleads, permanent preventers, or possibly a bumpkin, sheet horse, ensign staff, etc. The method of laying off and developing the stern chock is shown in Fig. 66, where the information given out by the mould loft is also indicated. In yachts with a short, wide counter, where there is more space, a transom can be fitted, to which the plank ends are screwed.

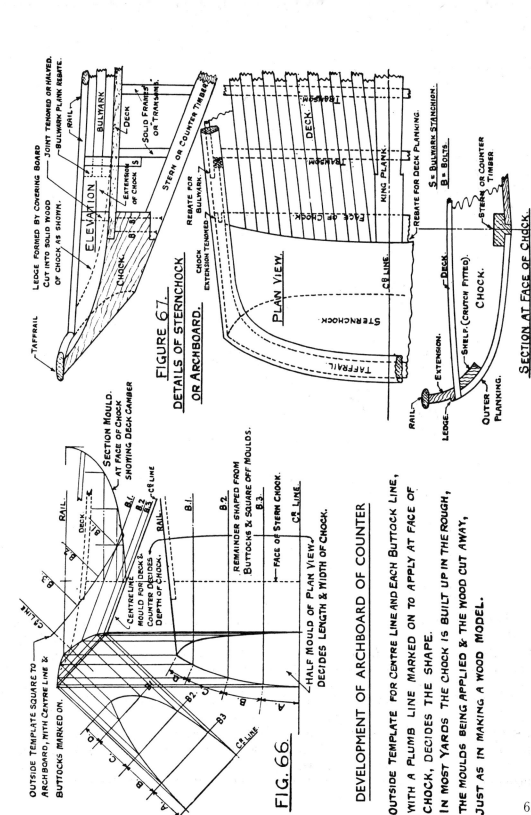

TAFFRAIL.

LEDGE FORMED BY COVERING BOARD
CUT INTO SOLID WOOD
AS SHOWN.

JOINT TENONED OR HALVED.

BULWARK PLANK REBATE.

RAIL.

BULWARK.

DECK.

SOLID FRAMES
OR TRANSOM.

ELEVATION.

EXTENSION
OF CHOCK. S

CHOCK.

B. B.

STERN OR COUNTER TIMBER.

TRANSOM.

DECK.

TRANSOM.

KING PLANK.

REBATE FOR DECK PLANKING.

S = BULWARK STANCHION.
B = BOLTS.

REBATE FOR
BULWARK.

CHOCK
EXTENSION TENONED.

PLAN VIEW.

FACE OF CHOCK.

STERNCHOCK.

C⃪ LINE.

TAFFRAIL.

FIGURE 67.
DETAILS OF STERNCHOCK,
OR ARCHBOARD.

RAIL.

EXTENSION.

SHELF. (CRUTCH FITTED).

CHOCK.

DECK.

STERN OR COUNTER
TIMBER.

OUTER
PLANKING.

SECTION AT FACE OF CHOCK.

OUTSIDE TEMPLATE SQUARE TO
ARCHBOARD, WITH CENTRE LINE &
BUTTOCKS MARKED ON.

SECTION MOULD.
AT FACE OF CHOCK
SHOWING DECK CAMBER.

RAIL.

DECK.

C⃪ LINE.

B.I.

B.2.
B.3.

B.I.

B.2.

B.3.

CENTRE LINE.

MOULD FOR DECK &
COUNTER DECIDES
DEPTH OF CHOCK.

RAIL.

C⃪ LINE.

C⃪ LINE.

REMAINDER SHAPED FROM
BUTTOCKS & SQUARE OFF MOULDS.

FACE OF STERN CHOCK.

HALF MOULD OF PLAN VIEW.
DECIDES LENGTH & WIDTH OF CHOCK.

B.2.

B.3.

C⃪ LINE.

FIG. 66.

DEVELOPMENT OF ARCHBOARD OF COUNTER

OUTSIDE TEMPLATE FOR CENTRE LINE AND EACH BUTTOCK LINE,
WITH A PLUMB LINE MARKED ON TO APPLY AT FACE OF
CHOCK, DECIDES THE SHAPE.
IN MOST YARDS THE CHOCK IS BUILT UP IN THE ROUGH,
THE MOULDS BEING APPLIED & THE WOOD CUT AWAY,
JUST AS IN MAKING A WOOD MODEL.

67

Chapter 4

Masts and Fittings. The modern style is to build the complete mast of aircraft quality spruce or aluminium alloy. The separate pieces of timber are scarphed together using resin glue.

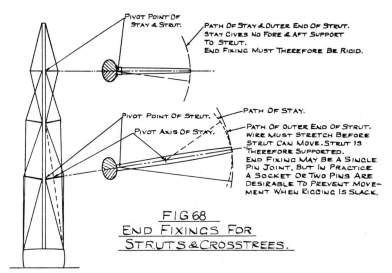

FIG 68
END FIXINGS FOR
STRUTS & CROSSTREES.

Aluminium alloy masts, especially extruded ones, are very good. They may be tapered by cutting a 'vee' out in the longitudinal direction and welding up, but with the masthead rig, that is headsails as well as mainsail running to the masthead, extra stiffness is required at the top, so no taper is given. Wood masts are sometimes made octagonal from the step up to just above the wedging at weather deck, above which the mast is round or streamlined, and in small yachts with bermudian sails, the section of mast is often as shown by Fig. 70. This section of mast is also often made hollow. A modern version for ocean racing yachts is clearly shown by Fig. 71. The thickness of the walls of a hollow mast should be about one-fifth of the diameter, or if not round, one-fifth of the max. diameter. The diameter of a mast is dependent upon the righting moment of the boat and the rig. Notice that the duty of the mast, and the way in which

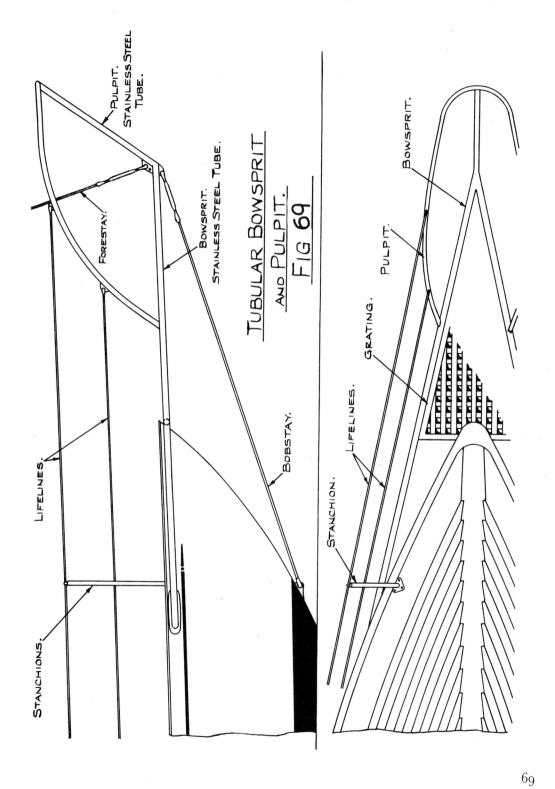

PULPIT. STAINLESS STEEL TUBE.

FORESTAY.

BOWSPRIT. STAINLESS STEEL TUBE.

LIFELINES.

STANCHIONS.

BOBSTAY.

TUBULAR BOWSPRIT.
AND PULPIT.
FIG 69

BOWSPRIT.

PULPIT.

GRATING.

LIFELINES.

STANCHION.

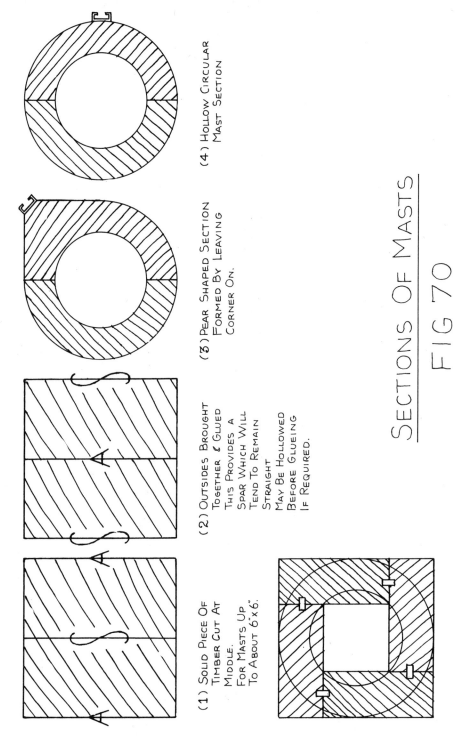

(1) Solid Piece Of
Timber Cut At
Middle.
For Masts Up
To About 6"x 6".

(2) Outsides Brought
Together & Glued
This Provides A
Spar Which Will
Tend To Remain
Straight
May Be Hollowed
Before Glueing
If Required.

(3) Pear Shaped Section
Formed By Leaving
Corner On.

(4) Hollow Circular
Mast Section.

Hollow Construction
Method Using Four
Pieces Of Timber Recommended
For Timber Economy.

Sections Of Masts

FIG 70

70

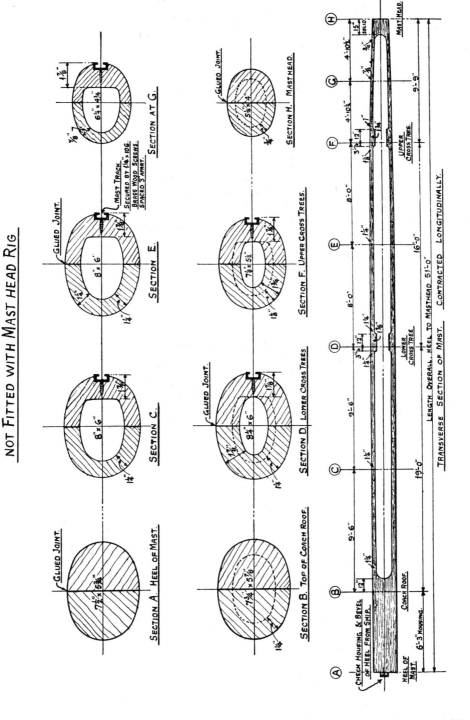

Figure No. 71

Details of Mast Construction for an Auxy. Sloop of about 11 Tons

Not Fitted with Mast Head Rig

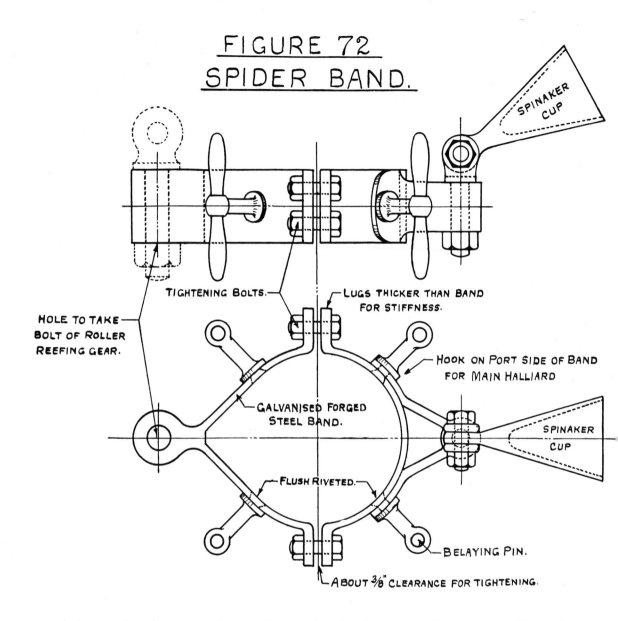

FIGURE 72
SPIDER BAND.

SPINAKER CUP

TIGHTENING BOLTS.

LUGS THICKER THAN BAND FOR STIFFNESS.

HOLE TO TAKE BOLT OF ROLLER REEFING GEAR.

HOOK ON PORT SIDE OF BAND FOR MAIN HALLIARD

GALVANISED FORGED STEEL BAND.

SPINAKER CUP

FLUSH RIVETED.

BELAYING PIN.

ABOUT 3/8" CLEARANCE FOR TIGHTENING.

it is stayed and supported naturally require that its largest diameter should be about midway between the deck and the lower crosstrees, above and below which it may be tapered down. A graph of the proportions of masts is given at the end of this book. When stepped, masts are usually set to an inclination aft, or rake. This rake varies with the rig, usual figures being $\frac{3}{8}$ in. per ft. for a ketch, $\frac{1}{2}$ in. per ft. for a schooner, and $\frac{1}{8}$ in. per ft. for a bermudian sloop rig.

Some short distance above the deck (dependent upon the layout of the vessel) there may be a 'spider' band, generally of galvanized wrought iron (see sketch, Fig. 72) which carries a suitable number of belaying pins and halyard hooks (these may be dispensed

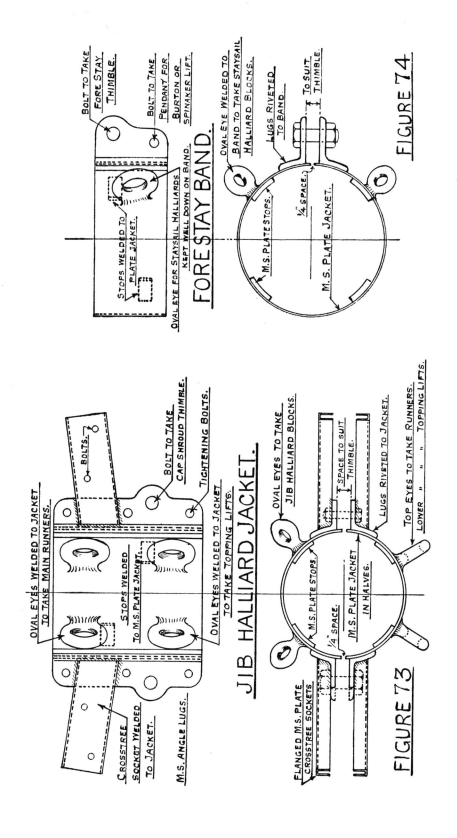

FORE STAY BAND.

BOLT TO TAKE FORE STAY THIMBLE.

BOLT TO TAKE PENDANT FOR BURTON OR SPINAKER LIFT.

STOPS WELDED TO PLATE JACKET.

OVAL EYE FOR STAYSAIL HALLIARDS KEPT WELL DOWN ON BAND.

OVAL EYE WELDED TO BAND TO TAKE STAYSAIL HALLIARD BLOCKS.

LUGS RIVETED TO BAND.

TO SUIT THIMBLE.

¼" SPACE.

M.S. PLATE STOPS.

M.S. PLATE JACKET.

FIGURE 74

JIB HALLIARD JACKET.

OVAL EYES WELDED TO JACKET TO TAKE MAIN RUNNERS.

BOLTS.

BOLT TO TAKE CAP SHROUD THIMBLE.

TIGHTENING BOLTS.

STOPS WELDED TO M.S. PLATE JACKET.

OVAL EYES WELDED TO JACKET TO TAKE TOPPING LIFTS.

CROSSTREE SOCKET WELDED TO JACKET.

M.S. ANGLE LUGS.

OVAL EYES TO TAKE JIB HALLIARD BLOCKS.

SPACE TO SUIT THIMBLE.

LUGS RIVETED TO JACKET.

TOP EYES TO TAKE RUNNERS.

LOWER " " TOPPING LIFTS.

M.S. PLATE STOPS.

¼" SPACE.

M.S. PLATE JACKET IN HALVES.

FLANGED M.S. PLATE CROSSTREE SOCKETS.

FIGURE 73

73

with when halyard winches are fitted), and also the gooseneck fitting or swivel for the inboard end of the boom. On the main mast of schooners a crutch for the fore boom is sometimes fitted here.

Mast mountings, by which term is meant all the various iron and steel bands, hoops and funnels necessary on a mast to attach and carry all the standing and running rigging, spars, etc., vary in such a vast and amazing manner that it will only be possible to describe them in general terms.

It is indeed surprising to reflect that during the very many years in which many thousands of small sailing yachts have been built, some standard of uniformity was not attained in this important matter, until recent years when with aluminium alloy masts at least this is to some extent being achieved because a small number of specialized firms are producing many hundreds of them.

Masts for Bermudian Rig. The jackets for the rigging are more or less equally divided along the length of the mast (see Figs. 77 and 78) and the whole of the rigging is secured to eyes, or between lugs on the jackets (in some racing yachts, for the sake of lightness, jackets and bands are largely replaced by light steel tangs, screwed to the mast, thickened up in way of the shackle eyes), to allow the track to have a clear run for the sail hanks to pass. Crosstrees are placed on each jacket, sometimes two or three sets, according to the size of the yacht, and the height of the mast.

At the top is a fitting with tangs, for eyes as required by the rig, which include jumper stays, masthead shrouds, backstay and boom topping lift and a sheave for the flag halyard, see Fig. 76. The mast jackets are generally made in halves, of light galvanized plate flanged or with vertical angle lugs riveted on, which form the joint when bolted together. The upper ends of the standing rigging (shrouds, cap shrouds, forestay, etc.) are worked with hearts or thimbles, which are shut between these angle lugs, or double tangs, and a large bolt passed through. The crosstree sockets are made of light galvanized steel plate, flanged and bent to the necessary shape and riveted and welded to the jacket. The other necessary eyes for runners, halyards, lifts, etc., are forgings riveted to the jacket; oval eyes with large palms and a good number of small rivets, but the more modern practice is to simply bend a piece of round iron to the required oval size, and weld it direct to the jacket without a palm. Stops should be welded or riveted inside the jacket, consisting of small rectangular pieces of iron, which, being let into the wood of the mast when fitted, prevent the jacket from pulling down under the tension of the shrouds, halyards, etc. A sketch of typical mast jackets is given in Figs. 73, 74, 75 and 76.

For some years now there has been a growing tendency on the smaller yachts, in order to lessen the weight aloft, to abandon the old style of forged steel mast bands in favour of much lighter fabricated mast jackets of very thin steel plate, relying more upon welded tangs to accommodate the various stays, shrouds, halyards, etc. Typical examples are shown by Fig. 75 and 76. Notice the projection on the masthead fitting to carry the standing preventer clear of the mainsail headboard, also the through bolts for the main halyard sheave, and for the shroud tangs. The jackets proper are made to conform to whatever shape is adopted for the mast section. All of these mast mountings should, of course, be galvanized.

Under the deck, at the foot of mast, it is necessary to fit pillars and stays, to transmit

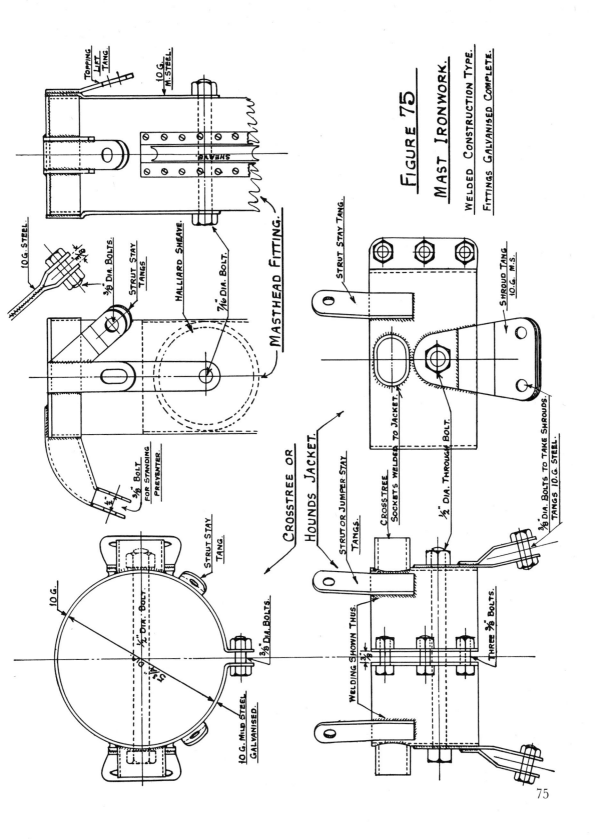

TOPPING
LIFT
TANG.

10 G.
M. STEEL.

10 G. STEEL

3/8 DIA. BOLTS.

STRUT STAY
TANGS

HALLIARD SHEAVE.

7/16 DIA. BOLT.

3/8 BOLT
FOR STANDING
PREVENTER

1/2"

STRUT STAY
TANG.

10 G.

1/2" DIA. BOLT.

3/8 DIA. BOLTS.

10 G. MILD STEEL
GALVANISED.

MASTHEAD FITTING.

CROSSTREE OR
HOUNDS JACKET.

STRUT STAY TANG.

SHROUD TANG
10 G. M.S.

CROSSTREE
SOCKETS WELDED TO JACKET.

1/2" DIA. THROUGH BOLT.

3/8 DIA. BOLTS TO TAKE SHROUDS.
TANGS 10 G. STEEL.

THREE 3/8 BOLTS.

STRUT OR JUMPER STAY
TANGS.

WELDING SHOWN THUS.

FIGURE 75

MAST IRONWORK.

WELDED CONSTRUCTION TYPE.

FITTINGS GALVANISED COMPLETE.

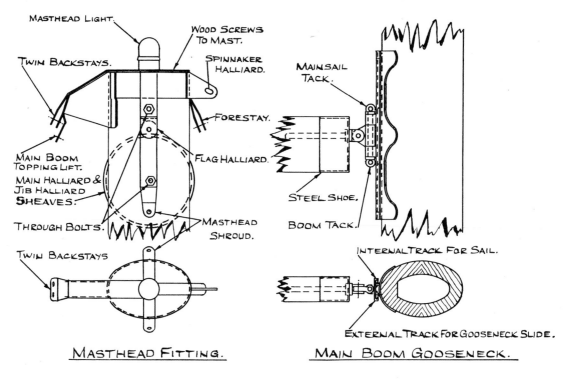

MASTHEAD LIGHT.
WOOD SCREWS TO MAST.
SPINNAKER HALLIARD.
TWIN BACKSTAYS.
FORESTAY.
MAIN BOOM TOPPING LIFT.
FLAG HALLIARD.
MAIN HALLIARD & JIB HALLIARD SHEAVES.
THROUGH BOLTS.
MASTHEAD SHROUD.
TWIN BACKSTAYS

MASTHEAD FITTING.

MAINSAIL TACK.
STEEL SHOE.
BOOM TACK.
INTERNAL TRACK FOR SAIL.
EXTERNAL TRACK FOR GOOSENECK SLIDE.

MAIN BOOM GOOSENECK.

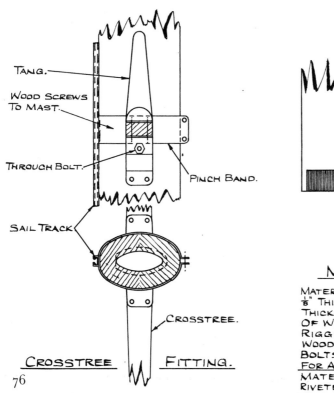

TANG.
WOOD SCREWS TO MAST.
THROUGH BOLT.
PINCH BAND.
SAIL TRACK.
CROSSTREE.

CROSSTREE FITTING.

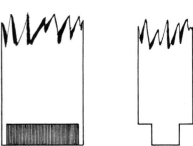

HEEL TENON.

FIG 76.
MAST FITTINGS.

MATERIAL, GALVANISED MILD STEEL $\frac{1}{8}$" THICK.
THICKENED LOCALLY BY MEANS OF WELDED DISCS IN WAY OF RIGGING PINS.
WOOD SCREWS TO MAST & THROUGH BOLTS AS INDICATED.
FOR ALUMINIUM ALLOY MASTS, MATERIAL, STAINLESS STEEL.
RIVETED TO MAST.
THROUGH BOLTS RETAINED.

76

the pull of the principal halyards from the deck to something more solid, and a very common practice is to fit a Y-headed pillar under the halyard or tackle eyes, diagonally across to a stout iron band on the mast, which places the mast in compression, so relieving the deck of a large part of the stress. With reel-on halyard winches, these pillars become unnecessary.

Masthead Rig. The essence of this rig is its simplicity, although the fittings, especially at the masthead, are somewhat complex. Runners are not used and are replaced by twin standing backstays from masthead to the quarters, clear of the boom. See Fig. 78.

At the masthead, provision must be made for twin backstays, boom topping lift, masthead shrouds, flag-halyard sheave, forestay with spinnaker-halyard eye above, a sheave for the main halyard and another for the jib halyard. These two sheaves may be angled, so that the main halyard groove is on the centre line at the aft side and the jib halyard groove on the centre line at the fore side.

At the crosstrees provision is made for shrouds, in the form of forked tangs. On the crosstrees at the lower shrouds, provision may be required for signal halyards, the spinnaker lift and floodlights for the deck. Below this a track is required for the spinnaker boom slider. The main boom gooseneck fitting often includes a track on the mast for taking down and may be fitted with a roller reefing gear.

The mast heel fitting with aluminium alloy masts, which takes the full mast thrust, may be a wooden plug with a tenon worked on, or better still a casting riveted to the mast.

The masthead and crosstree fittings should have a bolt passed right through them and the mast, to take the main load.

The fittings shown in Fig. 76 suit wood or aluminium alloy masts, except that with the latter the bands on the crosstree fittings may be eliminated and rivets are used instead of wood screws; galvanized steel fittings are used for wooden masts and stainless steel for aluminium alloy ones. Special care must be taken to ensure that the tangs are thickened in way of the standing rigging timble pins, to suit the bearing load. It is very important that the two sides of fork tangs are symmetrical about the centre line of wire, see Fig. 76, so that equal loading is taken in each tang. If the arrangement is one side straight and the other side knuckled, all of the load will be taken on the straight side only and the pin will be in single shear instead of double, giving only half strength.

Wooden masts of the type shown in Fig. 71 have been very successful in practice. Hollow, with a glued joint on the athwartship centre line, walls thickened in way of mast bands and track, solid in the heel with a tenon cut on.

Extruded aluminium alloy masts of streamlined or elliptical section are formidable rivals to the wooden construction.

Standing Rigging. Comprises that part of the rigging whose function it is to stay or support the masts, etc. against the various stresses to which they are subjected. In the type of vessel under notice the standing rigging is made of plough steel wire or stainless steel. The wires from which plough steel ropes are made have a tensile strength of about 100 tons per sq. in. The rigging must, of course, be galvanized. Stainless steel is a modern improvement.

The importance of spread has been recognized from early times, and it was once common practice to secure the maximum spread by setting up the shrouds on to

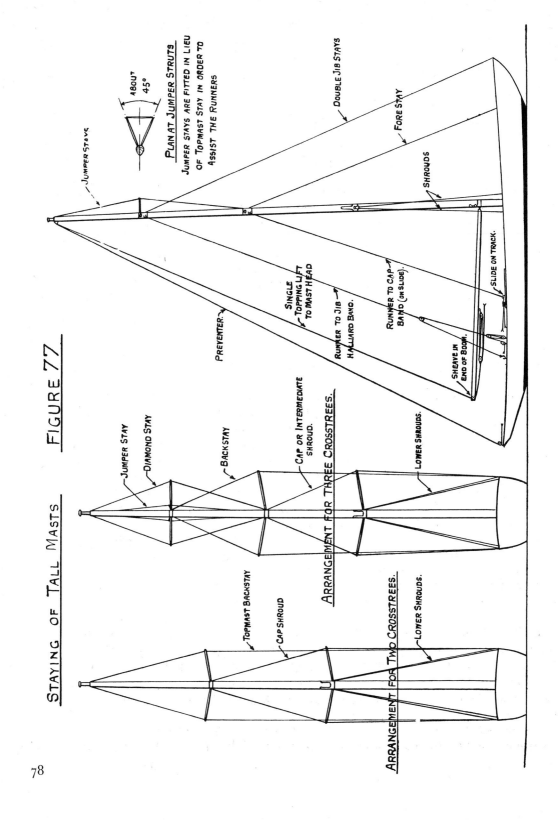

STAYING OF TALL MASTS   FIGURE 77

PLAN AT JUMPER STRUTS
JUMPER STAYS ARE FITTED IN LIEU
OF TOPMAST STAY IN ORDER TO
ASSIST THE RUNNERS

ABOUT 45°

JUMPER STAYS

DOUBLE JIB STAYS

FORE STAY

SHROUDS

PREVENTER.

SINGLE
TOPPING LIFT
TO MAST HEAD

RUNNER TO JIB
HALLIARD BAND.

RUNNER TO CAP
BAND (ON SLIDE).

SLIDE ON TRACK.

SHEAVE IN
END OF BOOM.

JUMPER STAY

DIAMOND STAY

BACKSTAY

CAP OR INTERMEDIATE
SHROUD.

LOWER SHROUDS.

ARRANGEMENT FOR THREE CROSSTREES.

TOPMAST BACKSTAY

CAP SHROUD

LOWER SHROUDS.

ARRANGEMENT FOR TWO CROSSTREES.

projecting platforms called 'channels' outside the hull, but now, with stronger materials available and vessels of greater breadth proportions, channels are seldom used.

Standing rigging is useless unless it is set up very taut and kept taut; and in order to ensure and facilitate this, rigging or stretching screws are used. These consist of a threaded body or bottle, carrying two screwed ends, with right- and left-handed threads, terminating in a double jaw, an oval worked eye, or a drilled eye, as may be required to suit the particular attachment. A turn or two with a tommy bar or a spanner will tighten or slacken the screw rapidly and efficiently, owing to the opposite threads. In yachts the body is often made of polished gunmetal with galvanized steel screws and ends, but a modern tendency is to use stainless steel or monel metal for the whole of the fitting. Tensile strength of screw under the thread must approximate to the strength of the wire.

Very tall masts require to be stayed on a girder principle, i.e. the stays must be spread out by means of spreaders or 'crosstrees', which serve the double purpose of giving the necessary spread or angle to the upper part of the stay, and supporting the mast at the crosstree by the resultant push caused by the tension on the stay (see Fig. 77).

All vessels require these crosstrees for the masthead shrouds and they are usually made of American or Canadian elm or aluminium alloy. One method is to set up the masthead shroud and the intermediate shroud on two eyes close together in the chainplate, the intermediate shrouds being in line with the centre of mast and the masthead shrouds being aft. The masthead shroud being carried in a scotchman at the outer end, and the intermediate shroud in a slot at the centre, or at a given length from the mast. Sometimes this is a fitting on the side of the crosstree; small wire lifts are sometimes fitted to the crosstrees to prevent them from tripping should a man stand on them when aloft.

A rough and ready rule to determine the size of rigging is that the strength of the standing rigging on one side should be enough to lift the displacement of the vessel.*

The bobstay, where fitted, is the strongest piece of standing rigging in the ship, with the forestay next in size, followed by the main (or lower) shrouds, intermediate shrouds and runner pendants all the same size, then the masthead shrouds, topmast forestay and backstay. The differences in size are most pronounced in the larger vessels, say 200 tons or so, and in the smallest yachts tend to round up into a smaller number of different sizes. In schooners the triatic stay is about the same size as the lower shrouds, or a trifle larger.

The adoption of masthead rig (see Fig. 78) in order to set large Genoa jibs, creates a heavier loading at the masthead and increased rigging sizes here are therefore required. For the comparatively small type of yacht to which this book applies, all of the standing rigging is often the same size, except that at the masthead. In modern practice with bermudian sails the tendency is to have short booms and employ double backstays set up permanently with rigging screws, at the quarters on the stern. Notice that with standing backstays clearance must be provided for a reasonable amount of lift on the outer end of the boom when coming about (see Fig. 77). Sometimes, in order to attain this with a single backstay a bumkin is fitted, which, of course, must be stayed down under the counter. Double forestays are often fitted for convenience in changing headsails. Care should be taken to keep them far enough apart for the sail hanks to clear. Where a mast is exceptionally high 'diamond stays' are frequently fitted, to avoid having too many

*A graph of standing rigging sizes is given at the end of this book.

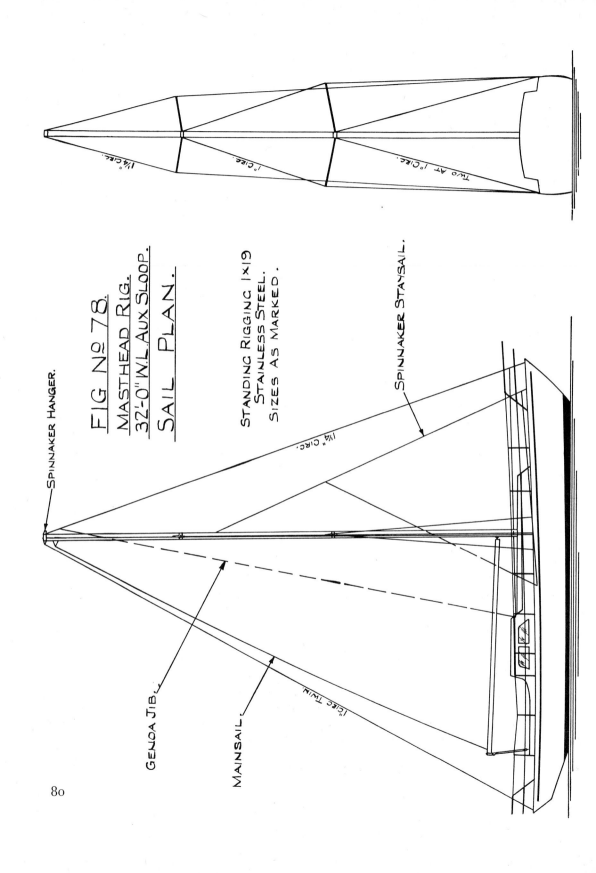

FIG No 78.
MASTHEAD RIG.
32'-0" W.L. AUX SLOOP.
SAIL PLAN.

STANDING RIGGING 1×19
STAINLESS STEEL.
SIZES AS MARKED.

SPINNAKER HANGER.

SPINNAKER STAYSAIL.

GENOA JIB.

MAINSAIL.

80

stays coming down to the deck. Jumper stays are also fitted in place of the topmast forestay when a spinnaker is to be set below the masthead.

Running Rigging. Comprises all the various tackles, purchases and falls required for the convenient working of the sails, spars, boats, etc., in fact, all wires, ropes, or line which are movable, or 'running'. Lloyd's Rules merely require that all masts, spars and rigging be in good order, and sails in sufficient number and in good condition; consequently the rig and the materials of the rigging are usually at the discretion of the owner, designer, or the skipper. Where great strength is required rather than extreme flexibility, such as for topping, lifts, halyard whips, sheet pendants, runner and preventer tackles, staysail tack, etc., flexible steel wire rope is used, galvanized of course, and having six strands of nineteen wires each (6 × 19).

This wire has a tensile strength of about 90 tons per sq. in. of the steel employed and will run reasonably well round sheaves $4\frac{1}{2}$ times the circumference of the rope. Where greater flexibility is required rope is used, either Italian hemp or Terylene; the latter is more flexible than hemp and is therefore used for most running and sundry purposes and is the stronger. Coir rope is made from the tough, fibrous husk of the coconut, and may be used for heavy towlines, fenders, etc. Sisal is a cheaper substitute.

It is hardly necessary to point out that the sizes used, and the strength of the various ropes required, depend entirely on the size and rig of the vessel and the purpose for which she is built. Assume as an example a yacht of about thirty tons, built for cruising. If rigged as a gaff cutter, her sails and spars would be on the whole larger and heavier than if rigged as a ketch or schooner; a bermudian rig in either case makes the rigging lighter due to the absence of the heavy gaff and its accompanying halyards, blocks, etc., and to the easy running of the sails on mast tracks, etc.

Owners, designers, etc. over the years develop special running rigging arrangements, such as that for spinnakers, etc., together with various mechanical fittings. Inevitably the successful ones are adopted as standard equipment, such as small sheet winches, runner levers or tracks, sheet tracks, gates in mast tracks, spinnaker slides, etc., and descriptions can only be attempted in very general terms. A series of sketches is given in Figs. 79, 80, 81 and 82, of the principal running rigging and fittings for a typical bermudian yacht. See Fig 112 for a halyard winch with wire stowage drum. In Figs. 83, 85, and 86 are various sketches of boom rigging. A long detailed description is unnecessary, as the sketches speak for themselves, but notice a few points in these sketches where variations often occur.

The halyard for a flying jib needs a winch with a very powerful purchase, because when the jib is set flying, i.e., is not on a stay, and there is no tack tackle the sail can only be tautened by the halyard. Runner purchase is fitted with a lever to take in the slack, instead of blocks and tackle, and jib and staysail sheets on a deck track, in line with the sheet, with a movable hank or slider which can be pinned in any desired position. The combination of upper and lower runners to one tackle, although very convenient in many cases, is not really the best practice, because it is very difficult to get both parts equally taut. It is better if possible to have a standing backstay as described on p. 79; for larger vessels the old idea of separate runners is still good practice.

In schooners the topping lift for the fore boom is often suspended from the main mast, in which case it must be attached to boom end, and only a single lift need be fitted, also

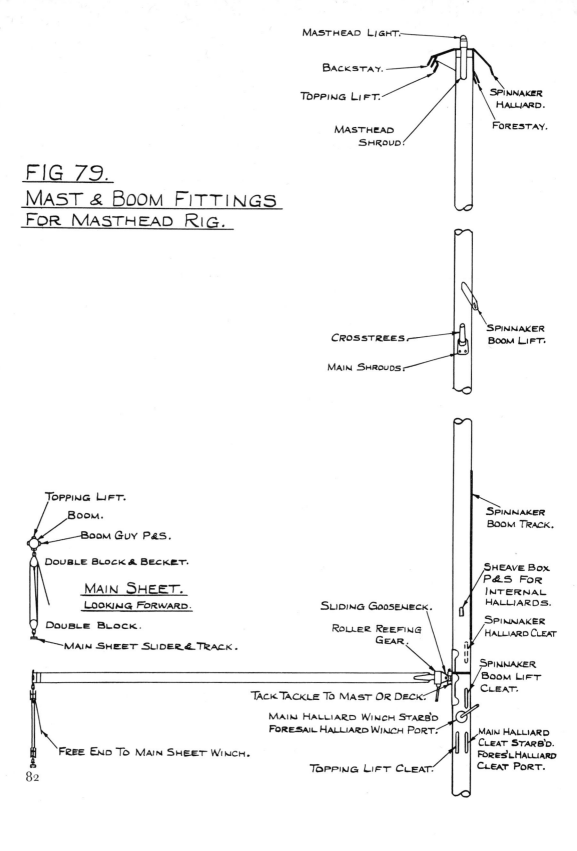

MASTHEAD LIGHT.

BACKSTAY.

TOPPING LIFT.

SPINNAKER HALLIARD.

MASTHEAD SHROUD.

FORESTAY.

FIG 79.
MAST & BOOM FITTINGS
FOR MASTHEAD RIG.

CROSSTREES.

SPINNAKER BOOM LIFT.

MAIN SHROUDS.

TOPPING LIFT.

BOOM.

BOOM GUY P&S.

DOUBLE BLOCK & BECKET.

MAIN SHEET.
LOOKING FORWARD.

DOUBLE BLOCK.

MAIN SHEET SLIDER & TRACK.

SPINNAKER BOOM TRACK.

SHEAVE BOX P&S FOR INTERNAL HALLIARDS.

SLIDING GOOSENECK.

ROLLER REEFING GEAR.

SPINNAKER HALLIARD CLEAT

SPINNAKER BOOM LIFT CLEAT.

TACK TACKLE TO MAST OR DECK.

MAIN HALLIARD WINCH STARB'D FORESAIL HALLIARD WINCH PORT.

FREE END TO MAIN SHEET WINCH.

TOPPING LIFT CLEAT.

MAIN HALLIARD CLEAT STARB'D. FORES'L HALLIARD CLEAT PORT.

82

FIG 80.
TYPICAL DECK PLAN
FOR THE OCEAN RACER.

① FAIRLEAD P&S.
② EYEPLATE FOR SPINNAKER SHEET (OR BOOM AFTER GUY) P&S.
③ BACKSTAY DECK PLATE P&S.
④ ENSIGN STAFF SOCKET.
⑤ CLEAT.
⑥ HELMSMANS SEAT.
⑦ STEERING WHEEL.
⑧ COMPASS.
⑨ SPINNAKER SHEET WINCH P&S.
⑩ MAINSHEET TRACK.
⑪ MAINSHEET WINCH.
⑫ FUEL FILLING FITTING.
⑬ BILGE PUMP.
⑭ SEAT LOCKER P&S.
⑮ GENOA SHEET WINCH P&S.
⑯ COMPANIONWAY SLIDING HATCH.
⑰ TRACK FOR GENOA SHEET LEADS & MAIN BOOM GUYS P&S.
⑱ FORESAIL SHEET LEAD TRACK P&S.
⑲ BAFFLE TYPE VENT.
⑳ BAFFLE TYPE VENT.
㉑ LOWER SHROUD PLATE P&S.
㉒ MASTHEAD SHROUD PLATE P&S.
㉓ INTERMEDIATE SHROUD PLATE P&S.
㉔ LOWER SHROUD PLATE.
㉕ BAFFLE TYPE VENT.
㉖ BAFFLE TYPE VENT.
㉗ GRAB RAIL. P&S.
㉘ GRAB RAIL.
㉙ SAIL HATCH.
㉚ CLEAT P&S.
㉛ SAMPSON POST.
㉜ FAIRLEAD P&S.
㉝ EYEPLATE FOR SPINNAKER BOOM FORE GUY P&S.
㉞ PLATE FOR FORESTAY & FORESAIL TACK.

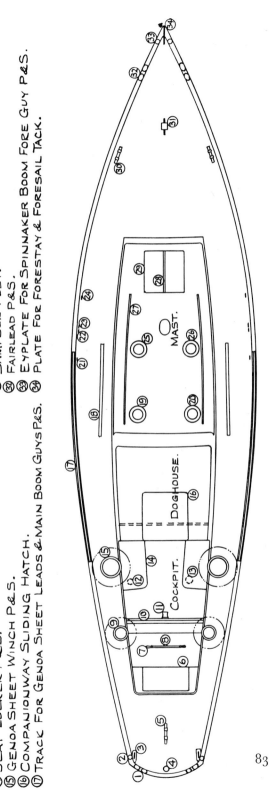

83

FIG 81.
SPINNAKER RIGGING ETC.,
FOR THE OCEAN RACER.

① SPINNAKER HALLIARD.
②   "   BOOM LIFT.
③   "   "   OR POLE.
④   "   "   FORE GUY.
⑤   "   "   AFTER GUY.
⑥   "   SHEET.
⑦   "   LEE FORE GUY (SLACK)
⑧ SNATCH BLOCK.
⑨ SPINNAKER SHEET WINCH.
⑩ GENOA SHEET WINCH.

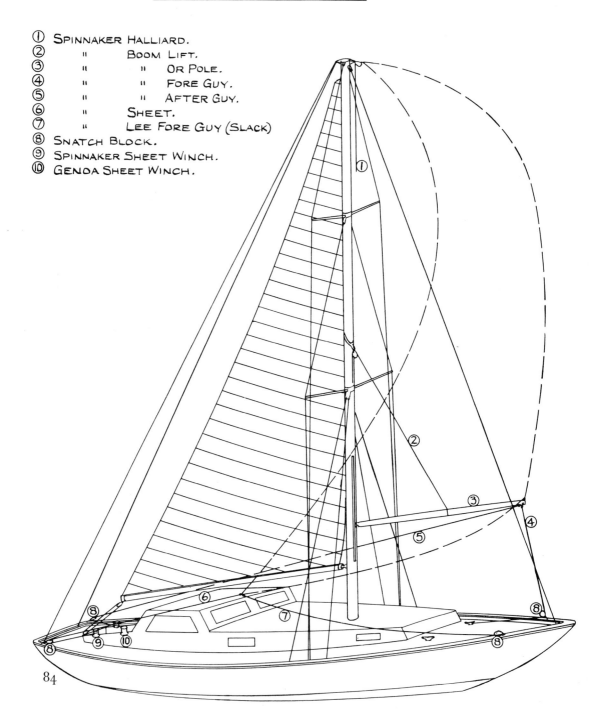

84

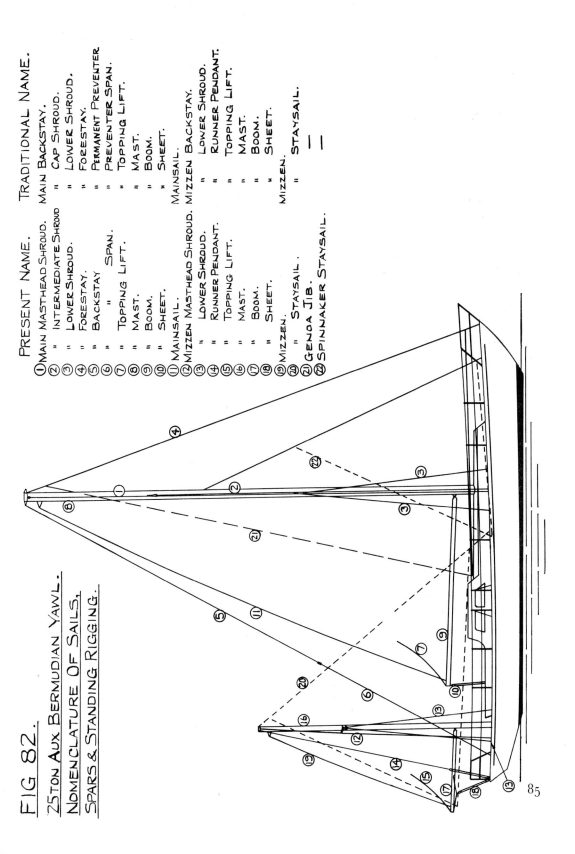

FIG 82.

25 TON AUX BERMUDIAN YAWL.
NOMENCLATURE OF SAILS,
SPARS & STANDING RIGGING.

PRESENT NAME.	TRADITIONAL NAME.
① MAIN MASTHEAD SHROUD.	MAIN BACKSTAY.
② " INTERMEDIATE SHROUD.	" CAP SHROUD.
③ " LOWER SHROUD.	" LOWER SHROUD.
④ " FORESTAY.	" FORESTAY.
⑤ " BACKSTAY	" PERMANENT PREVENTER
⑥ " " SPAN.	" PREVENTER SPAN.
⑦ " TOPPING LIFT.	" TOPPING LIFT.
⑧ " MAST.	" MAST.
⑨ " BOOM.	" BOOM.
⑩ " SHEET.	" SHEET.
⑪ MAINSAIL.	MAINSAIL.
⑫ MIZZEN MASTHEAD SHROUD.	MIZZEN BACKSTAY.
⑬ " LOWER SHROUD.	" LOWER SHROUD.
⑭ " RUNNER PENDANT.	" RUNNER PENDANT.
⑮ " TOPPING LIFT.	" TOPPING LIFT.
⑯ " MAST.	" MAST.
⑰ " BOOM.	" BOOM.
⑱ " SHEET.	" SHEET.
⑲ MIZZEN.	MIZZEN.
⑳ " STAYSAIL.	" STAYSAIL.
㉑ GENOA JIB.	—
㉒ SPINNAKER STAYSAIL.	—

85

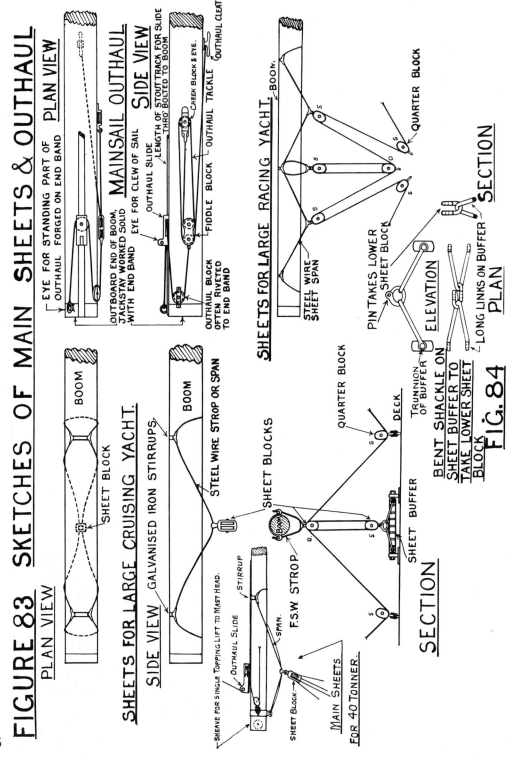

FIGURE 83   SKETCHES OF MAIN SHEETS & OUTHAUL

MAINSAIL OUTHAUL

PLAN VIEW

EYE FOR STANDING PART OF OUTHAUL FORGED ON END BAND

SIDE VIEW

OUTBOARD END OF BOOM, JACKSTAY WORKED SOLID WITH END BAND

EYE FOR CLEW OF SAIL

OUTHAUL SLIDE

LENGTH OF STOUT TRACK FOR SLIDE THRO' BOLTED TO BOOM

CHEEK BLOCK & EYE.

OUTHAUL CLEAT

OUTHAUL TACKLE

FIDDLE BLOCK

OUTHAUL BLOCK OFTEN RIVETED TO END BAND

SHEETS FOR LARGE CRUISING YACHT.

PLAN VIEW

BOOM

SHEET BLOCK

SIDE VIEW   GALVANISED IRON STIRRUPS.

BOOM

STEEL WIRE STROP OR SPAN

SHEAVE FOR SINGLE TOPPING LIFT TO MAST HEAD.

OUTHAUL SLIDE

STIRRUP

SPAN.

F.S.W. STROP

SHEET BLOCK.

MAIN SHEETS FOR 40 TONNER.

SHEETS FOR LARGE RACING YACHT.

BOOM

STEEL WIRE SHEET SPAN

QUARTER BLOCK

PIN TAKES LOWER SHEET BLOCK

ELEVATION

TRUNNION OF BUFFER

BENT SHACKLE ON SHEET BUFFER TO TAKE LOWER SHEET BLOCK

SECTION

LONG LINKS ON BUFFER

PLAN

FIG. 84

QUARTER BLOCK

DECK

SHEET BLOCKS

SHEET BUFFER

SECTION

86

a boom crutch can be shipped in mainmast spider band, and gallows for the fore boom dispensed with.

Main and staysail halyards in ocean racers are usually internal, entering the mast just above the headboard in the case of the mainsail and leaving just above the winch (see Fig. 79) which is preferably of the reel-on type to stow the wire. This arrangement does not put any upward pull on the deck as experienced with the old block and tackle purchase.

Blocks. In the type of vessel under notice the blocks are a very important part of the vessel's outfit, and require the greatest care when preparing the block list, to ensure suitability for the purpose they are intended, as regards size, material, and fitting.*

Tufnol blocks have almost completely ousted other types on yachts. They consist essentially of Tufnol cheeks and sheaves with stainless steel bindings and sheave pins. Eyes and swivels, etc. are of Superston. They are manufactured by a number of firms and specials are obtainable provided sufficient delivery time is allowed. The sizes are determined to suit the size of rope, for example a block for nylon or hemp rope needs thicker sheaves of smaller diameter than for wire, but a block for wire rope needs to be stronger size for size to suit the wire strength.

The principal wear on ropes comes from unsuitable blocks, badly set sheaves, and excessive loads. If there is insufficient room in the 'swallow' the rope will chafe and wear on the outside. If the blocks are very small, the wear of the rope internally will be increased. The size of the rope selected should be larger than is needed to bear the stress, thus postponing renewals.

In calculating pull exerted on a tackle for a given loading, a friction allowance of 8 per cent accumulative should be made for each sheave in the purchase. Some approximate figures are as follows:

Tackle		1 single	2 single	S & D	2 D	D & T	2 T
Ratio	$\dfrac{\text{Pull on running part}}{\text{Load lifted}}$	1.08	0.56	0.39	0.31	0.25	0.22

Where S = single block D = double block T = treble block.

Add a further friction allowance accumulative for each lead sheave at a rate of 8 per cent for 180° encirclement. This shows that the number of lead sheaves should be kept to a minimum.

The pull in the luff tackle purchase sketched in Fig. 87 may be calculated thus:

Load to be lifted = 150 lb. Double and single blocks.
Pull (using ratio given in table)
$$= 150 \times 0.39$$
$$= 58.5 \text{ lb.}$$

This should just produce movement.

As previously observed, the correct description of a block when ordered is most important. The lay or direction in which the block is to face when in position, and the

* A sample block list is given at the end of this book. See table 111.

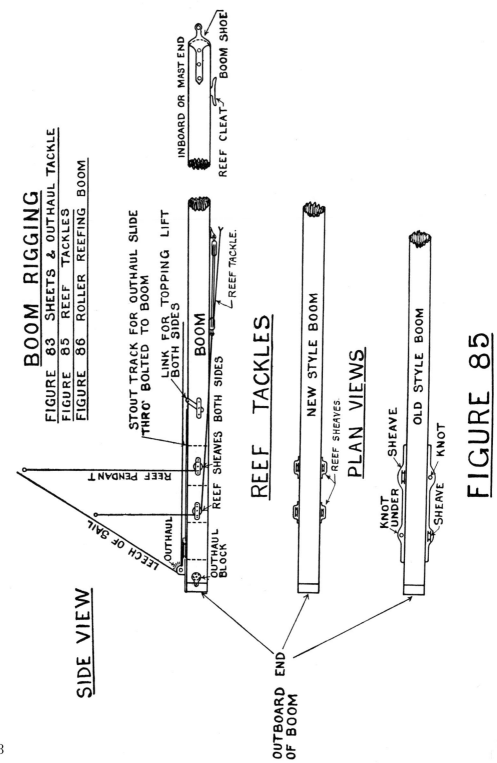

BOOM RIGGING

FIGURE 83 SHEETS & OUTHAUL TACKLE
FIGURE 85 REEF TACKLES
FIGURE 86 ROLLER REEFING BOOM

INBOARD OR MAST END

REEF CLEAT

BOOM SHOE

BOOM

REEF TACKLE.

STOUT TRACK FOR OUTHAUL SLIDE
THRO' BOLTED TO BOOM

LINK FOR TOPPING LIFT
BOTH SIDES

REEF SHEAVES BOTH SIDES

REEF PENDANT

OUTHAUL

LEECH OF SAIL

OUTHAUL
BLOCK

SIDE VIEW

REEF TACKLES

NEW STYLE BOOM

REEF SHEAVES.

PLAN VIEWS

OLD STYLE BOOM

KNOT
UNDER SHEAVE

SHEAVE KNOT

OUTBOARD END
OF BOOM

FIGURE 85

fitting it is attached to often decide the method of fitting the shackle. Normally the shackle is fitted with its pin at right-angles to or 'across' the axis of sheave, this being the most convenient way to forge the strop of the block (see Fig. 88). If this is required it is sufficient to simply specify shackle, but if it is necessary to have the shackle pin parallel, or 'in line' with the sheave pin, it must be specified as 'reversed shackle'.

This is often required to ensure the falls of a tackle being in line with the hauling part, as, for instance, in the sheet block sketched in Fig. 89. If the shackle is required to be fitted with its jaw uppermost, then 'upset shackle' or 'reversed upset shackle' must be specified. When a shackle eye only is required, it must be clearly stated whether a 'drilled' eye or a 'worked' eye is wanted. A drilled eye is stronger than a worked eye because the pin bears equally throughout its thickness, also it is less trouble to make. Upset shackles are usually worked into the eye of block, but if it is intended to reeve a shackle in, then an oval eye must be specified.

Types of hooks vary largely and should be clearly defined in accordance with requirements. Loose hooks are generally used for handy billy and deck watch tackles, and for the lower block of the fish tackle, usually with a small eye for a tripping line worked at the back of hook. Stiff hooks, 'front' or 'side', are not used much on small sailing yachts, but swivel hooks are often fitted to the lower blocks of davit falls, when there are rings fitted in the boats, and sister or clip hooks are sometimes used in jib halyards. For all heavy lifts shackles should be used in preference to hooks.

Where swivel eyes or swivel hooks are required, it is advisable to order somewhat larger blocks than actually necessary in order to gain increased strength in the swivelling parts. Swivel eye blocks are used for main sheet quarter blocks, jib purchase, topping lift purchase, preventer backstays, etc., and for boats' falls when there are hooks in the boats.

Snatch blocks have a hinged part in one cheek which can be opened and the rope laid in, thus avoiding the tedious business of reeving. They are used as lead blocks for the hauling parts of any tackle to be diverted.

Deck Fittings. All woodwork about the deck, such as skylights, companions, seats, lockers, pin rails, etc., are best of teak, well varnished. All ironwork, such as shroud plates, windlass or capstan, compressor, bollards, mast fittings, etc., should be galvanized, but it may be remarked here that there is a growing tendency amongst the more luxurious class of yacht to replace galvanized iron or steel by stainless steel, or nylon-coated mild steel.

The general disposition of all deck fittings should be carefully schemed out and arranged on a deck plan of the vessel, see Fig. 80, keeping in mind the primary requirements of working and mooring and/or anchoring the vessel. The first items to arrange should be the main sheet track, sheet leads and bonnets and the cleats for belaying the sheets. Positions of headsail sheets are usually settled in collaboration with the sailmakers, and the positions of runners and preventers are taken from the rigging plan for the fore and aft direction, their transverse position being in the covering board where they have the maximum spread, and where they can be bolted to the shelf.

If the runners are worked by levers their positions must be arranged, and if there are runner tackles along the deck care must be taken to see that there is sufficient drift between the blocks and runner sheaves. Sheet winches must be placed in line with the leads from the bonnets or quarter blocks to their respective cleats.

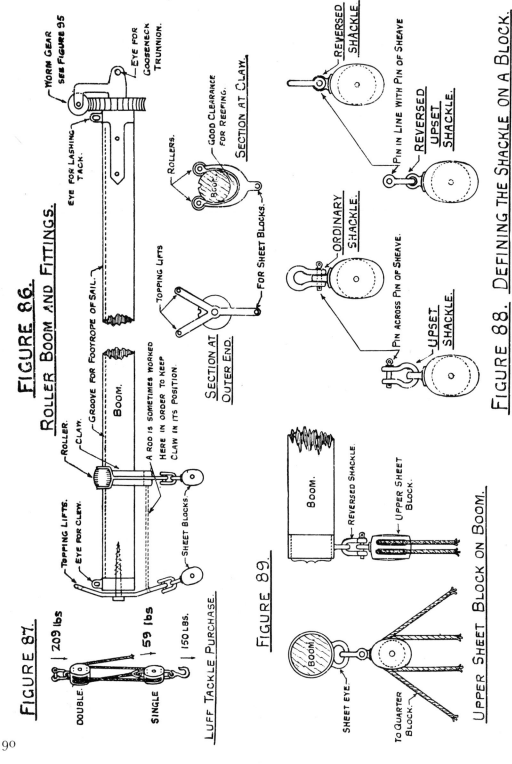

FIGURE 86.
ROLLER BOOM AND FITTINGS.

WORM GEAR SEE FIGURE 95

EYE FOR GOOSENECK TRUNNION.

EYE FOR LASHING TACK.

ROLLERS.

GOOD CLEARANCE FOR REEFING.

BOOM.

SECTION AT CLAW.

TOPPING LIFTS.

FOR SHEET BLOCKS.

SECTION AT OUTER END.

GROOVE FOR FOOTROPE OF SAIL.

BOOM.

ROLLER.

CLAW.

A ROD IS SOMETIMES WORKED HERE IN ORDER TO KEEP CLAW IN ITS POSITION.

TOPPING LIFTS.

EYE FOR CLEW.

SHEET BLOCKS.

FIGURE 87.

209 lbs

59 lbs

150 LBS.

DOUBLE.

SINGLE.

LUFF TACKLE PURCHASE.

FIGURE 88. DEFINING THE SHACKLE ON A BLOCK.

REVERSED SHACKLE.

REVERSED UPSET SHACKLE.

PIN IN LINE WITH PIN OF SHEAVE

ORDINARY SHACKLE.

PIN ACROSS PIN OF SHEAVE.

UPSET SHACKLE.

FIGURE 89.

BOOM.

REVERSED SHACKLE.

UPPER SHEET BLOCK.

BOOM.

SHEET EYE.

TO QUARTER BLOCK.

UPPER SHEET BLOCK ON BOOM.

90

Davits must be arranged to suit the boats to be carried and to allow for them to be worked without fouling the shrouds, runners, etc., taking care that their heights when stowed do not interfere with the boom.

Those deck fittings which are subject to a heavy pull, such as main sheet track, quarter blocks, sheet bonnets, pin rails, halyard eye bolts and hooks, should always be arranged to bolt through beams if possible or failing this, through good chocks between the beams, as described on p. 52. Runner fittings and bowsprit shroud eyeplates are usually bolted through the shelf, with packing or eking pieces fitted between the deck and shelf as required (see p. 52).

Several sketches of deck eyeplates and eyebolts are given in Fig. 98, notice that those which have to take a strong fore and aft pull are fitted with toes which are let down into the deck and help to take some of the stress off the bolts. Cleats, of which a sketch is given in Fig. 64, should stand in the line of the deck planks. The after fairleads are usually placed on the taffrail, see p. 66, but the forward fairleads should be kept forward of the whiskers if, as is sometimes the case, these should be placed well aft, so that mooring lines can be led forward without interference. Bollards are not usually fitted in small sailing yachts, their function being fulfilled by stout cleats in suitable positions. The catheads, on the fore deck, are fitted square to the ship's side, on a specially strengthened bulwark stanchion, if there are bulwarks, if not, somewhat after the style sketched in Fig. 60. At one time, it was usual to provide either a sheet buffer (see Fig. 83 and 84), or a sheet horse with a rubber block at each end, but modern practice in small yachts is to revert to a plain oval eye or track on deck for the main sheet, well bolted to a beam, and pillared below if possible.

Rig and Sails. The rig adopted for a yacht is a matter which rests entirely with the owner, who, of course, is influenced in his decision by the purpose he has in view, whether racing, off shore, or deep-sea cruising, or just a day boat. There are four rigs in common use, the cutter—the accepted definition of a sloop is a cutter with a single head sail—ketch, schooner and yawl.

Sloop rig is most popular for the smallest yachts, yawl and ketch rigs being used to reduce the size of sails in larger yachts and to provide the useful facility, for cruising, of a mizzen. Schooner rig is, of course, most suitable for the largest yachts.

All of these types may be either bermudian or gaff-rigged or a combination of both for two-masted vessels, but the bermudian rig is most favoured on account of the saving in top hamper, and the increased efficiency. Gaff-headed sails require topsails to complete the sail area, which involves more running gear and labour and, when sailing, the gaff falls off to leeward, and the net result is about the same shape as a well cut bermudian sail. Vangs to prevent this do not find favour with yachtsmen, the reason probably being that the height of gaff is too great and the beam too small for vangs to be of practical use. Square sails in small yachts are very uncommon (except for yachts undertaking ocean voyages), but are often fitted in the larger vessels for running before the wind, to avoid gybing a spinnaker, but for sailing in light airs genoa jibs and yankee jib topsails are very popular.

Sails are made from flax canvas, cotton cloth, Terylene, Dacron, etc., of varying weights to suit the purpose and size of the sail. For instance, a storm trysail would obviously be of much stouter material than a jib topsail. Sailmaking is a highly specialized business

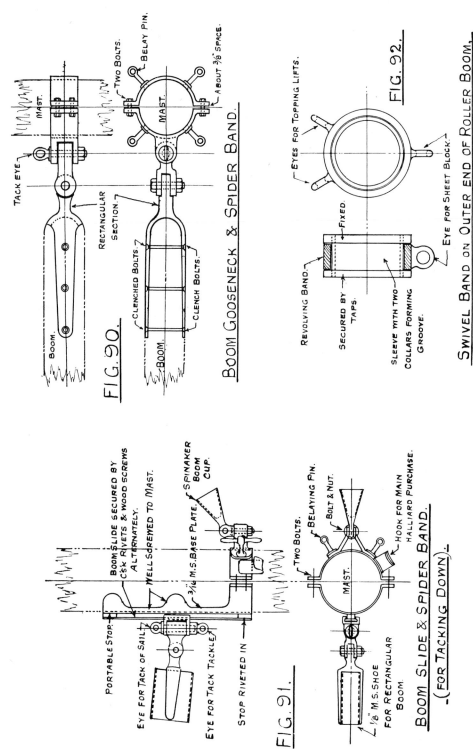

TACK EYE.

MAST.

TWO BOLTS.

BELAY PIN.

MAST.

ABOUT ⅜ SPACE.

RECTANGULAR SECTION.

CLENCHED BOLTS.

BOOM.

CLENCH BOLTS.

BOOM.

FIG. 90.

BOOM GOOSENECK & SPIDER BAND.

EYES FOR TOPPING LIFTS.

EYE FOR SHEET BLOCK.

FIG. 92.

REVOLVING BAND.

FIXED.

SECURED BY TAPS.

SLEEVE WITH TWO COLLARS FORMING GROOVE.

EYE FOR SHEET BLOCK.

SWIVEL BAND ON OUTER END OF ROLLER BOOM.

TO TAKE SHEET & TOPPING LIFTS.

SOMETIMES USED FOR SHEET ON ORDINARY ROUND BOOM.

BOOM SLIDE SECURED BY C'SK RIVETS & WOOD SCREWS ALTERNATELY.

WELL SCREWED TO MAST.

SPINNAKER BOOM CUP.

3/16 M.S. BASE PLATE.

PORTABLE STOP.

EYE FOR TACK OF SAIL.

EYE FOR TACK TACKLE.

STOP RIVETED IN

FIG. 91.

TWO BOLTS.

BELAYING PIN.

BOLT & NUT.

HOOK FOR MAIN HALLIARD PURCHASE.

MAST.

⅛" M.S. SHOE FOR RECTANGULAR BOOM.

BOOM SLIDE & SPIDER BAND.

(FOR TACKING DOWN).

92

requiring very great knowledge, skill and experience, the actual cut being as important as workmanship and materials, and it may be remarked here that in selling a boat, the fact of the sails being made by a reputable firm carries full weight. Flax canvas is used for heavy or storm sails, Egyptian cotton cloth is considered good for light sails, American cotton cloth being considered next best, but for racing yachts each of the synthetic materials such as nylon, Terylene, Dacron, etc., has in turn been accepted as the last word in sail material, only to be eclipsed as a later one has been marketed.

Sails from natural materials are made up of strips (or cloths) sewn together, the commercial widths being 12, 15, and 18 in. wide. In small yachts the cloths are almost invariably 12 in. wide. Close seams are necessary to keep stretch to a minimum. With the synthetic materials which are 'heat set' during manufacture, sails are subject to stretch to a much smaller degree, so may be made from wider cloths of say 34 to 36 in. wide.

The 'lay' or direction of the cloths in the different sails is subject to variation, but good practice is represented by the sketches in Fig. 99. The seams are usually machine sewn, except in very large and heavy sails, when hand sewing is employed which is, of course, more expensive. The best type of machine sewing is known as the cross-stitch, thus: $\wedge \wedge \wedge \wedge \wedge$, which is more suitable for the stretch of sails. The stretching of new cotton sails should be a gradual process and only undertaken in fine weather; too sudden or violent stretching spoils the shape of sails, and further, it is not advisable to reef down until after the sails have had a fair chance of stretching. Tanned sails, which are seldom used in yachts, are of doubtful utility as a preservative for long life, but are of undoubted value as a protection against wet and damp. One of the advantages of the synthetic materials is their resistance to the effects of dampness.

The life of cotton sails is lengthened considerably if care is taken to see that they are dry when stowed. Before putting sails away for the winter it is good practice to scrub them with fresh water, and then thoroughly dry them before storing.

There is a wide choice of colours with the synthetic materials and a feature of any assembly of sailing yachts nowadays is the bright array of colours displayed, especially with spinnakers.

Bermudian sails are cut with a considerable round-out in the leach, and to prevent this rounded leach from curling, light battens are sewn into pockets in the sail, the higher ones being square to the leach, but the lower ones in the vicinity of the reefs being in line with the reefs.

Roller reefing has been described on p. 98, but ordinary reefing requires a row of reef points for tying down the sail to the boom. There are two methods in use, the fixed point, where the points are permanently knotted in the sail, and the loose point or lacing type, where holes only are provided, the latter type being mainly used in the larger yachts. Bolt ropes of best tarred Italian hemp are worked round the edge of sail, in small yachts along foot, luff and partly along upper and lower extremities of leech. Head boards of aluminium alloy are used in bermudian mainsails and spinnakers, being sewn to the head of the sail, with the bolt rope passing round in a groove (see Fig. 100).

Spars and Fittings. The heavier spars for cruising boats are usually made of Oregon pine, whilst the lighter racing boat spars are made of aircraft quality spruce.

Aluminium alloy spars, especially within the ocean racer range, are in wide use, either built up from sheets or of extruded section with taper worked as required. Made by specialist firms, complete with stainless steel fittings riveted on, they are a sound proposition.

Booms have no fixed practice as to their sections; passing fashions show us in use streamlined and pear-shaped sections, round, rectangular, triangular, 'Park Avenue' and roller booms. Round booms are the majority, streamlined and pear-shaped are seldom seen, rectangular sections make a nice looking and simple hollow boom, roller booms are popular in small types for quick and easy reefing.

Present practice is to stretch the foot of the sail very tight, and to facilitate this a track is fitted along the top of the boom, which the sail hanks engage and slide on. The boom is attached by a gooseneck fitting at one end to the mast, and secured by a sheet at the other end. Its greatest diameter is nearest to the outer end, and should be about $\frac{1}{4}$ in. for every foot of the length for a round boom, tapering at each end the outer end being the larger of the two and it should be fish-bellied. Note that in schooners the fore boom, which is short, should be of stouter diameter than the above proportions would give, 5/16 in. per foot of length being about right.

In the present-day rare event of a loose-footed sail being used, a round boom is the proper style, with its greatest diameter at the main sheet, which is a strop or band round the boom, the other mountings being similar to those to be described later. The inner end of the boom is fastened to the mast by a species of universal joint which also has an oval eye for taking the tack shackle. There are many ways of making this gooseneck, but good types for a small vessel are given by Figs. 76 and 90. Notice that the joint allows the boom to be freely swung up and down (topped), as well as athwartships, thus permitting it to be adjusted to any point of sailing. The band is usually made in halves for convenience in fitting and clamped round the mast and bolted. The lugs for the bolts should be stout and have good fillets to prevent bending when tightening up the bolts. Angle bar lugs make a good job here but are not so sightly as forgings.

On the outboard end of the boom is a band to which is secured a moderate length of larger-size track to take the outhaul slide, which consists of a sliding block or carriage, embodying a sheave for the outhaul to pass round, and jaws with a bolt passed through to take the clew of the sail. The end band also carries an eye on one side for the standing end of the outhaul, and a cheek block on the other side for the running part of outhaul pendant (see sketch, Fig. 83). The outer bight of the main sheet span sometimes comes on this band. The topping lifts and reef cleats are spaced as arranged on the sail plan, also fittings for the sheet spans. The reefs were at one time arranged with a standing end passed through a hole in the cleat on one side, held by a knot underneath (see Fig. 85) up through the reef cringle, and down the other side and round a sheave to the reef tackle, which thus pulled on one part only. The present practice is to work the reef with two sheaves, one each side of boom, the reef pendant having two thimbles to which the reef tackle is shackled, thus pulling on both parts at once.

Fittings for the sheets vary greatly, depending somewhat upon the rig, and largely upon the size of vessel. Two methods for large yachts are sketched in Figs. 83 and 84, and a method for roller booms in Fig. 79. In small yachts with an ordinary boom it is quite common to fit the sheet horse or buffer directly under the end band of the boom, which carries an athwartship worked oval eye to take the upper sheet block, or a swivel band with eye, as sketched in Fig. 92.

The foot of the sail is held down to the boom by sliding hanks working on a track

94

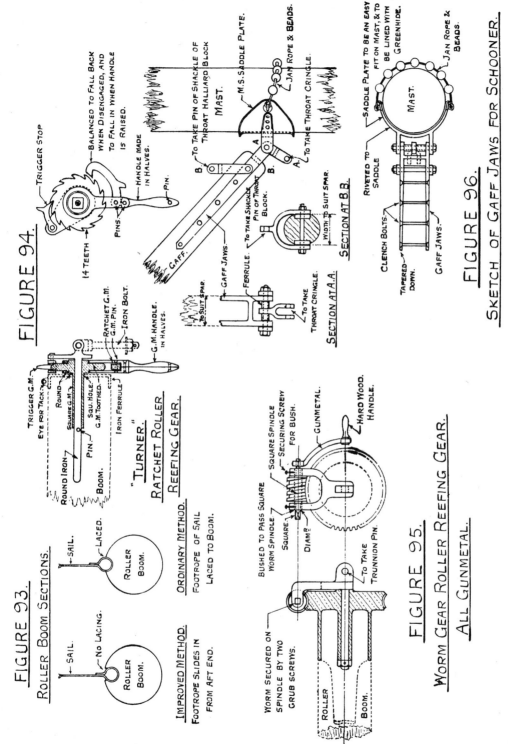

FIGURE 94.

TRIGGER STOP

14 TEETH

BALANCED TO FALL BACK WHEN DISENGAGED, AND TO FALL IN WHEN HANDLE IS RAISED.

HANDLE MADE IN HALVES.

PIN.

PINS.

B. TO TAKE PIN OF SHACKLE OF THROAT HALLIARD BLOCK.

M.S. SADDLE PLATE.

MAST.

JAN ROPE & BEADS.

TO TAKE THROAT CRINGLE.

A.

A.

B.

TO TAKE SHACKLE PIN OF THROAT BLOCK.

GAFF.

GAFF JAWS.

FERRULE.

TO SUIT SPAR.

WIDTH TO SUIT SPAR.

SECTION AT B.B.

SECTION AT A.A.

TO SUIT SPAR.

TO TAKE THROAT CRINGLE.

FIGURE 96.

SADDLE PLATE TO BE AN EASY FIT ON MAST, & TO BE LINED WITH GREENHIDE.

JAN ROPE & BEADS.

MAST.

RIVETED TO SADDLE.

CLENCH BOLTS.

TAPERED DOWN.

GAFF JAWS.

SKETCH OF GAFF JAWS FOR SCHOONER.

FIGURE 93.

ROLLER BOOM SECTIONS.

SAIL.

LACED.

ROLLER BOOM.

SAIL.

NO LACING.

ROLLER BOOM.

IMPROVED METHOD.
FOOTROPE SLIDES IN FROM AFT END.

ORDINARY METHOD.
FOOTROPE OF SAIL LACED TO BOOM.

"TURNER."
RATCHET ROLLER REEFING GEAR.

TRIGGER G.M.
EYE FOR TACK.

RATCHET G.M.
G.M. PIN.

IRON BOLT.

ROUND G.M.

SQU. HOLE.
G.M. TOOTHED.

SQUARE G.M.

PIN.

ROUND IRON.

BOOM.

IRON FERRULE.

G.M. HANDLE.
IN HALVES.

FIGURE 95.

WORM SECURED ON SPINDLE BY TWO GRUB SCREWS.

BUSHED TO PASS SQUARE WORM SPINDLE.

SQUARE SPINDLE.

SECURING SCREW FOR BUSH.

SQUARE.

DIAMR.

GUNMETAL.

HARD WOOD HANDLE.

TO TAKE TRUNNION PIN.

ROLLER.

BOOM.

WORM GEAR ROLLER REEFING GEAR.
ALL GUNMETAL.

95

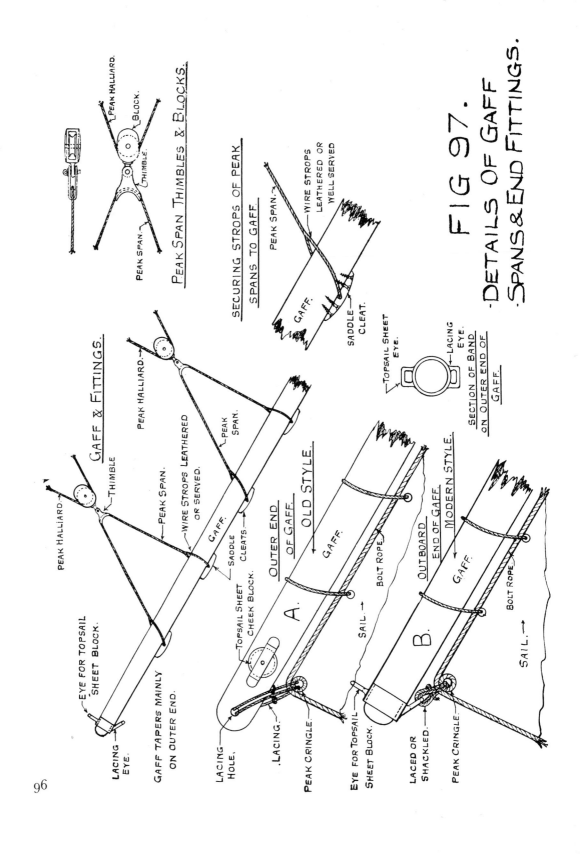

PEAK SPAN THIMBLES & BLOCKS.

PEAK HALLIARD.
BLOCK.
THIMBLE.
PEAK SPAN.

SECURING STROPS OF PEAK SPANS TO GAFF.

PEAK SPAN.
WIRE STROPS LEATHERED OR WELL SERVED
GAFF.
SADDLE CLEAT.

TOPSAIL SHEET EYE.
LACING EYE.
SECTION OF BAND ON OUTER END OF GAFF.

FIG 97.
-DETAILS OF GAFF SPANS & END FITTINGS.

GAFF & FITTINGS.

PEAK HALLIARD.
THIMBLE
PEAK SPAN.
PEAK SPAN.
WIRE STROPS LEATHERED OR SERVED.
GAFF.
SADDLE CLEATS.
TOPSAIL SHEET CHEEK BLOCK.

PEAK HALLIARD.

EYE FOR TOPSAIL SHEET BLOCK.
LACING EYE.
GAFF TAPERS MAINLY ON OUTER END.

OUTER END OF GAFF. OLD STYLE.

A.

GAFF.
BOLT ROPE.
SAIL
LACING HOLE.
LACING.
PEAK CRINGLE.
EYE FOR TOPSAIL SHEET BLOCK.

OUTBOARD END OF GAFF. MODERN STYLE.

B.

GAFF.
BOLT ROPE.
SAIL.
LACED OR SHACKLED.
PEAK CRINGLE.
SAIL.

96

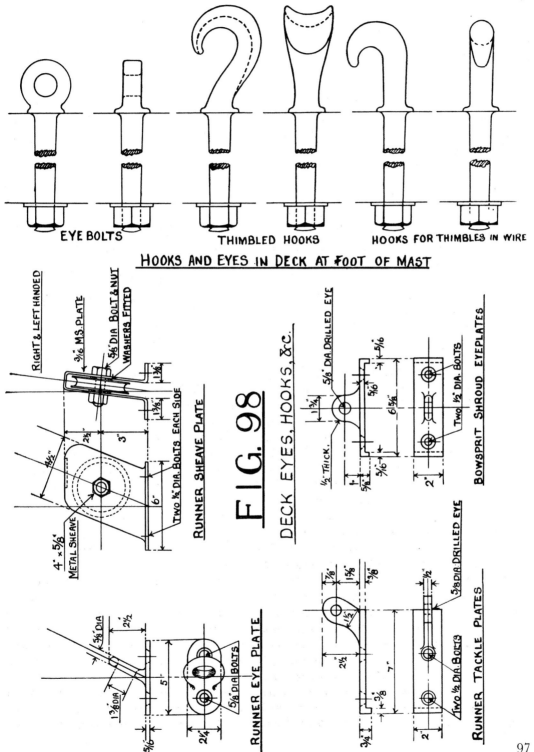

EYE BOLTS   THIMBLED HOOKS   HOOKS FOR THIMBLES IN WIRE

HOOKS AND EYES IN DECK AT FOOT OF MAST

FIG. 98

DECK EYES, HOOKS, &c.

RUNNER SHEAVE PLATE

RIGHT & LEFT HANDED
3/16 M.S. PLATE
5/8 DIA. BOLT & NUT WASHERS FITTED
1 3/8
1 3/8
3"
2 1/2"
4 1/2"
6"
4" × 5/8" METAL SHEAVE
TWO 1/2" DIA. BOLTS EACH SIDE

RUNNER EYE PLATE

5/8 DIA
2 1/2
1 3/8 DIA
5"
2 1/4
5/16
5/8 DIA BOLTS

BOWSPRIT SHROUD EYEPLATES

5/8 DIA. DRILLED EYE
5/16
1 3/4
1/2 THICK.
1"
5/8
5/16
5/16
6 5/8"
Two 1/2 DIA. BOLTS
2"

RUNNER TACKLE PLATES

5/8 DIA. DRILLED EYE
7/8
1 5/8
1 3/8
1 1/2
2 1/2
3/8
3/4"
7"
1/2
Two 1/2 DIA BOLTS
2"

97

fastened along the top of the boom by screws, and stretched tightly by the outhaul tackle. Roller booms should be tapered slightly so that the sail will roll on without puckering because, of course, the shape worked into the sail makes its girth at centre greater than at the luff. The following diameters were used for a boom 18 ft. long: 4 in. at forward end, $4\frac{3}{4}$ in. at middle, 5 in. at after end. The foot of the sail is stretched taut along the boom by lashing to an eye on the outer end. This form of boom is used for quick and easy reefing, the sail wrapping round the boom, which is turned by a worm and wormwheel winch, or a ratchet gear at the mast end of boom (see Figs. 94 and 95), which embodies a bolt for shipping in the mast band, letting the boom slew athwartships. At the outer end of the boom is a spindle with a revolving 'Y' fitting to take the topping lifts and sheets, and sometimes, disposed along the boom is one, or perhaps two, claw fittings (see sketches, Figs. 79 and 86) for the sheet blocks.

Gaff is the name given to the spar which extends and supports the head of a four-sided or quadrilateral sail. In its working position a gaff is high aloft, and as it must be hoisted up and down, it follows that it should be as light a spar as its duty permits. The gaff differs from the boom in the fact that it is supported along its length by the several spans of the peak halyards, therefore the amount of taper is less. Its middle diameter should be about 7/32 in. for every foot of the length, tapering down at the jaw end to about 90 per cent, and at the outer end to about 80 per cent of its middle diameter. Gaffs are usually round and the figures quoted are for a hollow spar.

The gaff is required to travel up and down the mast, to slew in the transverse direction and to hinge up and down, and to achieve all this an elaborate fitting, commonly referred to as the gaff jaws, is necessary. A good type is sketched in Fig. 96. The plate saddle transmits the thrust of the gaff to the mast, the jan rope and parrel balls prevent the gaff from surging away, the bridle or stirrup for the throat halyard block adjusts itself to all angles of the gaff when hoisting, and the loose links for the throat cringle do the same for the sail. The peak halyard spans are held in their places along the gaff by wood saddle cleats on the underside of the spar, as shown by sketch (Fig. 97).

The sail is laced to the gaff and is held out to its position by a lacing or earring through the peak cringle to the end of the gaff. At one time it was the practice to provide a lacing hole in the outer end of the gaff, with a cheek block for the topsail sheet, as shown at 'A' in Fig. 97, but a more modern style is to provide a steel band with two staple eyes, the lower one worked to a suitable angle to take the peak lacing, and the upper one to take the topsail sheet block, all as shown at 'B' in Fig. 97. As previously mentioned, the gaff creates a considerable thrust upon the mast when sailing, and should the gaff jaws be placed well below the runners, it is usually considered necessary to fit a strut stay here, to stiffen the mast against this thrust. This is more particularly the case in ketches and yawls, where the standing rigging of the mizzen mast consists of shrouds only, with no runners or preventer near the gaff jaws; then a strut or 'jumper' stay can be fitted with advantage. The strut itself is a short stout iron bar, with a groove in the outer end to take the wire stay, which is seized in, and the mast end can be either on a band or a saddle plate screwed to the mast. The lower end of the stay can be set up with a rigging screw, either to the spider band, or to an eyebolt in the deck at foot of mast.

The spinnaker boom is a light hollow spar which is used for booming out one corner of the large, light, roughly triangular sail, which is used for running before the wind. The length of spinnaker boom permitted by the Royal Ocean Racing Club without penalty,

98

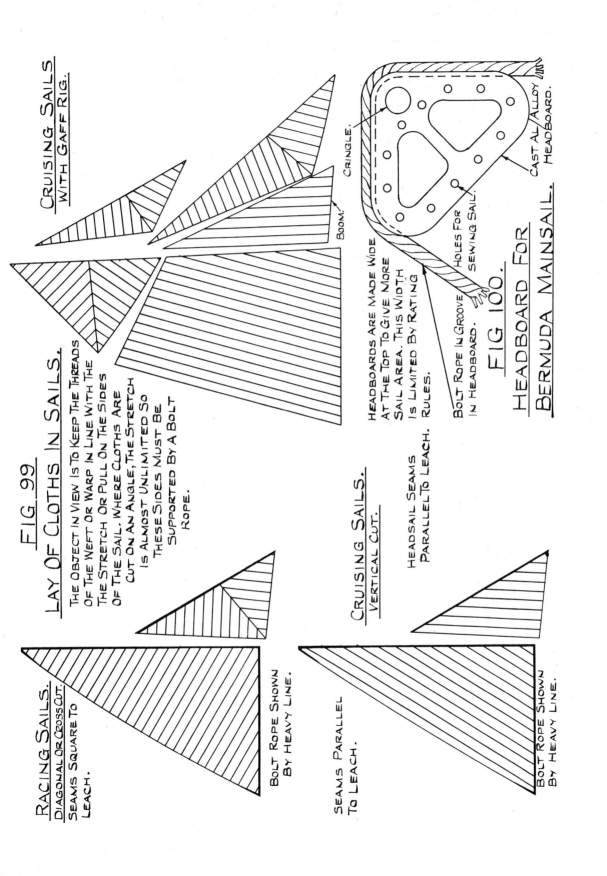

FIG 99

LAY OF CLOTHS IN SAILS.

The object in view is to keep the threads of the weft or warp in line with the the stretch or pull on the sides of the sail. Where cloths are cut on an angle, the stretch is almost unlimited so these sides must be supported by a bolt rope.

CRUISING SAILS.
WITH GAFF RIG.

BOOM.

CRINGLE.

RACING SAILS.
DIAGONAL OR CROSS CUT.

SEAMS SQUARE TO LEACH.

BOLT ROPE SHOWN BY HEAVY LINE.

CRUISING SAILS.
VERTICAL CUT.

HEADSAIL SEAMS PARALLEL TO LEACH.

SEAMS PARALLEL TO LEACH.

BOLT ROPE SHOWN BY HEAVY LINE.

HEADBOARDS ARE MADE WIDE AT THE TOP TO GIVE MORE SAIL AREA. THIS WIDTH IS LIMITED BY RATING RULES.

BOLT ROPE IN GROOVE IN HEADBOARD.

HOLES FOR SEWING SAIL.

CAST AL. ALLOY HEADBOARD.

FIG 100.

HEADBOARD FOR BERMUDA MAINSAIL.

is the length from the foreside of mast to where the line of the luff of the foremost headsail cuts the deck or bowsprit. Suitable diameters for this spar are indicated in Table I and it is usually made of silver spruce, or aluminium alloy for the sake of lightness. The inboard end is sometimes fitted into a cup provided for it on the mast band, see Fig. 91, but usually it has a hook fitting instead, and in racing yachts it is often fitted on a track so that the heel of boom may be adjustable. Especially in racing boats, spinnaker booms are now made double-ended, with quick-release fittings for attaching to the mast slider. The outer end is attached to the tack and is provided with forward and after guys. The spinnaker lift or sling is held in place on the boom at the half-length to assist balance when shipping the boom. The spinnaker lift is rove through a block aloft. See Fig. 81.

Chapter 5

Joinery Work. Broadly speaking, the term joinery work embraces all the woodwork necessary to render the yacht habitable and convenient. It includes such items as cabin floors, linings, and bulkheads, doors, ladders and stairs, seats, lockers, berths, tables, wardrobes, and furniture in general, all panelling, deckhouses, skylights and companions, cockpit floors and seats, and the making and fitting of all numerous small items that go to make a well-fitted and comfortable yacht. Cabin floors have been dealt with under the heading of Cabin Sole (p. 54 et seq.) and Skylights and Companions on p. 48 and onwards.

A long detailed description of joinery work is absolutely impossible, because the variety of materials, styles, workmanship and finish that is possible would make any attempt at complete description futile, and extremely boring. But there are a few outstanding facts to notice. Materials, style and decoration are questions for the owner to decide on the basis of expense, but workmanship and finish range from the very best to the extremely rough. It may be safely assumed, however, that a first-class firm with a reputation to maintain, makes a really good job, naturally and as a matter of course, because apart from all other reasons, they employ foremen and workmen who have a high standard of attainment which they find difficult to depart from.

In racing boats, marine quality plywood single thickness from $\frac{1}{2}$ in. upwards is now the usual material for cabin bulkheads, but in high-class cruising yachts of a somewhat larger type, these are sometimes constructed of two thicknesses of $\frac{1}{2}$ in. 'Weyrock' with $\frac{7}{8}$ in. thick T. and G. between, with face-mounted mouldings to give a decorative effect, or more traditionally bulkheads are of two thicknesses of framing and panelling placed back to back, the total thickness being about $1\frac{5}{8}$ in. to $1\frac{3}{4}$ in. screwed to cants on cabin flat, and to the frames and the beams overhead. The scantlings for the latter two types of bulkhead construction may seem at first sight to be excessive, but for a height of about 6 ft. 6 in. and a large unsupported width they are only just adequate.

The doors are framed and panelled both sides in the usual manner, the thickness being $1\frac{1}{4}$ in., the general finish being polished or painted, according to the owner's wishes. A somewhat inferior job for bulkheads is where the framing is only single, showing the panel on both sides like a door, the thickness of the framing being about $1\frac{1}{8}$ in. This also may be polished if desired. A cheaper method is to make the bulkheads of ordinary tongued and grooved wood, vee jointed or otherwise, which may be either

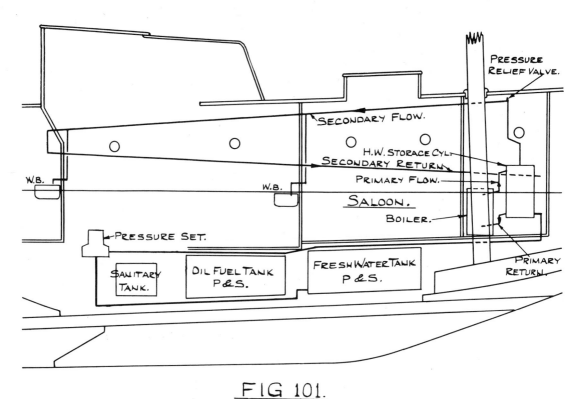

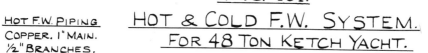

FIG 101.
HOT & COLD F.W. SYSTEM.
FOR 48 TON KETCH YACHT.

HOT F.W. PIPING
COPPER. 1" MAIN.
½" BRANCHES.

COLD F.W. PIPING
COPPER OR RIGID
P.V.C. ¾" MAIN.
½" BRANCHES.

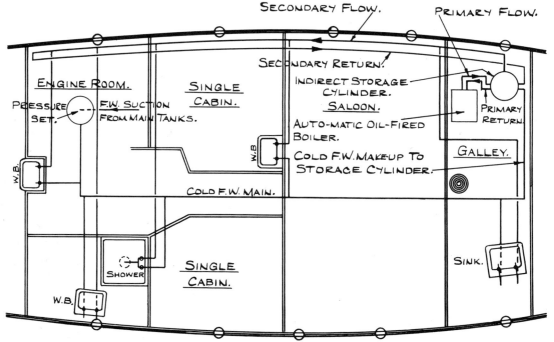

double and breaking joint, or single and fairly thick. It may be either painted or varnished, and the doors are framed and panelled, as before.

The ship's side lining in small yachts offers an even greater range of ideas. In very small yachts there is often none at all, but from about 10 tons upwards some form of lining is generally worked. A modern tendency is to use one of the many board substitutes now available, such as beaver board, Sundeala, Masonite, chipboard, etc. These may be decorated with mouldings as previously mentioned for bulkheads to give a panelled effect. A very durable and pleasing finish may be obtained by covering with plastic material glued on. It is, however, important that material actually recommended by the manufacturers for this purpose should be used, as the wrong type is liable to shrink badly and leave gaps at the seams. Rigid plastic material is also widely used, especially in galleys and bathrooms, where conditions are most exacting.

Ladders and stairs should be of hardwood, teak or mahogany, the treads being fitted with some form of non-slip tread or nosing. Deckhouses should be of the same wood as skylights and companions, properly framed and panelled, and with good strong coamings, well secured to the beams and carlings. In the best class of work the cockpit coamings, seats and risers, are all of hardwood to match the skylights, companions, etc.

The interior furniture may be simple and cheap, or lavish and expensive, according to the owner's taste and resources, but attention is directed to the remarks in the article on 'General Arrangement', p. 126, where the drawbacks consequent upon overcrowding the vessel with fittings of doubtful value are referred to. Somewhat similar objections apply to those devices which are too complicated and ingenious, because of the inherent tendency they all possess to go wrong at the most inconvenient moments.

Plumbing Arrangements. The pumping and plumbing arrangements in sailing boats under 50 feet are usually of a very simple character. As a rule there is no watertight bulkhead, the nearest approach to it being an oiltight floor at the fore end of engine-room, if the latter is aft; or at either end if the engine-room is amidships. Consequently, the bilge-pump suctions are only two or three in number, one to the engine-room and the other to the hold space, or spaces, as the case may be. They are of the deck hand pump type, with a discharge from the barrel through the vessel's side, the tail pipe or suction being led to the lowest part of the compartment and fitted with a rose, whilst the discharge is brought out through the vessel's side just below the waterline. Pump barrels to be twice diameter of tail pipe. Power-driven bilge pumps are not called for by Lloyd's in sailing and auxiliary craft below 75 feet.

The remainder of the plumbing may be briefly summarized as: (1) filling and discharging the fresh-water tanks; (2) the cold fresh-water supply to the baths and wash-basins; (3) the hot-water supply to the baths and wash-basins; (4) the drains from baths, wash-basins and galley and pantry sinks; (5) the W.C. system; (6) the hot-water radiator system (if fitted). Proper scuppers are not usually fitted in racing yachts, the common practice being to cut freeing ports in the bulwark or washrail. The fresh-water tanks are dealt with on p. 109 et seq., and typical sketches are given in Figs. 101 and 102.

Cold Fresh-water supply should be arranged as follows. In the ocean-racer class up to about 20 tons T.M., where there are only one or two wash-basins and one sink, a separate hand pump for each is most economical in weight and cost. There are available

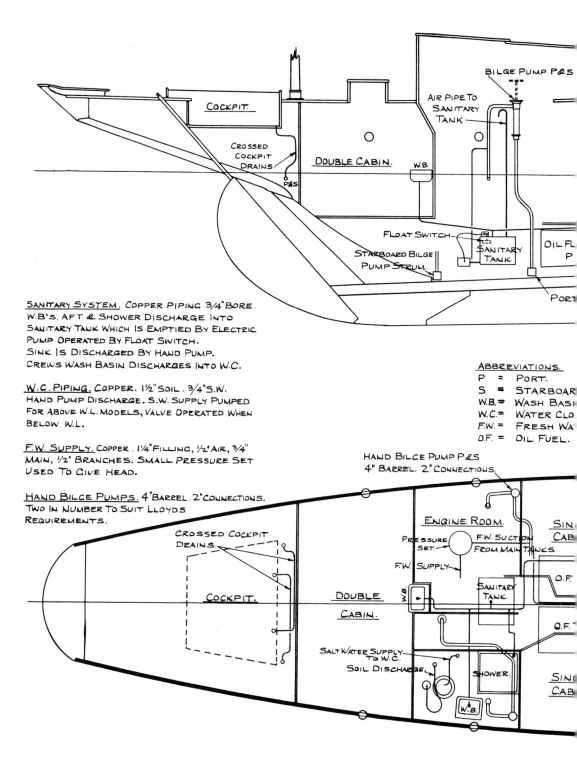

COCKPIT.

CROSSED
COCKPIT
DRAINS.

P&S

DOUBLE CABIN.

W.B.

BILGE PUMP P&S

AIR PIPE TO
SANITARY
TANK

FLOAT SWITCH

STARBOARD BILGE
PUMP STRUM.

SANITARY
TANK.

OIL FU
P

PORT

SANITARY SYSTEM. COPPER PIPING 3/4"BORE.
W.B.'S. AFT & SHOWER DISCHARGE INTO
SANITARY TANK WHICH IS EMPTIED BY ELECTRIC
PUMP OPERATED BY FLOAT SWITCH.
SINK IS DISCHARGED BY HAND PUMP.
CREWS WASH BASIN DISCHARGES INTO W.C.

W.C. PIPING. COPPER. 1½"SOIL. 3/4"S.W.
HAND PUMP DISCHARGE. S.W. SUPPLY PUMPED
FOR ABOVE W.L. MODELS, VALVE OPERATED WHEN
BELOW W.L.

F.W. SUPPLY. COPPER. 1¼"FILLING, ½"AIR, 3/4"
MAIN, ½" BRANCHES. SMALL PRESSURE SET
USED TO GIVE HEAD.

HAND BILGE PUMPS. 4"BARREL. 2"CONNECTIONS.
TWO IN NUMBER TO SUIT LLOYDS
REQUIREMENTS.

ABBREVIATIONS.
P = PORT.
S = STARBOAR
W.B. = WASH BASI
W.C. = WATER CLO
F.W. = FRESH WA
O.F. = OIL FUEL.

HAND BILGE PUMP P&S
4" BARREL. 2" CONNECTIONS.

CROSSED COCKPIT
DRAINS.

COCKPIT.

DOUBLE
CABIN.

ENGINE ROOM.

PRESSURE
SET.

F.W. SUCTION
FROM MAIN TANKS

F.W. SUPPLY

W.B

SANITARY
TANK.

SIN
CAB

O.F.

SALT WATER SUPPLY
TO W.C.
SOIL DISCHARGE.

SHOWER.

O.F.

W.B.

SIN
CAB

104

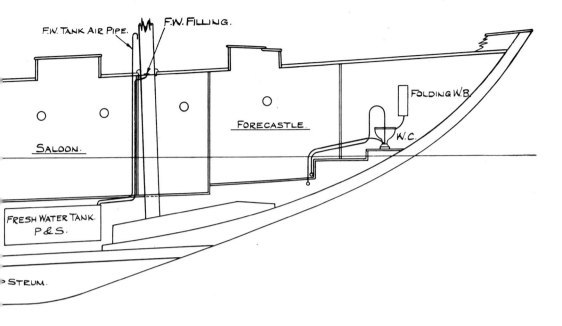

FIG 102
BILGE, SANITARY, W.C. & F.W SUPPLY PIPING.
FOR 48 TON KETCH YACHT.

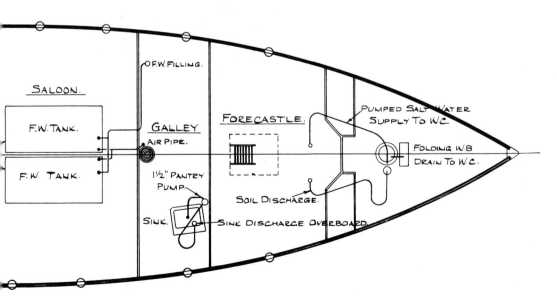

specially suitable 'rocker' pumps for this purpose, to draw direct from the main tanks.

With large cruisers, fitted with a battery and generator, an electrically driven pump operating a pressure cylinder is to be recommended for fresh-water supply, see Figs. 101 to 104. 'Pressure sets', as they are called, may be installed at any height, within the limitations of the pump suction lift; they are available in a wide range of sizes and are completely automatic. They can be supplied to give ample pressure at every tap.

Water Heaters. The hot-water supply in yachts of about 50 tons and upwards may be by means of an oil-fired or gas-fired boiler or from a coal-fired cooker if one of these is installed. The automatic oil-fired boiler is probably most convenient for a complete hot-water and radiator system in a yacht, especially when an oil supply is available from the propelling machinery tanks; it can be conveniently controlled to give a constant water temperature, which should not exceed about 165°F., otherwise furring will take place in the hot pipes.

Gas heaters are very suitable for one or two adjacent taps on a non-circulating system.

With a constant-burning coal-fired cooker, which is preferred by many yacht chefs, it is a measure of economy to use the waste heat for heating water. There is a disadvantage with this, however, and it is that there is no means of controlling water temperature, and if no water is drawn off for a while, it will boil and cause rapid furring in the hot pipes, to the extent of completely blocking them.

Hot-Water Systems. The most elementary hot-water system, as shown in Fig. 103, consists of a boiler, heating water in a storage cylinder by convection, with individual hot-water supply to wash-basins, etc., drawn direct by means of dead runs. The length of these runs must be kept to a minimum to avoid wastage of cold water being drawn off before hot water reaches the tap.

The next system shown in Fig. 104 consists of a boiler with primary circulation to a hot-water storage cylinder and a secondary circuit to run around the ship's side, to and from a point adjacent to the most remote hot tap. The storage tank should be kept as low as possible, but with the tank outlet not less than about 3 in. above the boiler inlet, in order to give maximum run to the secondary circuit. From the top of the storage tank the secondary circuit should rise vertically as high as possible, as this height determines the circulating force. There must then be a continuous slope in both the flow and return piping back to the storage tank. The piping should be pitched to enable it to vent to the expansion tank or radiators. A pitch of 1 in. in 10 ft. should be treated as a minimum on a boat from boiler to tank. If a downward run in the flow and return mains is not possible, a special 'circulator' pump may be fitted to force circulation, natural circulation is, in fact, seldom achieved.

It should be noted here that there is a common misconception that a pressure exerted on the system by a header tank or pressure set will help circulation in a closed system. This is not so; external pressure in a system does not cause any flow until a tap is opened.

The heating system shown in Fig. 105 is one employed in the large yachts where hot-water radiators as well as hot-water supply is required. It consists essentially of a boiler, usually oil fired with thermostatic control, a direct circuit for the radiators with a branch forming the primary circuit passing through a heating coil in the indirect cylinder. From the indirect cylinder an indirect secondary circuit is run around the ship for hot-water supply to wash-basins, showers, baths, sinks, etc., and heating to towel rails and linen cupboards. Cold-water supply is connected to the bottom of the storage cylinder on the secondary side. Make-up water to the radiator circuit is from a small tank positioned at the highest point of the system. By way of explanation, the radiator system is kept completely separate, as it is turned off in summer and tends to collect rusty water which must not be allowed to reach the taps. Also, it is taken direct from the boiler, as this water is required to be hotter than the supply to the taps, and as little water is lost from this system there can only be a small amount of furring. Towel rails and airing-cupboard coils must be connected to the hot water not the radiator circuit as these must not be turned off in summer.

A hot-water radiator system is seldom fitted in small sailing yachts, because it is quite possible to keep them satisfactorily warmed and aired by means of the galley and saloon stoves, which are cheaper to instal, and more convenient. In larger sailing yachts (50 tons and upwards) hot-water heating is often successfully installed, but it is costly and heavy, and requires careful layout to ensure satisfactory results.

The single pipe radiator system shown in Fig. 105 is most common for yacht work, being simple and economical in piping, but when necessary to make the temperature of each radiator the same a two pipe system is required.

Size of Boiler. This is determined for a combined heating and hot-water system by obtaining the sum of the following:

(1) Heat losses from spaces warmed.
(2) Heat required per hour at peak hot-water demand.
(3) A margin of 10 per cent to 15 per cent.

Heat losses (1) may be estimated by choosing a temperature difference between the inside and outside of spaces, say 65°F. inside minus 30°F. outside, making 35°F. and determining heat losses from standard published tables for glass, wood, steel, etc., based on the area of bulkheads, overheads, etc. A quick estimate may be made by working on a standard of $2\frac{1}{2}$ sq. ft. of radiator heating surface per 100 cu. ft. of space to be heated and then calculating heat transmission based on a temperature difference between the hot water and room air of, say, 100°F. (165°F.–65°F.). Figures for heat transmission of radiators are published by the makers. Heat demand per hour (2) may be calculated by making an allowance for each wash-basin, bath, shower, sink, etc., and partially off-setting this from hot water in the storage cylinder. The sum of (1) + (2) + (3) should be in units of B.T.U.s per hour and this may be used to determine the necessary boiler output, rated in the same units. A word of warning is called for here, as boilers have different ratings for different services. For instance a boiler used in a radiator system is rated at 4,400 B.T.U.s per hour per square foot of heating surface, while for a boiler used in a direct hot-water supply system, see Fig. 103, the rating is 11,000. For an indirect hot-water supply system, see Fig. 105, the rating is about 6,500.

These varying outputs are caused mainly by the temperature difference between the water entering the boiler and the water leaving it. With a radiator system practically no water is lost, so no cold is supplied; this gives a small temperature difference and small output. A direct hot water-supply system is supplied with a large amount of cold water, giving greater temperature difference and greater output. The combined radiator system and indirect hot-water supply would give a boiler rating of about 5,500, assuming each system to take about 50 per cent of the output.

Hot-Water Storage Cylinder. This may be of the direct type, see Figs. 103 and 104, or of the indirect type, see Fig. 105. The size may be determined by using the following method. Hot-water requirements for the peak period are satisfied by supply from boiler plus storage capacity. One or two hours may be allowed as the storage cylinder heating-up period. If a one-hour heating-up period is chosen, the storage capacity would be equal to the amount taken from the boiler per hour.

Example. Hot-water requirement = 100 gal. per hour, and a one-hour heating-up period
    is to be allowed.

Then capacity taken from boiler = 50 G.P.H.
         Storage capacity   = 50 G.P.H.

    Total water available in one
      hour peak period   = 100 G.P.H.

Heat to be supplied by boiler, allowing a temperature difference between cold water supplied and hot water used of $120°F. - 40°F. = 80°F.$, would equal $50 \times 10 \times 80 = 40,000$ B.T.U.s per hour.

Sanitary System. In the smallest type of yacht with wash-basins and sinks above the waterline, drainage may be direct overboard, or in order to reduce the number of sea fittings down to a minimum, wash-basins may be drained into W.C. pans.

With larger yachts, wash-basin and bath drains are often below or too close to the waterline for direct drainage, so some means of pumping must be employed. In order to keep the number of pumps and sea fittings to a minimum a sanitary tank is best employed, see Fig. 102, taking waste water from baths, showers and wash-basins. This can be pumped out automatically by fitting a float switch operating an electric pump. The galley sink is best discharged overboard separately, either drained or pumped, depending upon its height in relation to the waterline. This prevents the system from being overloaded and isolates the piping most likely to be blocked.

The W.C.s in a small sailing yacht must be of the under-waterline, or pump type, and to ensure satisfaction, a good and reputable make of W.C. should always be installed. If the W.C.s are more than 3 ft. below the waterline, or if a salt water flushing tank is fitted, water can be admitted to the pans by a push valve, or a foot-operated valve; but if not, the W.C.s must be of the type which pump in and pump out simultaneously by means of a double-acting pump. The discharge, or soil pipe, should be carried up above the waterline for a distance of about 2 ft. 6 in. to 3 ft., bent over, and brought down to discharge through the bottom at about the same distance below the waterline. By doing this, should any obstruction become lodged under the W.C. valves, flooding is prevented, even should the vessel take a considerable heel. The sea-water inlets should have sea-cocks fitted and should be situated forward of, and lower down than, the soil pipe discharge. Both soil pipes and salt-water inlets are usually lead pipes, the former 2 in., and the latter $1\frac{1}{4}$ in. bore. Lead pipes discharging below the waterline should be connected to the outer plank with a gunmetal flanged piece, but this is replaced by the sea-cock in the case of the salt-water inlet.

Plastic Piping. At the time of writing there is no plastic piping available which is capable of standing up to boiling water, although I would hasten to add that developments in the plastic field are such that I would not be surprised to see this remedied at any time.

If it is desired to make the maximum use of plastic materials for piping, polythene may be used for short lengths, such as W.C. soil pipes where bends are required, rigid P.V.C. for long straight runs such as cold fresh-water piping, as this material will stay straight without too many clips. It is advisable to use copper or steel for overboard discharges in the engine-room, where a slight fire might melt plastic piping and so allow the sea to flow in. Because of the fire danger, plastic is probably an unnecessary risk for fuel-oil piping also. All ship's side connections should be fitted with either stopcocks or non-return valves.

Fresh-Water Tanks. These are usually made of mild-steel plate and are galvanized after completion, usually about $\frac{1}{8}$ in. thick, and they may have either riveted or welded seams and joints. As a rule they are stowed in the hold under the saloon floor and, as owing to the sharp rise of floor in sailing vessels the space here is rather restricted, they must be shaped to conform to the section of the vessel in order to economize room. They must be of a size that will readily pass through the saloon skylight, and through a portable section or flush hatch, in the saloon floor. At the same time the capacity of each individual tank should be as large as circumstances permit, so as to save labour and material, i.e., if the matter is not properly gone into, three tanks might be fitted, whereas by careful measurement and calculation, the same capacity might have been obtained with two.

The actual capacity carried varies, of course, with the size and type of vessel; figures for typical cruising yachts being as follows: 9-ton sloop 30 gal., 19-ton sloop 80 gal., 48-ton ketch 270 gal., 65-ton ketch 450 gal., 134-ton ketch 2,000 gal. Fresh-water tanks should be properly stiffened inside to prevent any working in the large flat sides and tops, and if the tanks are exceptionally long or wide, a wash plate or diaphragm should be fitted to prevent excessive surging, also if the width is very great a diaphragm becomes necessary in order to reduce the free surface on the water when the tank is partially full, as this has a very adverse effect upon the stability.

Tanks are usually tested to a pressure of 5 lb. per sq. in., but if owing to the height of filling and air pipes, this pressure is likely to be exceeded in service, then tanks should be tested to twice the working pressure. The tanks must be properly secured in place, to obviate any danger of movement when the vessel rolls or pitches at sea. Usually strong posts are fitted from vessel's bottom to the cabin sole beams and the tanks are tommed and shored from the adjacent frames and beams. Manholes in large (handholes in small) tanks must be fitted, sufficient in number and so placed as to allow access to all interior parts of the tank for cleaning purposes, and these holes must be in accessible positions when the tanks are in their final stowed position. Manholes are usually an 'engineers' joint', i.e., a plate cover and rubber ring, stud bolted into a stiffening ring welded to the tank around the manhole. It is the usual practice to connect all of the tanks together with a levelling pipe, from which a fresh-water supply main is run. Each tank should have a shut-off cock fitted in an accessible position, so that in the event of leakage or trouble with any particular tank it may be shut off from the others. The filling pipe is usually run down from the deck on the port side, and connected into the levelling pipe. This reduces the number of connections to the tanks. A screw-down deck plate is fitted at the top of the filling pipe, and the water may be pumped in through a flexible hose or poured in through a funnel.

An air pipe must be fitted to each tank, and it is good practice to make these equal in area to the filling pipe. They may be run up independently, or combined into one large pipe, but in any case they should run up to a position above the filling plate and terminate in a pipe gooseneck bend, in a visible position, so that it may be seen when the tanks overflow; against the bulwark is not good practice in a sailing yacht, on account of the possibility of getting salt water down them, it is better to place them in the lee of a deck fitting. Sounding pipes are usually fitted in small yachts, although, of course, gauges may be fitted as an additional refinement. Fresh-water pipes are generally made of polythene in the smaller yachts, but in the larger ones the filling, air and main are galvanized mild steel and the branches copper, because of their smaller outside diameter and neater fittings.

Steering Arrangements. The arrangements for steering are of a very simple character, a long tiller being quite common in the smaller vessels, but some form of wheel gear is preferred. Power gears are very unusual in sailing vessels except in the very largest examples, where in some boats electric, or electric-hydraulic steering gears have been installed. In the type of vessel under notice the usual arrangement is a hand steering gear, with a wheel on deck, controlling some form of quadrant on the rudder head.

It is a very common practice to steer from a cockpit aft, so that the wheel is brought near the rudder stock. A drum on the steering-wheel spindle with a piece of flexible steel-wire rope captive, with one end running to the port side of the quadrant and the other to the starboard side, form the basis for steering gears on sailing yachts up to 100 tons or so. The steering wires must run in gunmetal lead sheaves suitably positioned. It must be remembered that the steering gear must be so arranged that clockwise movement of the steering wheel will cause the vessel to turn to starboard and vice versa for port turning. A sprocket is sometimes used in place of the drum, keyed to the steering-wheel spindle and a piece of roller chain shackled to the steering wires.

The area of rudder provided for small sailing yachts is relatively very large. If expressed as a fraction of the immersed longitudinal plane some actual figures are: 9 tons 1/9.6, 11 tons 1/12, 13 tons 1/10, 22 tons 1/13, 30 tons 1/14, 54 tons 1/12, 78 tons 1/12, 124 tons 1/14.7, 200 tons 1/18. The rudder area is not included in the area of the immersed longitudinal plane. Notice that the ratio decreases as the size of ship increases. The reason for this can be roughly put thus: with the increased tonnage there is increased length, and also greater length compared to the beam, actual figures being

Thames tons	13	78	200
Beams in W.L. length	3.1	3.3	3.7

Therefore the arm of the steering couple formed by the area of the rudder and the distance of the centre of effort of the rudder from the centre of lateral resistance, is greatly increased, and consequently a relatively smaller area of rudder becomes possible. Quickness and readiness to go about is a most important quality in a sailing yacht, and with this in mind the rudder should always be well immersed.

Classification. The fact that a vessel is classed is a guarantee to everybody connected with her that she is a sound well-constructed job, with scantlings and materials suitable for the size and purpose of the ship, and equipped in corresponding fashion. By having a vessel built to the rules and under the survey of any of the recognized classification societies, the owner is assured that his vessel conforms to a high standard of construction, and as it follows that, in order to maintain her class the vessel is subjected to periodical surveys, a high standard is kept up, the men who sail in her know that they have a sound vessel under them, and if at any time the owner wishes to sell, prospective purchasers have an independent guarantee that she is a well-built vessel, and in good condition. Also, it may be remarked here, that for insurance purposes classification carries its full weight, a high class meaning a low premium, whereas the fact of being unclassed would involve high insurance premiums.

Lloyd's class of A1 has for many years been proverbial as the symbol of perfection, but apart from Lloyd's Register there are other classification societies. Lloyd's Register of Shipping may be regarded as the oldest and most influential of all the classification societies, dating from about the middle of the eighteenth century, and classing about one-third of the total tonnage of the world.

Lloyd's highest yacht class is denoted by 100 A 1 Yacht ✠ LMC

To understand fully the implications of this notation, it is necessary to study carefully the rules and it is recommended that this should be done. It might however be useful to briefly mention the main points. The figure 1 indicates that a yacht's equipment of anchors, chain cables, hawsers and warps are of an approved standard. The symbols ✠ LMC show that the propulsion machinery has been surveyed at the makers' works during construction and has been satisfactorily installed. This machinery class may sometimes be virtually impossible to obtain especially with foreign machinery of mass produced manufacture. The symbols ★ LMC or LMC without ✠ or ★ are used to indicate this.

To retain her class in the Yacht Register, a yacht must undergo a Special Survey every four years with intermediate Biennial Surveys. At the age of twelve years and every eight years thereafter a more stringent Special Survey is required. Records of these surveys are made in the Register of Yachts. There are also Reclassification Surveys whereby a yacht can be restored to class after lapsing.

Machinery is also subject to periodical surveys as above.

It is possible to class yachts which have not been built under survey, application being made to Lloyd's Committee, who will direct a Special Survey to be made and drawings will be required for scrutiny.

Lloyd's have an established scale of fees which are based on the actual cost to the Society, and of course the time and travelling expenses of surveyors must be covered in these charges. Fees for surveys held at ports abroad are chargeable according to the nature and extent of the services rendered.

Ventilation. The ventilation of small yachts is most important for two reasons, one being the comfort and well-being of the persons aboard, and the other being the preservation in good order of the vessel herself, and her valuable contents. An ill-ventilated and stuffy boat can easily become 'smelly', and most unpleasant to live in, and

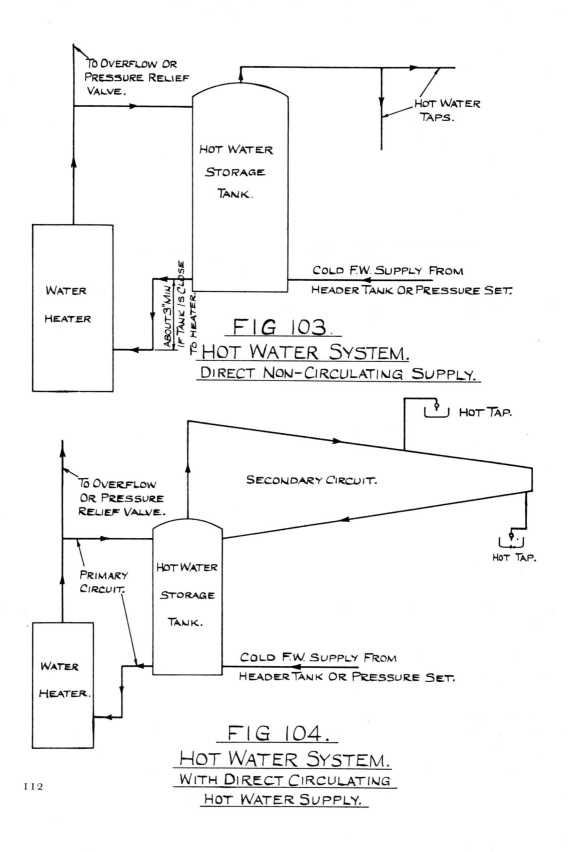

TO OVERFLOW OR PRESSURE RELIEF VALVE.

HOT WATER TAPS.

HOT WATER STORAGE TANK.

WATER HEATER

ABOUT 3"MIN IF TANK IS CLOSE TO HEATER.

COLD F.W. SUPPLY FROM HEADER TANK OR PRESSURE SET.

FIG 103.
HOT WATER SYSTEM.
DIRECT NON-CIRCULATING SUPPLY.

HOT TAP.

SECONDARY CIRCUIT.

TO OVERFLOW OR PRESSURE RELIEF VALVE.

PRIMARY CIRCUIT.

HOT WATER STORAGE TANK.

HOT TAP.

WATER HEATER.

COLD F.W. SUPPLY FROM HEADER TANK OR PRESSURE SET.

FIG 104.
HOT WATER SYSTEM.
WITH DIRECT CIRCULATING
HOT WATER SUPPLY.

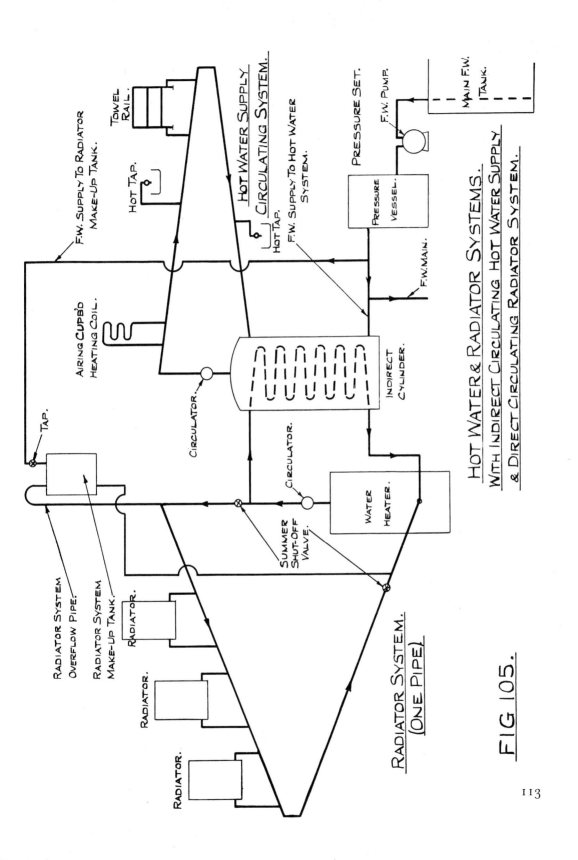

FW. SUPPLY TO RADIATOR MAKE-UP TANK.

TOWEL RAIL.

HOT TAP.

HOT WATER SUPPLY CIRCULATING SYSTEM.

HOT TAP.

FW. SUPPLY TO HOT WATER SYSTEM.

PRESSURE SET.

FW. PUMP.

MAIN FW. TANK.

PRESSURE VESSEL.

FW. MAIN.

AIRING CUPB'D HEATING COIL.

INDIRECT CYLINDER.

CIRCULATOR.

TAP.

CIRCULATOR.

CIRCULATOR.

SUMMER SHUT-OFF VALVE.

WATER HEATER.

RADIATOR SYSTEM OVERFLOW PIPE.

RADIATOR SYSTEM MAKE-UP TANK.

RADIATOR.

RADIATOR.

RADIATOR.

RADIATOR.

RADIATOR SYSTEM. (ONE PIPE)

HOT WATER & RADIATOR SYSTEMS.

WITH INDIRECT CIRCULATING HOT WATER SUPPLY & DIRECT CIRCULATING RADIATOR SYSTEM.

FIG 105.

113

lack of fresh air below causes damp, mildew, rot and various other unwelcome conditions.

It is found in small yachts of the type under consideration that sufficient ventilation can usually be obtained by the simple and ordinary means of cowl and mushroom ventilators, combined with reasonable skylights, without resorting to the use of electric fans and trunking, or any of the expensive methods necessary on larger vessels. A point to be borne in mind is that a free circulation of air must be allowed throughout the vessel; therefore the cabin sole (or lower deck) must not be fitted close out to the ship's side planking. If ceiling or side lining is fitted in the cabins there should be spaces, grilles, or some equivalent, so that air can get behind it; bathroom and W.C. doors should be similarly treated; in fact, every means possible adopted to secure fresh air everywhere and so avoid that musty damp atmosphere so often encountered below decks.

Ventilators in general may be made proof against rain and spray, but when solid water on the deck is to be reckoned with, the most effective part of a ventilator is its coaming height which positively prevents the shipping of water.

The next most effective method of keeping water out whilst providing ventilation is by the suitable use of baffles and a notable example of this type is the Tannoy ventilator. This is only about $1\frac{1}{2}$ in. high and circular in plan view and is most effective against rain and spray, but not against solid water over about $1\frac{1}{2}$ in. deep, so should be positioned clear of berths.

The French head vent combines coaming height with effective baffling and is therefore very effective. In this ventilator, see Fig. 106, the aperture at front in the hood is slightly larger, and cut lower, than the hole at back in the coaming, which in turn is slightly larger in area than the area of the vent coaming. Any water that enters at front is likely to drop through the drain holes before overflowing into coaming, and in practice these vents have been found quite effective in all types of vessel. They are usually made of steel plate, all welded.

The water box vent is a further variation combining coaming height with baffling, but is rather too bulky.

Another approach to this problem is by using the form which may be completely closed when severe conditions are expected, and are therefore mainly for use in harbour if mounted in an exposed position. Two examples of these are the cowl vent which should be fitted with a lift-off cowl on a fixed coaming with a plug for closing completely and the mushroom vent which may be screwed down tight. The cowl may be used to encourage air supply by turning into the wind, whilst the latter being very low in height is suitable for use in positions which must be kept clear for the use of ropes.

Ventilator arrangement on small cruisers and ocean racers should make use of the fact that the coachroof forms the coaming element necessary for complete watertightness, so most ventilators may be of the low, baffled type, fitted on top of the coachroof. This type has probably superseded the waterbox vent on these boats. Mushroom vents may be used for the forward and after peaks, where they must be screwed down in bad weather.

For larger yachts the following arrangements are made for natural ventilation. Goosenecks on the inside of bulwarks vent the hold spaces under the lower deck. These are made from galvanized steel pipe from $1\frac{1}{2}$ in. bore upwards.

Natural ventilation to the forecastle is achieved by using cowl vents, as is the natural supply to the engine-room.

114

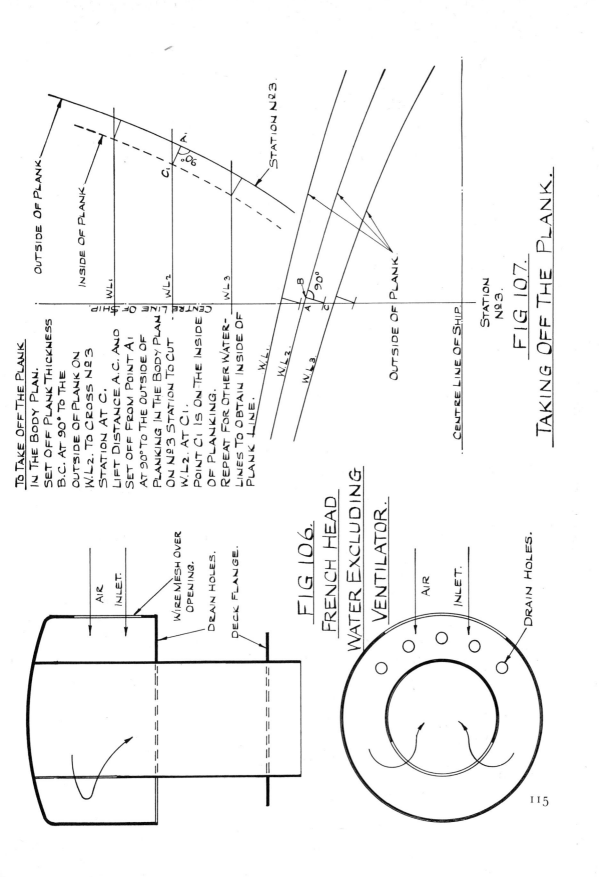

To Take Off The Plank.
In The Body Plan.
Set Off Plank Thickness
B.C. At 90° To The
Outside Of Plank On
W.L₂. To Cross Nº3
Station At C.
Lift Distance A.C. And
Set Off From Point A₁
At 90° To The Outside Of
Planking In The Body Plan
On Nº3 Station To Cut
W.L₂. At C₁.
Point C₁ Is On The Inside
Of Planking.
Repeat For Other Water-
Lines To Obtain Inside Of
Plank Line.

OUTSIDE OF PLANK.

INSIDE OF PLANK.

WL₁

WL₂

WL₃

CENTRE LINE OF SHIP.

STATION Nº3.

.06

A₁

C₁

90°

B

A

C

OUTSIDE OF PLANK.

W.L₁

W.L₂

W.L₃

CENTRE LINE OF SHIP.

STATION Nº3.

FIG 107.
TAKING OFF THE PLANK.

AIR

INLET.

WIRE MESH OVER OPENING.

DRAIN HOLES.

DECK FLANGE.

FIG 106.
FRENCH HEAD
WATER EXCLUDING
VENTILATOR.

AIR

INLET.

DRAIN HOLES.

115

Mushroom vents are used over W.C.s and bathrooms. In owner's and guests' accommodation aft, cowl vents are fitted where possible.

Forced ventilation to accommodation spaces and engine-room is achieved conveniently by using the in-line waterproof type of fan mounted above the weather deck with a French head on top. The fan forms a coaming whilst the French head provides the necessary baffling. Alternatively the space between deckhouse side and inside of panelling may be used to conceal trunking and the inlet or outlet formed in the deckhouse plating with a suitable internal baffle.

All openings leading to trunking should be covered with wire mesh or louvres, etc., to prevent the harbouring of vermin.

Natural ventilation is the oldest, simplest and cheapest, and can be the best system, if it is arranged properly, bearing the fact in mind that air which has been breathed is warmer than pure air, and rises to the top of a compartment. Therefore supply openings (cowls and their like) should be trunked low down and exhaust openings in the deckhead.

All ventilation openings must have an appropriate fitting on the weather deck, and whether it be cowl, mushroom, gooseneck, French vent, or skylight, it is highly important that the coaming, and its attachment to the deck, be strong and substantial, commensurate with the size of the fitting. Cowls should always be made to unship, and plugs or covers be provided for the coamings during heavy weather. It is good practice to make all ventilation coamings spigot through the deck as well as giving them a reasonable height. Notice here that the Ministry of Transport does not recognize any ventilator of less than 5 in. diameter, and although they have no jurisdiction over yachts, it has to be admitted that some small yachts have very inadequate ventilators, and it would seem desirable to make 3 in. diameter the minimum for any size of yacht.

Electrical Equipment. Almost all cruising boats are fitted with an auxiliary engine with integral generator, electric starter and battery. This is equivalent to the thin end of the wedge, as if there is a battery aboard, electric cabin lighting is the next logical step, followed by an electric log, direction-finding equipment, navigation and deck lighting, etc.

All of these appliances can be run off a 12-volt direct current which is the same used for auxiliary starting, so they form standard equipment even for the smallest cruisers. A radio receiver can, of course, be run off its own dry battery.

In larger yachts with more space and greater need for amenities, to the above list may be added some or all of the following. Radio telephone, radar, depth recorder, refrigerator, electric pumps for fresh-water supply and sanitary-tank discharge, ship's telephones, etc. These are suitable for running off a 24-volt D.C. supply and a suitable generating set is required, preferably diesel driven. The auxiliary engine starting battery would be separate and for the one purpose only, still charged by its own generator and all of the remaining electrical supply taken from the generator set. The use of a battery of sufficient size enables a quiet period to be achieved at night, with the generator shut down.

The ship's *battery capacity* is determined by the following means. *Battery capacity* (*ampere hours*) = *Night load* (*amps*) × 10. This allows a quiet period of ten hours.

The *generator output* must be sufficient to cope with the *maximum load demand + charging rate* measured in kilowatts.

A 24-volt installation is not suitable for running direct from the generator, without a battery.

There is a considerable range of additional electrical equipment available and in demand for the largest yachts, but this is not available for 24 volts D.C., so 110 volts D.C. is required, with generator set and battery. The additional equipment running off this voltage could include anchor windlass, capstan, boat hoist, automatic pilot, deep-freeze plant, bilge pump, dishwasher, food mixer, etc. The battery capacity and generator output are obtained as previously stated and the maximum load demand is when getting under way. Therefore *generator output = getting under way load + charging rate.*

Certain other appliances such as television, radiogram, air conditioning, etc., require an A.C. supply in order that standard units may be installed. One solution is the use of a rotary coverter, although a complete A.C. installation is probably the best method with such a wide use of electrical equipment. Batteries would then be of no use, so a continuously running alternator would have to be accepted. In a really large yacht this could be tolerated if space is allocated for effective sound insulation.

To sum up, the following installations are possible:

(1) The smallest.

12 volts D.C. using the engine starting battery. In some small yachts 6 volts D.C. is used, but this is not recommended owing to the higher ampere values.

(2) Increased range of electrical equipment.

24 volts D.C. with generating set and ship's battery.

(3) Full electrical equipment.

110 volts D.C. supply with generating sets, ship's battery and a rotary converter for any A.C. requirement.

(4) As an alternative to (3) a complete A.C. installation, with constant running alternator (day and night) and no main battery, although a small one is most essential for emergency lighting.

Battery stowage compartments must be well ventilated as an explosive gas is generated during charging and discharging, which must not be allowed to accumulate. With the smallest batteries this may be achieved by natural ventilation only, but larger ones giving off more gas must have forced ventilation. Electric fans for this purpose must be so arranged that the explosive gas does not pass around the motor because of the danger of sparking. The centrifugal type fan will prevent this and may be used for extraction or supply, but the axial flow type with exposed motor may be used for supply only, as only fresh air will then be in contact with the motor; a natural outlet should be arranged remote from the supply.

Battery trays for lead/acid batteries must be lined with G.R.P. or lead, a suitable sheet being 5 lb. per sq. ft. weight. Nickel/iron batteries with an alkaline electrolyte may have wooden or steel trays unlined, but there must be sufficient space allowed between battery and tray to keep any excess distilled water from contact with the bottom of the battery.

It is good practice to have the *switchboard* made up to Lloyd's requirements and it should, of course, be quite accessible.

The principal fittings required on a switchboard for the small type of vessel are as follows: Main dynamo switch, direct or to battery; voltmeter (switch and fuse in circuit with voltmeter): two ammeters (for charge and discharge); battery cut-out, and controlling switches and fuses for each outgoing circuit from the switchboard.

The circuits are simple in character; from main switch on the switchboard to a fuse box, with not more than seven lamps from one fuse. The wiring is simple, generally 5-ampere wire is used for lighting, single 3/.029 wire, T.R. sheathed in the accommodation and butyl insulated P.C.P. sheathed, braided with fire-resisting compound, in the engine-room. The wiring in the engine-room may be in conduit if desired, but it is not essential.

The wattage of the lamps used is selected to suit their position in the vessel, such as engine-room, owner's accommodation, crew's quarters, etc., but the total load should not exceed 5 amperes on the lighting cables. The lighting fuses are 5 ampere. Small fans can be run off the lighting system if required; apart from this each motor must have its own separate switch, fuse and wiring.

Auxiliary Propulsion. In the choice of diesel engines versus petrol engines the former are preferred when weight and space are not too severely limited. Below about 20 tons T.M. it is these two points which often dictate the use of petrol engines.

Shaft installation for deep-keel sailing yachts may be from one of the following alternatives.

(1) Centre line with aperture in rudder and a two-bladed propeller which should be fixed with blades vertical behind the sternpost when not in use. If the diameter is restricted a three-bladed propeller should be used.

(2) Single-screw side installation with 'A' bracket and three-bladed propeller. A right-hand propeller suits a shaft on the port side and a left-hand on the starboard side, assuming the shaft about parallel to the ship's centre line. If the centre line of shaft produced crosses the ship's centre line abaft her pivoting point, the right-hand propeller then suits the starboard side and the left-hand the port side. If this is carried out, the paddle effect of the propeller will act against the tendency to deviate from a straight course due to the line of action of the propeller thrust.

(3) Side installation with sterntube close to rudder stock, above top of rudder, see Fig. 15, the propeller being abaft the rudder. This has the advantage of producing the thrust close to the centre line of ship and means that the masking of the propeller is very slight, as this is a part of the yacht with a fine ending. A three-bladed propeller is most suitable and the remarks made in (2) regarding rotation still apply, but to a much reduced degree. The immersion must be watched, as it could be too little.

The general idea now is that propellers should be fixed for sailing and not allowed to rotate. A propeller rotating in neutral is liable to cause gearbox lubrication problems.

There are various types of propellers available designed to reduce drag, suitable for small boats. Among these the clam type is simplest; its blades will fold due to the forward motion of the boat, when the engine is not in use, and open out due to centrifugal force when the shaft is rotated. With this type, however, a yacht cannot motor astern. Another type is the automatic feathering propeller which will turn its blades fore and aft automatically when not in use, for minimum drag. This type also cannot be used for reversing. A third type is the reversing feathering propeller, the blades of which may be controlled from inboard to give three positions, which are ahead, feathered and for reversing. With this type the boat may be driven astern without having a reverse gearbox fitted on the engine.

Propeller R.P.M. In general the lower the R.P.M. the higher the propeller efficiency, but if this necessitates fitting a large reduction gear there will be a loss in efficiency here plus the increased weight and space and increased diameter of propeller and shafting which can be ill afforded in a sailing yacht. On balance, shaft rotation of 1,500 to 2,000 R.P.M. can be accepted and a propeller designed to suit. A stop should be fitted on the throttle at the top designed R.P.M. to prevent the engine from being overloaded.

Propellers. For satisfactory performance each propeller must have its diameter, pitch and blade area determined to suit the boat's speed and form, the engine R.P.M. and horsepower. There is no such thing as a propeller to suit an engine, it must suit the boat and engine together. For the same type of engine in different boats, widely different propellers would probably be required. For this reason the propeller characteristics must be determined by using specialist knowledge and data for the type of boat in question. An incorrect propeller forecast at the building stage could result in the propeller aperture or 'A' bracket being too small and perhaps impossible to correct without the expensive job of altering the shaft line.

Speed under power for any particular boat is best judged by the speed/length ratio $\frac{V}{\sqrt{L}}$ where

V = speed in knots;
L = length of waterline in feet.

If this ratio is taken as 1.2, so that $V = 1.2\sqrt{L}$, this will give a guide to what speed may be expected from the deep-keel type of sailing yacht without being too unreasonable. This gives about $6\frac{1}{2}$ knots for a 30 ft. waterline and about $7\frac{1}{2}$ knots for a 40 ft. waterline. At this speed, increased power is dissipated mainly in wave-making rather than increasing speed. A high trial speed for prestige purposes is bought at high price, if the result is that at a lower speed, giving reasonable range as dictated by fuel capacity, the propeller will be operating at reduced efficiency and will, in reality, be too small for the boat.

A very common misunderstanding is connected with the speed of sailing yachts when under power. There appears to be a strong opinion that because of the fine lines of sailing yachts they should be very easily driven, but, unfortunately, matters are not quite so simple as this. The principal resistance at low speeds is frictional or skin resistance, and if this is judged by wetted surface, the comparison between sailing and power yacht is very close thus:

Type of yacht	*Aux. ketch*	*T.S. motor yacht*	*Aux. schooner*	*T.S. motor yacht*
Thames tons	78	79	200	195
Wetted surface sq. ft.	1,173	1,170	2,252	2,140

When speaking of powering sailing yachts the word 'auxiliary' is unfortunate, because it instantly conveys the idea that it is of minor subsidiary importance, and therefore can be pushed well into the background. In the event, however, of a total absence of wind, with adverse tides, the auxiliary power becomes the only power, and the claim can fairly be made that the 'auxiliary' engine is of primary importance, and should be installed in a manner worthy of its undoubted value. Any person who has tried to correct minor engine troubles in a hurry, on a motor hidden away in an inaccessible position in a cupboard under a stair, will probably appreciate the reasons for the foregoing remarks.

Engine Seats. See also page 57. In all but the most lightly built craft it is quite good practice to bolt engines solid to their beds without the use of flexible mounts. This avoids the necessity of using flexible connections for all engine piping and flexible shaft couplings. The beds should be heavily constructed, well connected to frames and floors and run as far forward and aft as practicable. Weight saving should not be attempted here.

For fitting snugly just forward of the sternpost, which is the most advantageous position for single-screw installations, the vertical-type engine with bolting faces approximately at the same height as the crankshaft is most suitable. Holding-down feet on the engine and gear box should be in line, so that straight engine beds may be used. Horizontally opposed engines, being wider, must be positioned farther forward and possibly higher than the vertical type.

Twin-screw installations demand an engine space at or near amidships, to gain width and give a suitable line of shafting. This takes the best part of the ship, but is quite practical in steel sailing yachts when the space between and below them can be used for built-in tanks, with the engine beds on the tank crown.

The actual position of the engine in the yacht is a most difficult question. All sorts of contrivances have been tried, but it would appear that there are only two reasonable positions, both presenting various good and bad features. If the engine is placed on the centre line well aft, with a straight drive to a propeller in an aperture, the advantages seem to be that the engine is in a handy place for cockpit control, somewhat separated from the accommodation, shafting is of a minimum length, exhaust can be easily led clear of the steering position, centre-line drive is obtained, and the whole installation is kept within a reasonable space. Certain disadvantages are that it is sometimes difficult to get the engine low enough to obtain proper propeller immersion, accessibility is very poor due to the fining in of the after end, and the space occupied by the engine can be made in a sailing yacht one of the best cabins in the vessel. Also with the fine lines of the after end, it is very difficult to arrange a belt drive off the engine for anything in the nature of a dynamo, pump for hydraulic windlass, etc.

The other position referred to is a few feet forward in the widest part of the boat where it can go hard down on top of the keel. This position allows the propeller to be low enough to be well immersed. The main disadvantage is that this position is usually in the way of the main cabin, but quite satisfactory cabin arrangements can be made to suit this position, usually by making the engine off centre. This enables a passage to be arranged on the opposite side. The shaft can be angled so that either a side or centre-line installation of propeller becomes possible. The exhaust pipe is usually run across to the nearest side and then aft to the transom.

Electric starting equipment is a great advantage and should always be fitted, together with remote control; the hand starting gear should be an emergency method only. Special lubrication arrangements are necessary, as it is often necessary to place the engines of sailing yachts on a fairly steep rake. Engine-driven bilge pumps are seldom fitted in these boats, and silencers are usually of a very simple character, water-jacketing or water-injecting being about the only refinements in common use.

Painting. The fouling of a vessel's bottom is caused by marine growths of a weed and animal nature, the former congregating near the waterline, and the latter on the lower parts of the hull. At one time copper sheathing was much used for covering the bottoms of wood ships. Copper corrodes but little under the action of sea water, but a notable feature is that when this metal is immersed in sea water, a constant process of exfoliation, or formation of soluble poisonous salts of copper is taking place, which, in washing off, effectually prevents the adhesion of weeds, shell fish or other marine growths. Therefore sheathing with copper not only prevents fouling, but protects the planking from the attacks of worms, a necessity for vessels using tropical waters. But remember that copper and iron or steel must not upon any account come into contact when immersed in sea water, or they would form a strong galvanic battery, resulting in the rapid wasting away of the iron or steel, so that wooden vessels which are to be coppered must be fastened throughout with non-ferrous metals.

As a substitute for coppering there are many good anti-fouling compositions on the market for coating ships' bottoms, the function of which is to kill these marine organisms while in their early stages. The principle of these anti-fouling compositions is that by the slow but constant solution of the poisonous matters (mainly copper and mercury) which they contain, the bottom of the vessel is kept in an antiseptic condition, making it most difficult for the minute organisms which cause fouling to obtain the initial footing necessary for their growth and development. Therefore the anti-fouling coat is constantly wasting away, and requires frequent renewal, and a good priming coat is essential.

A good painting specification for a small yacht is roughly as follows:

Topsides. One coat of fillers, three coats of priming, one coat of enamel.
Bottom. Two coats of priming, one coat of anti-fouling undercoating and one coat of anti-fouling.
Decks. Planed and scraped for scrubbing.
Brightwork. Spars, covering boards, king plank, rails, companions and skylights, and all other brightwork, four coats of synthetic varnish.
Interior of hull. Bilge up to cabin sole, three coats of bitumastic solution. Above cabin sole, three coats of priming, and one of non-condensation.
Cabin decoration. Bulkheads, furniture, etc., three coats of priming and one coat of enamel of approved colour.

To obtain the best and most satisfying results, there are various elementary rules to be observed in painting, such as: good brushes should always be used. Painting should always be done in fine, settled weather, and on an absolutely dry surface. Rain, frost and dew will spoil wet paint. Be sure that varnishing will dry before evening. The secret of good painting is the rubbing down after every coat of priming or undercoating. It is good practice to coat the boot-top with a special boot-top paint that will not be affected by the weather or the water, there being various good makes, and a choice of colours available. Care should be taken never to paint or varnish both sides of new wood in positions where air cannot freely circulate; to do so is a sure inducement to dry rot.

Chapter 6

Thames Tonnage. In England it is the usual practice to judge the size of a yacht by her Thames Measurement Tonnage. This system of tonnage measurement was adopted by the Royal Thames Yacht Club in 1854 as an approximate representation of internal capacity of a yacht, and consequently, an indication of her size. It was adopted by the Yacht Racing Association in 1878, and as stated, is now used by everyone connected with yachts and yachting as an index to relative size. To those accustomed to think in terms of displacement, deadweight, or gross and net tonnage, Thames measurement at first seems strange and crude, but with a few years' experience and a reasonable amount of data, it becomes apparent that it is a sound basis for all sorts of transactions. The rule is as follows: from the length (measured from the foreside of stem to the after side of sternpost on deck) deduct the breadth (extreme), multiply the result by the breadth, and the product by the half-breadth, and divide by 94. The expression is therefore:

$$\frac{(L-B) \times B \times \frac{1}{2}B}{94}$$

This tonnage is given in Lloyd's Register of Yachts for all British yachts, and amongst its other uses, serves as a good basis for valuation, laying-up fees, etc. Where the sternpost does not extend up to the deck, the length is taken to the centre of the rudder head, and any part of a ton is taken as a ton. Recently Lloyd's Register have given a ruling that a part of a ton up to one half is to be neglected and one half and over taken as one ton, so that there is a certain amount of ambiguity in the measurement. The safe thing is therefore to express T.M. in tons and decimals of a ton.

Notice here that the Board of Trade figures for tonnage must not be used for computing Thames tonnage, because they measure the length to inside of stem, and in a wood yacht this makes quite a difference, and the reduced tonnage obtained by such a figure is likely to lead to dispute. There is obviously no direct relationship between Thames tonnage and displacement, but a rough proportion can easily be established as an inspection of the tabulation of actual cases given below will show:

		Sloop	*Sloop*	*Sloop*	*Ketch*	*Ketch*
Thames	tons	11	13	19	48	65
Displacement	,,	8.9	11.25	15.75	42.1	61.4
Gross	,,	8.72	10.53	15.28	37	47.48
Net	,,	7.25	9.36	14.33	28	30.61

These figures are typical of modern sailing yachts, but cannot in any way be applied to full power yachts.

Coefficients of Fineness. One of the peculiar features of small sailing yachts is the very small values of the block coefficient of fineness of displacement, the coefficient of fineness of immersed midship section, and the prismatic coefficient. This is a point which is not actually within the scope of this work, but it is mentioned, because there is a lot of misconception on the subject, the popular idea being that sailing yachts are very much finer than power yachts, and that it is proved by their relative coefficients. But is it? Look at the following comparisons:

	80-ton ketch	*80-ton T.S.M.Y.*
Block coefficient	.257	.453
Midsection coefficient	.47	.742
Water plane coefficient	.696	.684
Prismatic coefficient	.548	.61
Wetted surface	1,173 sq. ft.	1,170 sq. ft.
Breadth	17 ft. 6 in.	15 ft.
Draught	8 ft. 6 in.	4 ft. 10½ in.
Length/breadth	3.26	5.35
Breadth/draught	2.06	3.09

The two most striking features are the differences in the relationship between the proportions of length to breadth, and breadth to draught. There is nothing in the water-plane coefficient and the wetted surface, but the great difference in the block coefficient is accounted for by the difference in draught and the fact that, in a sailing yacht, the block coefficient must be measured to the underside of keel because of its bulk, and this goes for midship section coefficient also. Therefore, remembering that nearly all sailing yachts of the type we have under consideration have a hollow section towards the keel, these two coefficients are not capable of comparison with a power yacht at all. The true comparison lies in the first two elements mentioned: the L/B factor indicates that the sailing vessel is by comparison stumpy and short, and the B/D factor shows that any fineness in the shape of the section is more than offset by the disproportionate draught. Consequently we are forced to the obvious conclusion that each type must have its own necessary features, and that comparisons of this sort are not only invidious, but useless as well.

Inside Ballast. Although there is a sharp division of opinion on the question of whether inside, or loose ballast, should or should not be carried in small vessels, there is no doubt that in larger yachts it is favoured by the professional skippers, who declare that a small alteration in trim will often greatly improve the sailing qualities of a vessel. This may be due to the corresponding movement in the position of the centre of lateral resistance, making the vessel more ardent, or slack, as the case may be, perhaps improving the readiness to come about in tacking, or reducing lee helm if the vessel is too slack.

If all this is true of large yachts, it should be equally true of small ones, and in any case, if there is a reasonable amount of loose ballast to move about, it saves expense in the event of future alterations to the ship. Suppose, for instance, a larger and heavier engine should be fitted, then, to keep the trim right it would certainly be cheaper to move or take away loose ballast, than it would be to cut out a piece of the lead keel and insert wood. Or if the owner should decide to have larger headsails, or perhaps shorten the boom and lengthen the luff, the centre of effort of the sail plan would move forward and a change of trim is indicated, and is easily achieved if there is loose ballast to adjust. Finally, if any benefit should be considered likely by so doing, the vessel can be lightened by the amount of inside ballast carried. The slight reduction of metacentric height, or loss of stiffness, caused by not having all the weight of ballast outside, can be ignored, except in the case of closely matched racing boats.

Improved performance could be due to the movement of longitudinal centre of buoyancy (L.C.B.), following a change of trim and this would probably be a very rewarding field for experimental tank research, as it has been shown* that in power-driven vessels a position of L.C.B. away from the optimum results in a large increase in resistance, and in sailing boats with their large ballast keel, there would be no difficulty in placing the L.C.B. in the optimum position. An example taken from the data given by Sir Amos L. Ayre for power-driven vessels is as follows:

L.B.P. = 36.0 ft. V = 6 knots $V/\sqrt{L}$ = 1.00.
L.C.B. 2 per cent forward of optimum. Increase in resistance = 18 per cent.
L.C.B. 2 per cent aft of optimum. Increase in resistance   = 2 per cent.
2 per cent of 36.0 ft. = 0.72 ft.

These figures must not be used for sailing boats, but there could be a similar phenomenon with them.

The Building Board. In some yards it is the practice when building wooden yachts, with sawn or grown frames, to use during erection a permanent datum line, which may be called for want of a better term, the 'building board'. Its purpose is to enable the workmen to fit and erect the framing, stem and stern timbers correctly, both for length and height, in a convenient and ready manner. It consists of a length of boarding about 9 × 1 in., straight on the top edge, and equal in length to the vessel (see Fig. 109). The frame spaces and numbers, together with lines indicating the crossings of stem and stern are drawn upon it, and it is set up level, or to the building declivity, with its top edge at the waterline height, and a little to one side, so as to pass by the stern and stem. It is made on the loft floor, and a height batten is supplied with it, giving distances to the outline, and to beams at centre. By using a short straight edge the waterline can be

*Sir Amos L. Ayre, *Transactions of the North East Coast Institution of Engineers and Shipbuilders*, Vol. 64.

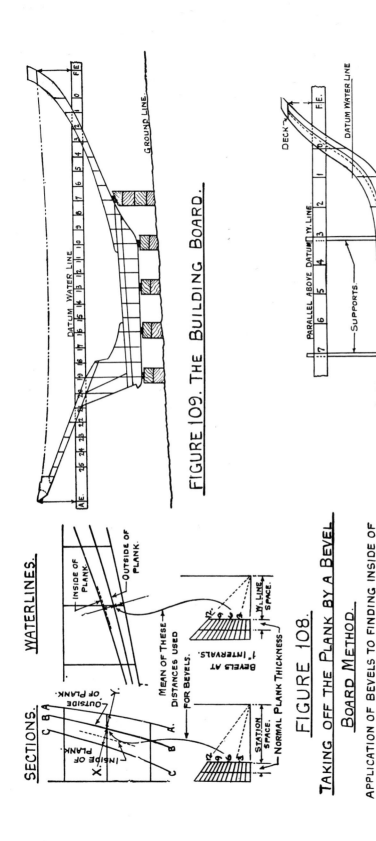

FIGURE 109. THE BUILDING BOARD.

FIGURE 110. MODIFIED BUILDING BOARD FOR SETTING UP
AN OVERHANGING STEM ON A WOODEN VESSEL.

WATERLINES.

SECTIONS.

FIGURE 108.

TAKING OFF THE PLANK BY A BEVEL
BOARD METHOD.

APPLICATION OF BEVELS TO FINDING INSIDE OF
PLANKING. STATION SPACE BEVELS USED FOR
SECTIONS OF BODY, AND WATERLINE SPACE BEVELS
FOR WATERLINES. METHOD IS BEST APPLIED IN
ONE VIEW OR PLANE ONLY, USING THREE SECTIONS
OR WATERLINES, SO THAT A MEAN BEVEL MAY BE USED.

125

levelled transversely, and individual frame heights checked, in addition to facilitating the usual plumbing and horning operations. A modified form of this building board is often used for setting up an overhanging stem on a composite or wooden vessel (see Fig. 110).

General Arrangement or Layout. Every experienced owner has his own idea of an ideal layout, which is almost bound to differ in many respects from that of most other owners; so that, although in these small yachts the limitations are very severe, yet there is no accepted standard and it is truly surprising to see the many different methods that are devised from time to time to utilize the available space.

It must be remembered that a man building a yacht is riding his hobby, and also that what one sailing man considers perfect, several other sailing men would be prompt to condemn for various reasons, based largely upon their own opinions and experience. This is all perfectly natural, but, as mentioned elsewhere, the indubitable fact remains that the man who is paying has the absolute right and privilege of having just exactly what he wishes.

These remarks apply to the man having a 'one off' boat, but with the advent of moulded construction, both plywood and fibreglass, the need to standardize has arisen for economy reasons and the market for the standard boat discovered.

Cooking, washing, sleeping and W.C. facilities should never be too cramped, the cockpit and chart space must be adequate. Sail stowage and wardrobe space must not be forgotten. In the ocean racer or cruising type up to about 15 tons T.M., a headroom of 5 ft. 10 in. on the centre line under the beams is just about acceptable; 6 ft. is good unless the owner happens to be 6 ft. plus tall. Berths 6 ft. 3 in. long, by 2 ft. 3 in. wide or 2 ft. wide, if the boat's flare helps space available, are acceptable and with two-tier bunks, 2 ft. 6 in. bottom to bottom is about minimum and this does not allow sitting up. Doors to W.C. and forecastle should not be less than 1 ft. 9 in.; for the companionway door 2 ft. is good. The W.C. space should have at least 2 ft. 6 in. of width, more if a wash-basin is required on a side bulkhead. W.C.s may be fitted on a 6 in. to 8 in. step to raise them and therefore enable them to be moved outboard when on the ship's side. 1 ft. 6 in. is about the minimum distance required to squeeze by an obstruction (and this means turning sideways), except at knee height at settee and table ends when 6 in. to 9 in. may be worked to. Wash basins 2 ft. 7 in. high to top. Tables 2 ft. 6 in. to top with 1 ft. 9 in. minimum length allowed for each person, 2 ft. is better; the Admiralty figure of 1 ft. 6 in. is too small. It probably allows for part of the crew being on watch. Chair height to suit 2 ft. 6 in. high table is 1 ft. 6 in., settee height may be less for comfort at 1 ft. 4 in. with depth back to front not less than 1 ft. 6 in. or more than 1 ft. 9 in. Sail hatch 2 ft. by 2 ft. Galley working surfaces 3 ft. high. Companionway steps are about right at 8 in. rise, a step in the cabin sole should not exceed 8 in. If these quoted standards are reduced, the people using the boat will notice it to their disadvantage.

Variations in Construction. These are not always definite enough in character to merit the term of different methods, but they may be roughly listed as follows: composite, semi-composite, carvel, clencher, double-skin, laminated, longitudinal framed and moulded plywood and fibreglass. This work being intended to be descriptive of the constructional methods in general use for wood yachts of from 8 to 80 tons, the

126

standard practice has been more or less adhered to, with only occasional references to other methods. Of these variations in construction, some are good, some not so good, some old and well tried, some new and practically untried—as far as the test of time is concerned, at all events.

Speaking generally, and leaving all-steel construction out, the construction that has been here described is undoubtedly the best for the range of tonnage mentioned above. A notable, time-honoured and most successful variation is *Composite Construction* and anyone who has had the privilege of inspecting one of the old clipper ships or some of the beautiful composite yachts, produced by designers like Fife, Mylne, or Nicholson, cannot fail to be greatly impressed by the strength and lightness of their building.

The composite method of construction was introduced about the year 1860, when the demand for longer and lighter ships defeated the strength capabilities of the all-wood construction of the period. Although the old wooden ships possessed great beam and depth, yet when they reached a length of about 200 ft. they proved to be longitudinally weak, and used to hog very badly. This was due to the impossibility of making really strong joints between the great multitude of pieces of wood which made up the whole structure, and to the enormous weight of the stem and stern structures. Furthermore, the weight of the structural material of their hulls was a very large percentage of their total displacement, and out of all proportion to the actual standard of strength and stiffness attained. Consequently some improvement was very necessary, and as iron construction was at that time fairly well advanced, it was obvious that a combination of the increased strength of iron with the advantages of wood was the answer to the problem. Hence the term composite; and later on, with the introduction of steel, further improvements became possible, and the modern composite vessel is a very fine job indeed.

In addition to the reasons stated above, a further inducement for bringing out composite ships was the China tea trade. The Suez Canal was opened about 1870, and previous to this all vessels making the China voyage had to go round the Cape. The steamers of the period could not make this long voyage pay, so the tea trade was conducted with larger sailing ships, the famous China tea clippers; and as the profits of the voyage depended largely upon a quick run home, it was essential to have copper sheathing in order to ensure a clean bottom for the return trip. Wood ships of the size and lightness required could not be built, and iron ships, wood sheathed and coppered, were too costly. Consequently the composite system was adopted, and there followed a succession of the finest examples of square-rigged ships that were ever built, and their voyages are nautical history. After the Suez Canal was opened, the tea trade was taken up by steamships, and although the composite ships were eminently satisfactory in every respect, particularly in the matter of durability, yet they were very costly; and with the introduction of steel the improvements in steam, and the general advance in size, they died out except with fishing boats. But for sailing yachts of the larger sizes it remains very suitable indeed, and is frequently employed; in fact, it should be preferred to the all-wood construction for any sailing vessel of over 100 tons.

A true composite vessel has steel frames, reverse frames, floors, beams, beam knees, bulkheads, etc., and a steel keel plate (with garboards in the larger yachts), steel keelsons, side stringers, bilge strake, sheer strake, and deck stringers, and in the larger vessels, a system of diagonal tie plates between the sheer and bilge strakes, and across the deck between the stringer plates. The keel, stem, sternpost, outer planking, decks, bulwarks, etc., are all of wood. Thus the main strength of the ship's framing, both transverse and longitudinal, is derived from the steel members of the structure, the wood is simply a closing-in medium completing the form and stiffness, and keeping the water out.

It is naturally not a cheap method of construction for the actual amount of work is increased, more trades are involved, it is more difficult to fit the planking on account of the plating, particularly over the diagonal tieplates, and the time required for building is longer. The frame spacing has to be close, because of the danger of the plank seams working between the frames, and loosening the caulking. It is more suitable for large yachts than small ones, one reason for this being that longitudinal strength is not so difficult to obtain in small vessels, and it may also be noted here that in large yachts it is advisable to avoid the use of large grown wooden frames or timbers (which are difficult to find), a direct result being that more internal space is available. Moreover, as mentioned elsewhere, a small composite yacht built to Lloyd's Rules is inclined to turn out rather heavy.

A modern tendency, in yachts of 30 tons and upwards, is to use a sort of semi-composite construction, often referred to in shipyards as 'bastard composite'. Here the frames, reverse frames, floors, beams, beam knees, centre and side keelsons, side stringers and structural bulkheads are of steel, but there are no longitudinal strakes of plating, except perhaps a partial sheer-strake and stringer in way of the masts and standing rigging, to take the place of clamps, lodge knees, etc. Consequently the longitudinal strength is very little improved, and the system is not good enough for yachts of large size. The principal advantages gained appear to be a slight saving in weight, space, and cost, by the substitution of steel for the large and bulky double timbers, wood beams, bilge stringers, etc., and by dispensing with the mass of heavy iron floors, hanging knees, lodge knees, etc. Below 30 tons it is very convenient to use steel for frames, beams, floors, side stringers and mast step, and wood for the remainder.

Some small sailing yachts are built upon *Boat Principles* of construction; that is with bent or steamed timbers, closely spaced and crossing the keel, with oak floors worked across in way of the lead. The outer planking is worked carvel fashion and caulked, and the hull usually terminates in some form of transom stern. This boat construction makes a light and cheap job of the hull, but is really only suitable for yachts of up to about 20 tons yacht measurement, and even then some grown oak or steel frames are required, especially at the mast.

Double Skin construction has been used for many years, for many types of vessel, both large and small. Not only the skin planking, but the decks and bulkheads may be similarly constructed. Amongst the advantages claimed for the double-plank system are greater strength and stiffness for decreased weight of material, less liability to leakage, and a smoother surface because no caulking is necessary. It is a somewhat expensive method, and is a favourite style of build for high-class motor launches, naval pinnaces and similar craft. High-class yachts' lifeboats of the past used to have their buoyance tank casings thus constructed. It is a rather heavy and costly method for small boats, but it can be, and is, successfully applied to quite sizeable vessels, and makes a very strong job. When more than two skins are used, it comes into the laminated category.

It should be remarked here that, in the event of damage to the planking, double-skinned or multiple-skinned vessels are much more difficult to repair, and correspondingly expensive. The outer skin is usually laid fore and aft, and is about three-fifths the total thickness, the inner skin (the remaining two-fifths) being generally at an angle across it, and laying aft. Consequently a double-skinned boat is very frequently referred to as being 'diagonal built'. But this is not always so: the inner skin may be fore and aft also, breaking joint of course with the outer skin, or, if the vessel is longitudinally framed it may be at right-angles to the keel; but generally speaking, it is considered to be a stronger method to lay the inner skin at an angle of 45 deg.

The usual practice is to coat the outer surface of the inner skin with boiled linseed oil and stretch oiled calico over it before the outer skin is worked. When planking up, the inner skin is first tacked into place, and then, as the outer skin goes on, both skins are through fastened to the frames. Between the frames, the two skins are fastened together with square copper nails, clenched inside on copper rooves. Finally the seams and nail pits are puttied. Decks can be constructed in the same manner, and a double diagonal deck, with the two thicknesses glued together, make a particularly strong deck, but it does not possess the handsome appearance of a properly laid and caulked deck. The completely weather-resisting type of marine ply can probably be said to have replaced double-skinned planking, especially for decks and hull planking for chine boats.

With reference to laminated construction, laminated methods are usually resorted to in an endeavour to avoid the trouble of finding, and the labour of working, large and heavy material. By far the most important feature of laminated work is the connection between the various layers, thicknesses, or lamina; they must be thoroughly well glued, bolted, or riveted together, so as to prevent each one sliding endwise on its neighbour when under stress.

A beam made up of detached horizontal layers is very deficient in strength and rigidity, and similarly any component part of a wood vessel's structure is also deficient, unless fastened in such a thorough manner that this sliding tendency is met and prevented. So far as the shell and deck planking is concerned, this sliding motion is partly retarded by the frictional resistance of the caulking; in composite ships the diagonal bracing helps against it, and in diagonal-built vessels, the inner skin; but, when frames, beams and other items of structure are built up in layers, it becomes a point of the first importance. It should, however, be stated that, for the type of yachts described in this work, neither double skins nor laminations are much used (except that laminated frames are favoured).

Longitudinal Construction. This system is extensively used for launches, small semi-composite power yachts, and various other types of small power craft. It is also used to a slight extent for small wood sailing yachts and appears to offer several small advantages. Described very briefly, it consists of a series of widely spaced steel web frames, or extra strong sawn frames, on which are fitted longitudinal members, extending all fore and aft. On these an inner skin is laid diagonally and an outer skin fore and aft. The deck may be constructed in the same way, and if so, is usually double with both skins laid diagonally. This system makes a very strong and rigid construction if carried out properly, and is also fairly light, but not cheap. The centre-line structure, i.e., keel, stem, sternpost, etc., are as for an ordinary wood yacht, and the longitudinal framing is usually of some sort of pine, with its greatest dimension athwartships, excepting the shelf.

Moulded Construction, which is carried out in wood or fibreglass, has now made its mark. It is, however, dependent for economy reasons on the standard design or should it be said, the One Design. A top class design is the first essential and the prototype should be given suitable trials and modified as required. There is additional capital outlay on the

129

mould, on a suitable building for moulding the hulls, which is permanently occupied until the mould is broken up and on obtaining and holding together reliable operatives, there being no pool of experienced labour to draw from for this new industry, especially with regard to fibreglass construction. The economic reasons against the one off now and one off in twelve months' time are apparent.

The hulls can be made lighter, strength for strength, than with traditional construction. Transverse framing can be eliminated in dinghies and kept to a minimum in sailing yachts when cabin bulkheads may be moulded in to act against the racking stresses of the mast. A very efficient type of hull can, in fact, be evolved.

It must of course be recognized that the timber used for moulded-plywood construction has not been proved as comparable with teak, English oak, pitch pine, etc., in lasting qualities, so there must be grave doubts that plywood boats will keep their value as they age. The ageing qualities of glass fibre hulls is also an unknown factor when thinking in terms of ten to fifteen years and over.

An illuminating slant on the above is furnished by the old *Trincomalee*. This old vessel was built at Bombay in 1817, and those who are curious enough to look, will find her listed in Lloyd's Yacht Register for 1932, as the yacht *Foudroyant*, ex H.M.S. *Trincomalee*. The writer remembers her quite well at Cowes some fifty years ago, and a rare old-fashioned packet she was indeed. Yet at the end of 115 years of a no doubt strenuous existence we find her listed officially as a yacht; under jury rig, it is true, but still a yacht. The great point to be noticed, however, is that the old *Trincomalee* was probably built of East India teak, and not glued shavings, if such an appalling definition is permissible.

Specialization. Although there are still very large numbers of traditional sailing yachts being built when most of the work is carried out by the one builder, it is now possible due to the setting up of firms dealing with specialized parts of boats, to build in the following circumstances. The 'builder' may buy out, a standard hull from one firm, a ballast keel cast to suit from another, tanks from another, mast complete with fittings, completed standing rigging, blocks and steering gears from other different firms. This means that at least seven firms plus the 'builder' can now be involved in work which is normally carried out by one builder.

Mechanical Fittings. As is only to be expected in this mechanical age, the modern tendency amongst yachtsmen is to utilize all sorts of mechanical equipment, labour-saving and safety devices; some made possible by modern engineering progress, some developed in racing experience, others borrowed from general ship practice and adapted to small sailing yachts, the value of them being assessed by the owner in the light of his own ideas and experience. A brief notice of the most important of these should be of interest.

Halyard and Sheet Winches, which have been several times referred to elsewhere in this work, are not at all a new innovation, but their present-day form bears small resemblance to the old fashioned type. Their great advantage, of course, is that one man can do the work of two or three men in less time, also the majority of them are self-holding, and they do away with the cumbrous and laborious block and tackle, pully-hauly work. There are roughly speaking, two main types; the first taking a capstan-like form for placing on the deck for sheets, the second with a wire stowage drum for fitting

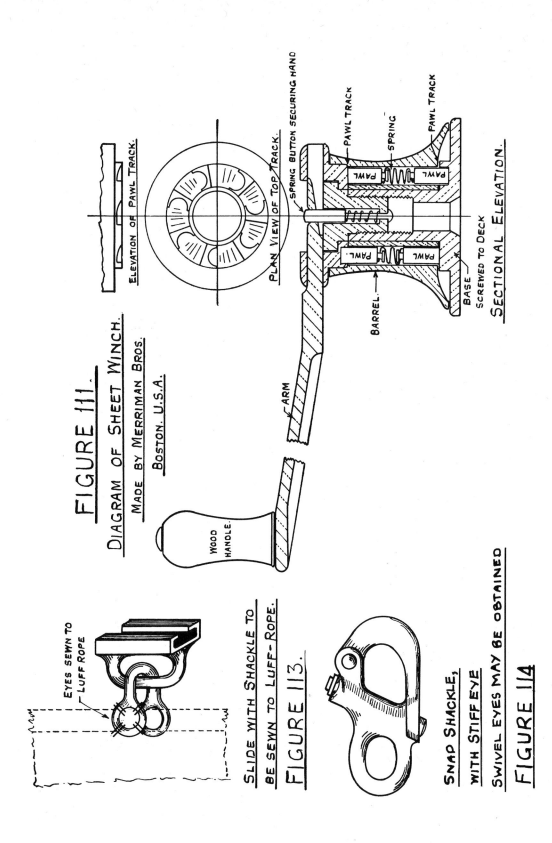

FIGURE 111.

DIAGRAM OF SHEET WINCH.

MADE BY MERRIMAN BROS.

BOSTON. U.S.A.

ELEVATION OF PAWL TRACK.

PLAN VIEW OF TOP TRACK.

SPRING BUTTON SECURING HAND

PAWL TRACK

SPRING

PAWL TRACK

PAWL

PAWL

BASE
SCREWED TO DECK

SECTIONAL ELEVATION.

BARREL.

PAWL

PAWL

ARM

WOOD
HANDLE.

EYES SEWN TO
LUFF ROPE

SLIDE WITH SHACKLE TO
BE SEWN TO LUFF-ROPE.

FIGURE 113.

SNAP SHACKLE,

WITH STIFF EYE

SWIVEL EYES MAY BE OBTAINED

FIGURE 114

FIGURE 112. SKETCH OF HALLIARD WINCH AS MADE BY CAMPER & NICHOLSONS LTD, SOUTHAMPTON.

For Direct Drive Handle is Applied at "A."
" Geared " " " " "B."

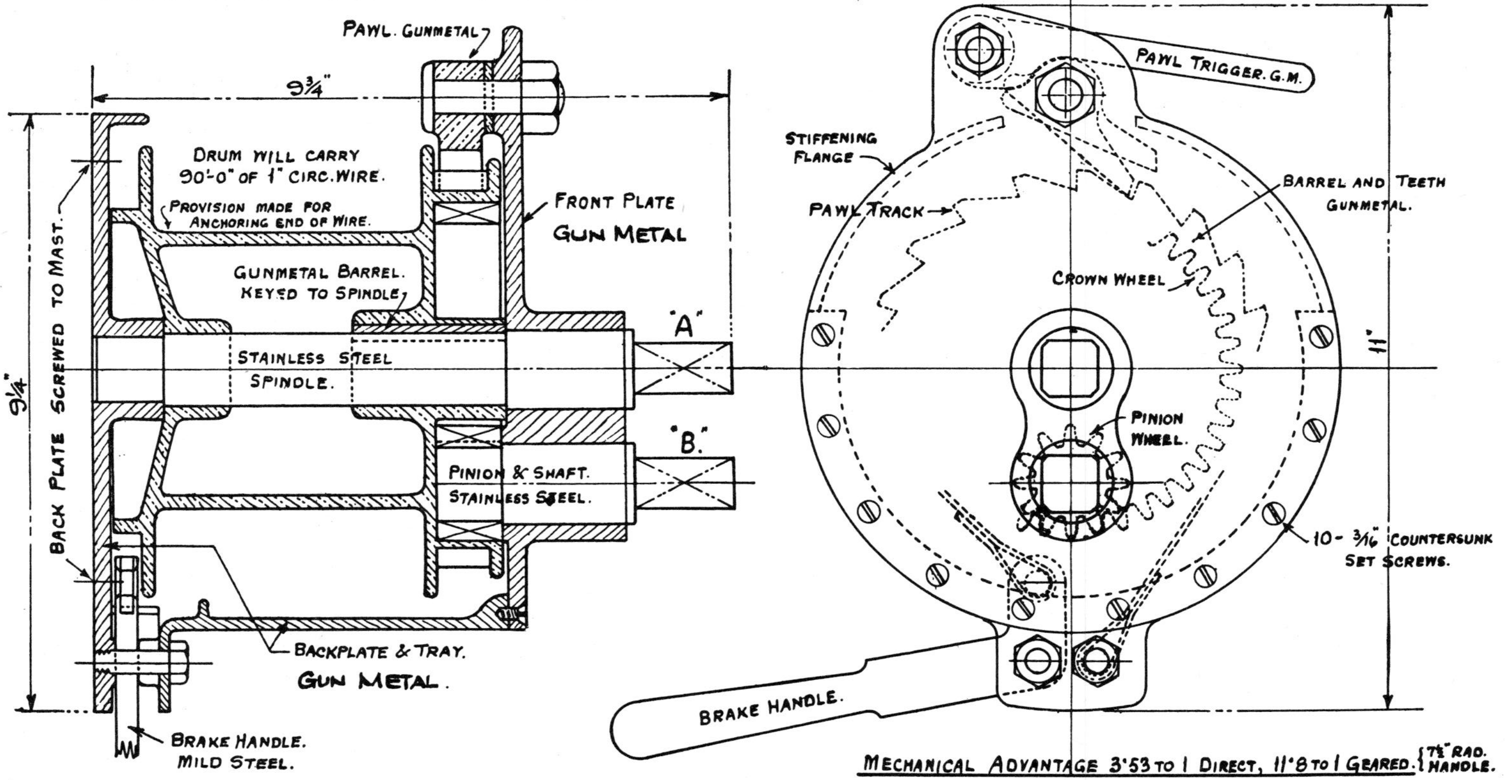

PAWL TRIGGER. G.M.

BARREL AND TEETH GUNMETAL.

10 - ³⁄₁₆ COUNTERSUNK SET SCREWS.

CROWN WHEEL

PINION WHEEL

STIFFENING FLANGE

PAWL TRACK

BRAKE HANDLE.

MECHANICAL ADVANTAGE 3·53 TO 1 DIRECT, 11·8 TO 1 GEARED. ⁷⁄₈″ RAD. ½ HANDLE.
GEAR RATIOS 1 TO 1, AND 3·3 TO 1.

"A."
"B."

FRONT PLATE GUN METAL

PINION & SHAFT. STAINLESS STEEL.

PAWL. GUNMETAL.

DRUM WILL CARRY 90'-0" OF 1" CIRC. WIRE.

PROVISION MADE FOR ANCHORING END OF WIRE.

GUNMETAL BARREL. KEYED TO SPINDLE.

STAINLESS STEEL SPINDLE.

BACKPLATE & TRAY. GUN METAL.

BRAKE HANDLE. MILD STEEL.

BACK PLATE SCREWED TO MAST.

132

to the mast for main and jib halyards, etc. There are many good types on the market, of various sizes and powers, the larger sizes being generally geared internally to give a large power ratio, but the smaller sizes having only the power ratio given by the radius of the handle divided by the radius of the drum or barrel, 8 to 1 being a common ratio. Their self-holding property is generally obtained by incorporating some form of pawl and pawl track, which can be readily released for the purpose of paying out. Fig. 111 shows a very small and compact type of sheet winch made by Merriman Bros. of Boston, U.S.A., and Fig. 112 a good type of halyard winch made by Messrs. Camper & Nicholsons Ltd., at Southampton, who also make about fifteen different sizes and types for various uses and requirements.

Pulpits at stem head were found valuable in ocean racing, and have been adopted as standard in cruising yachts. They are, generally, only suitable for vessels without bowsprits, and the idea is that they provide safety and freedom to work in changing headsails at sea. They generally take the form of a light stainless steel tube enclosure right at the stem head around the head or jibstays, about 27 to 30 in. high, and about 30 in. long in the fore and aft direction, against which a man may brace himself and keep both hands free. In vessels having bowsprits it is good practice to provide a sort of net below the spar, by fitting foot ropes laterally between the bowsprit shrouds and the bobstay. A practice tried in some small racing yachts is the short tubular bowsprit, over which a pulpit is fitted (see Fig. 69).

In yachts which have large headsails set on the outer stay, it is advisable to fit some form of 'quick-release gear' to the inner or forestay.

Most sailmakers recommend for the luff or hoist of the mainsail the use of that type of sliding hank which incorporates a form of shackle to be sewn to the luff-rope (see Fig. 113). These may be bought either of aluminium alloy hank and stainless steel shackle or galvanized iron and they save the chafe of seizings and prevent the slide from tilting and jamming on the track, which may be either external or internal.

Chafe is one of the chief enemies of the long-distance cruising man, and means should be adopted to counteract or entirely obviate it wherever possible. The usual methods are to fit anti-chafe coverings on topping lifts, runners and any other wires and ropes likely to contact the sails, to fit soft rubber caps to the ends of the crosstrees, and revolving wood covers to the lower ends of shrouds in way of the fore-sheets, etc.; also to serve carefully all wires and ropes likely to chafe against each other. Standing rigging which crosses in contact should be seized together.

Snap Shackles which are claimed to be as strong and secure as a shackle, and as quick as a hook, are a type of fitting which is in general use. A sketch is given in Fig. 114, showing the usual form, but various types may be obtained. They are extremely useful for genoa and balloon jib and spinnaker halyards and sheets, for use with blocks, and in fact wherever a strong and quick attachment is required.

Other Fittings. It is sometimes required, for various reasons, to step the mast on deck. Some of these reasons may be, either to pass under bridges, etc., for convenience in attending to masthead fittings, to avoid obstruction below deck, and so forth, but the point to remember is that if the mast is stepped on deck, the large thrust caused by its

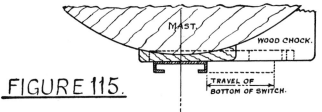

FIGURE 115.

SKETCH OF MAST TRACK SWITCH AND MAGAZINE TRACK FOR TRYSAIL.

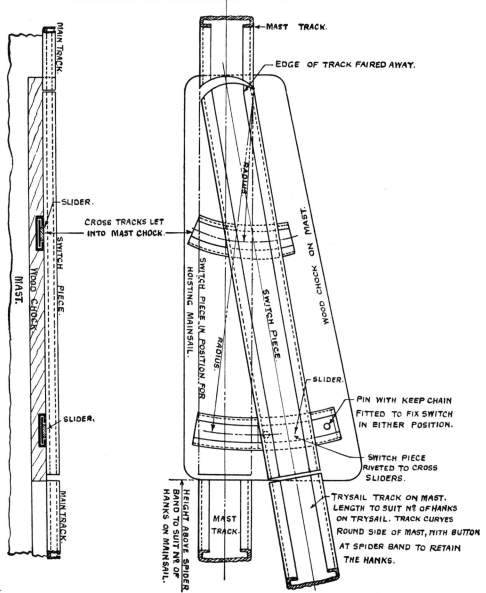

134

weight, and the tension of the taut shrouds, stays, etc., must all be borne by the deck, which should be stiffened accordingly. The most effective method of stiffening is by fitting an underdeck pillar concentric with the mast.

A convenient method for bending a trysail is by introducing, just above the boom, switch points and a siding for a trysail track. This enables the mainsail to be lowered, and the trysail to be set with the absolute minimum of time and trouble. The arrangement is clearly pictured in Fig. 115, where it will be noticed that the trysail magazine track must be long enough to house all the trysail hanks. The siding from the switch to the magazine track curves round to the side of the mast.

Some owners who go in for deep-sea cruising like to have some form of additional buoyancy in their tenders, so as to give them more or less the qualities of a life-boat. This may be done by fitting copper or plastic buoyancy tanks, by the use of cork slabs, plastic foam, buoyant fenders, and similar means.

Variable pitch propellers seem to be an ideal worth aiming at for use with sailing boat auxiliaries, as they offer several advantages; firstly, the heavy and cumbersome reverse gear can be eliminated, thereby saving weight, space and cost. Secondly, propeller drag when sailing can be reduced to the minimum by feathering the propeller blades when the engine is not being used. Thirdly, the maximum efficiency can be obtained from the engine, as the blades can be adjusted to exactly the correct pitch for the power developed and the speed possible. This last point is of interest, because it means that when both sail and motor are in use, the pitch can be adjusted to suit whatever speed can be attained under these conditions. Thus the full power of the engine can still be utilized, which would not be so in the case of a propeller with fixed pitch, which would, of course, be designed to give the correct load to the engine under power only. Some patent propellers in common use go a long way towards this, but the infinite pitch variation is often lacking (see page 118).

Electrochemical Damage in Yachts. Lloyd's have become greatly concerned about the harm which can occur in wood yachts due to the effects of electrochemical action. They consider that not enough attention has been given to the type of metal used for plank fastenings, and that the use of dissimilar metals for fastening structural members is incorrect. Rapid deterioration of planking around the fastenings has occurred, which is of course a serious matter.

First discoloration, then softening, and finally perishing of the wood fibres round the fastenings take place. This is caused by an electrochemical action between two dissimilar metals, and the condition is aggravated by the wider range of timbers and the lighter scantlings now in use.

Bronze through fastenings in steel floors, with wood saturated with sea water, form an electrolytic cell, and chemical alkaline concentrations are built up at the bronze fastenings, with acid concentrations at the steel.

Most timbers resist acid, but the alkaline concentration causes the timber to deteriorate. The combination of bronze, steel, and certain timbers should therefore be avoided. Teak and pitch pine are superior in resistance to mahogany, cedar, and oak.

It is to be noted that this chemical action, once started, continues even when the yacht is not afloat. If timbers having low resistance to alkaline attack are in conjunction with dissimilar metals some insulation precautions are necessary.

135

Chapter 7

Glass-Reinforced Plastic Boats   ·   Advantages
The Material   ·   Comparative Properties
Moulds   ·   Methods of Construction
Notes from Lloyd's Rules   ·   Repairs

Glass-Reinforced Plastic (G.R.P.) Boats. A complete section of boatbuilding in itself and already the subject of many publications, to which the reader is referred for more detailed information, G.R.P. construction appears to have an assured future. This chapter is intended to give a broad introduction to some of the terms and general methods of moulding involved in reinforced plastic construction.

At one of the early National Boat Shows, several good examples of this construction were exhibited, see Figs. 116 and 117, ranging from small dinghies to larger boats including a 26 ft. 3 in. L.O.A. bermudan sloop, a 20 ft. motor cruiser and 24 ft. lifeboat. In the same year a Portsmouth firm received the order for the Southampton Trinity House Pilots' 31 ft. boarding launch *Jessica*, with plastic hull, deck of plywood with teak overlay, English oak beams and beam shelf, plywood superstructure.

Since then considerable numbers of dinghies and motor cruisers have been built, as well as deep-keel sailing boats. One of the G.R.P. hulls is shown in some detail in Fig. 122 (see back endpapers) and 123. The size of motor cruiser constructed has risen to between 60 and 70 ft.

It is believed that with most of these boats the cost of the mould necessitates quantity production for economy reasons. Above these sizes and up to about 120 ft. length it is claimed that economic building can be carried out on a 'one off' basis, see p. 129. This certainly provides a challenge for an owner to place an order and a builder to design and construct such a craft.

Advantages. The advantages of G.R.P. are well known and consist mainly of—
being immune from marine borers,
impervious to corrosion, rotting and wastage by electrolysis,
high strength/weight ratio, helped by the avoidance of corrosion allowances
    necessary with steel,
practically non-absorbent,
fire-resisting qualities may be obtained locally in way of engine spaces,
    etc., by the use of fire-retarding paint and/or additives to the resin system,
no precautions are necessary against excessive condensation,
shaping is much less limited than with wood, steel, or aluminium alloy,
repairs are exceptionally easy,
maintenance is at a minimum.

FIGURE 116.

WATERCRAFT L.T.D.
24'-0" LAMINATED GLASS FIBRE LIFEBOAT.
M.O.T. APPROVED.

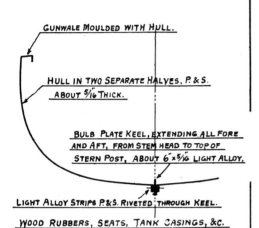

GUNWALE MOULDED WITH HULL.

HULL IN TWO SEPARATE HALVES, P. & S.
ABOUT 5/16" THICK.

BULB PLATE KEEL, EXTENDING ALL FORE
AND AFT, FROM STEM HEAD TO TOP OF
STERN POST, ABOUT 6" x 5/16" LIGHT ALLOY.

LIGHT ALLOY STRIPS P. & S. RIVETED THROUGH KEEL.

WOOD RUBBERS, SEATS, TANK CASINGS, &C.

LLOYDS EXPERIMENTAL.
54'-0" HULL IN "DEBORINE" FIBRE GLASS BY
HALMATIC L.T.D, FINISHED OFF BY TOUGH BROS. L.T.D.
3/8" THICK SKIN, 1 LAYER SCRIM, 6 LAYERS 2 OZ. MATT.
FLOOR INTEGRAL WITH SHELL, HOLLOW FRAMES TOP-
HAT SECTION, CONTINS FROM GUNWALE TO GUNWALE.

FRAME HOLLOW SECTION 1/8" THICK; THIN
GAUGE LIGHT ALLOY INSIDE FRAME.
FLOOR 1/4" THICK.
3/8" THICK HULL.   NO HEAT USED IN
"DEBORINE" PROCESS. FEMALE MOULD IN TWO HALVES.
FRAMES 15"/18" SPACING, CONTINS ACROSS FLOORS. WOOD
FALSE KEEL, DECK & BULKHS. BRASS STERN TUBE SLEEVE.

HERBERT WOODS L.T.D
9'-6" x 4'-4" FIBRE GLASS DINGHY.
SHELL ABOUT 3/16" THICK, MOULDED IN ONE PIECE.
TRANSOM 3/8" THICK.
WOOD STERN KNEE.

AIR MINISTRY.
FIBRE GLASS DINGHY HULL IN ONE PIECE.

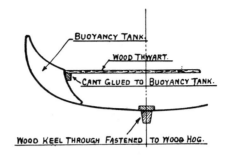

BUOYANCY TANK.
WOOD THWART.
CANT GLUED TO BUOYANCY TANK.

WOOD KEEL THROUGH FASTENED TO WOOD HOG.

TODD.
20'-0" GLASS FIBRE CABIN CRUISER.
HULL IN ONE PIECE, ABOUT 3/16" THICK.

COACH ROOF, MOULDED BEAMS.

CABIN TOP, MOULDED STIFFENING.

BOATS & ENGINES.
7'-6" TO 10'-6" DINGHIES EXHIBITED.

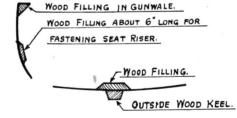

WOOD FILLING IN GUNWALE.
WOOD FILLING ABOUT 6" LONG FOR
FASTENING SEAT RISER.

WOOD FILLING.

OUTSIDE WOOD KEEL.

KEMPS SHIPYARD L.T.D
BERMUDA SLOOP. 26'-3" O.A. 20'-0" W.L.
CANOE BODY. WOOD FIN KEEL. WOOD RUBBERS.
MOULDED FRAMES, ABOUT 12" CENTRES,
CONTINS ACROSS FLOORS.
No MAST STEP OR SPECIAL STIFFENING IN WAY OF
SAME WAS FITTED.

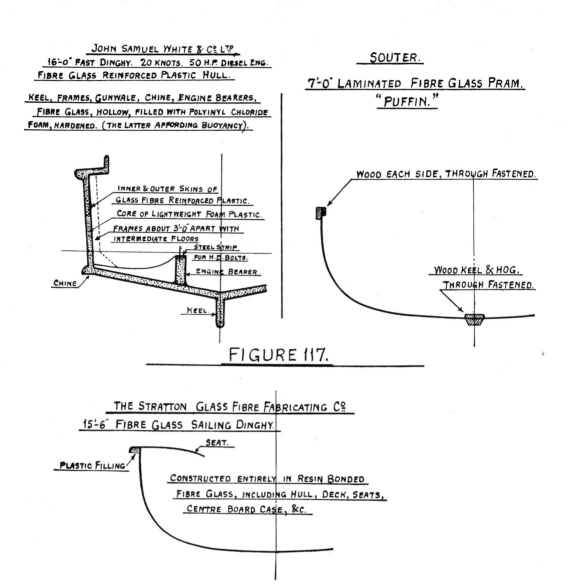

JOHN SAMUEL WHITE & Cᵒ Lᵀᴰ
16'-0" FAST DINGHY. 20 KNOTS. 50 H.P. DIESEL ENG.
FIBRE GLASS REINFORCED PLASTIC HULL.

KEEL, FRAMES, GUNWALE, CHINE, ENGINE BEARERS,
FIBRE GLASS, HOLLOW, FILLED WITH POLYINYL CHLORIDE
FOAM, HARDENED. (THE LATTER AFFORDING BUOYANCY).

INNER & OUTER SKINS OF
GLASS FIBRE REINFORCED PLASTIC.
CORE OF LIGHTWEIGHT FOAM PLASTIC.
FRAMES ABOUT 3'-0" APART WITH
INTERMEDIATE FLOORS.
STEEL STRIP
FOR H.D. BOLTS.
ENGINE BEARER.

CHINE

KEEL

SOUTER.

7'-0" LAMINATED FIBRE GLASS PRAM.
"PUFFIN."

WOOD EACH SIDE, THROUGH FASTENED.

WOOD KEEL & HOG.
THROUGH FASTENED.

FIGURE 117.

THE STRATTON GLASS FIBRE FABRICATING Cᵒ
15'-6" FIBRE GLASS SAILING DINGHY.

SEAT.

PLASTIC FILLING

CONSTRUCTED ENTIRELY IN RESIN BONDED
FIBRE GLASS, INCLUDING HULL, DECK, SEATS,
CENTRE BOARD CASE, &C.

The Material. The resin system may consist of polyester resin, catalyst and accelerator, to which may be added colour pigment, fillers and thixotropic agents, etc. Polyester is a thermohardening or thermosetting plastic material, which after the initial action of required heat and pressure cannot be changed in shape by the application of more intense heat or higher pressure. Hand lay-up produces 25 per cent to 30 per cent glass content by weight. The glass reinforcement is usually chopped strand mat made from 2 in. strands and is used for boats, car bodies, etc. The mat is available in weights of 1 oz., $1\frac{1}{2}$ oz., 2 oz., and $2\frac{1}{2}$ oz. per sq. ft. Short chopped strands with special filled resins known as 'dough' are used for castings, etc.

Polyester Resins. Esters are formed by the reaction of an acid and an alcohol. Complex esters are known as polyesters. The raw material generally originates in the coal-tar and petroleum industries.

A catalyst must be added to the polyester resin to promote the formation of the chemical links which are the characteristics of the thermosetting plastics.

The accelerator increases the hardening rate and this is necessary when resins are required to set at room temperature.

Thixotropic agents are added to enable laying up to be carried out on sloping, vertical or overhead surfaces. They prevent the resin from running off. Their proper use will have little effect on the strength of the laminate. Fillers may be used to—

reduce cost,
improve abrasion resistance,
improve surface hardness,
improve fire resistance,
reduce exotherm, which is the liberation of heat due to chemical reaction during
   manufacture.

Release Agent. A suitable release agent must be applied over the working surface of the mould, to prevent sticking from causing surface faults.

Gel coat is the coat of resin applied first in the hand lay up process. After it has been applied, no resin or glass mat is added until it has 'gelled' or surface hardened. It is applied to form a resin surface on the outside of the hull to prevent soakage of water along the glass fibres; it also prevents the glass from being rolled through. Thixotropic additives are used, as are flexibilizers which prevent star shakes from forming.

Comparative Properties. As a matter of interest it may be admissible to give the following comparison of physical properties:

	Mild steel	Alumi-nium alloy	Spruce	Glass cloth laminate	Glass mat laminate (25%–30% glass)
Ultimate tensile strength lb./sq. in.	67,200	38,000	10,000 to 11,000	20,000 to 27,000	12,000 to 14,000
Specific gravity	7.86	2.7	0.512	1.72	1.5
Weight lb./cu. ft.	490	169	32	107	94
Modulus of elasticity	29×10^6	10×10^6	1.6×10^6	2.8×10^6	0.9×10^6 to 1.2×10^6

Moulds. Contact laminating by hand lay up, see Fig. 118. This is the process most commonly used for boat construction and is probably the one most suitable for the largest sizes. It consists mainly of a female mould of plywood built up on ribbands and

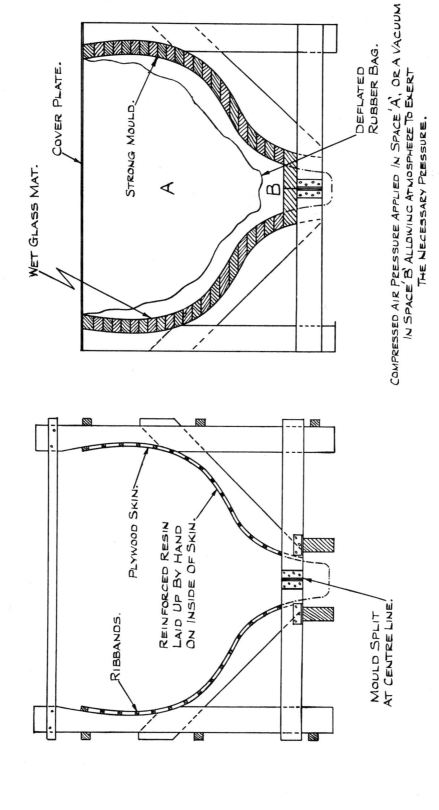

COVER PLATE.

WET GLASS MAT.

STRONG MOULD.

A

B

DEFLATED RUBBER BAG.

COMPRESSED AIR PRESSURE APPLIED IN SPACE 'A', OR A VACUUM IN SPACE 'B' ALLOWING ATMOSPHERE TO EXERT THE NECESSARY PRESSURE.

FIG 119.

PRESSURE MOULDING USING A RUBBER BAG.

PLYWOOD SKIN.

REINFORCED RESIN LAID UP BY HAND ON INSIDE OF SKIN.

RIBBANDS.

MOULD SPLIT AT CENTRE LINE.

FIG 118.

MOULD FOR CONTACT LAMINATING BY HAND LAY UP.

transverse sections. The process makes use of the materials, etc., just described, that is, a parting agent is coated on the ply mould followed by the gel coat and successive layers of glass mat in turn coated with resin and rolled in by hand to ensure that the mat is properly impregnated.

Frames and longitudinals are moulded in, mainly of top-hat section, with the aid of aluminium alloy formers. Only the outside has a good finish, which is determined by the finish of the plywood mould. The inside of the laminate is rough. Plywood bulkheads can be very conveniently moulded in with glass mat angles impregnated with resin, bonded to the shell and bulkhead. The mould is almost certain to be in two halves, split on the centre line, to facilitate the removal of the laminate. A hull with tumblehome could not be removed from a one piece mould because it would not lift out.

Pressure moulding using a rubber bag, see Fig. 119, requires a solid female mould into which the mat and resin, etc., is laid up as above. Pressure is applied either from the outside, by compressed air, or by applying a vacuum pump between rubber bag and mould and so using atmospheric pressure.

Matched die pressure laminating, see Fig. 120, in which wet mat is placed on a male mould and pressure applied by means of a matching female mould.

Vacuum laminating, see Fig. 121. Dry mat is laid on the male mould, the female mould is positioned to give required thickness. A vacuum is applied at the keel, drawing resin from reservoirs at the sheer line, which saturates the mat.

There are numerous possible faults with glass-reinforced laminating, as with the more common boatbuilding materials. They can be avoided mainly by careful control and inspection, during and after moulding. Among these faults are—

variation in thickness,
crazing and cracking of resin,
resin-rich and resin-starved areas,
surface faults,
etc.

Methods of Construction. In the smallest dinghies the shell is made sufficiently rigid to avoid the use of any stiffening, except at keel and gunwale. Stiffening here may take the form of resin glass doublings, with or without the use of resin glass dough to give depth, or recessed mouldings forming semi-circular shaped stiffeners as in pressed steel work. It should be noticed that the equivalents of bent timbers of wooden dinghies are not required.

With larger boats the disposition of strength members closely follows that of normal construction in steel, except that more longitudinal framing is introduced. We therefore have doublings at centre line and sheerline, in the form of extra layers of glass mat or a resin glass dough filling to give extra thickness, transverse and longitudinal framing of top-hat section, floors and additional transverse stiffening provided by web frames or bulkheads bonded to the shell.

Lloyd's 'Provisional Rules for the Construction of Reinforced Plastic Yachts' have gone beyond anything at present built. They cover full power, sailing and auxiliary yachts between 20 and 120 ft. in length and up to a breadth of 24 ft., which is approaching a Thames Measurement of 300 tons. This is considered to be about the economic limit of the reinforced plastic hull, as for steel yachts the steel corrosion allowance at this

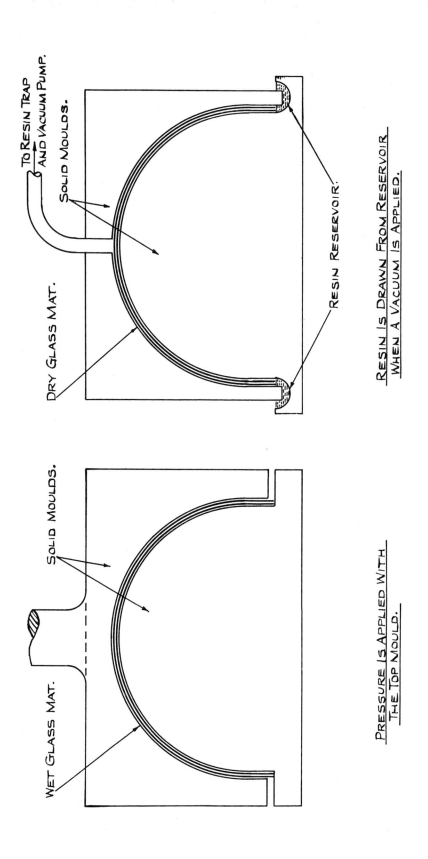

TO RESIN TRAP AND VACUUM PUMP.

SOLID MOULDS.

DRY GLASS MAT.

RESIN RESERVOIR.

RESIN IS DRAWN FROM RESERVOIR WHEN A VACUUM IS APPLIED.

FIG. 121.

VACUUM LAMINATING.

SOLID MOULDS.

WET GLASS MAT.

PRESSURE IS APPLIED WITH THE TOP MOULD.

FIG 120.

MATCHED DIE PRESSURE LAMINATING.

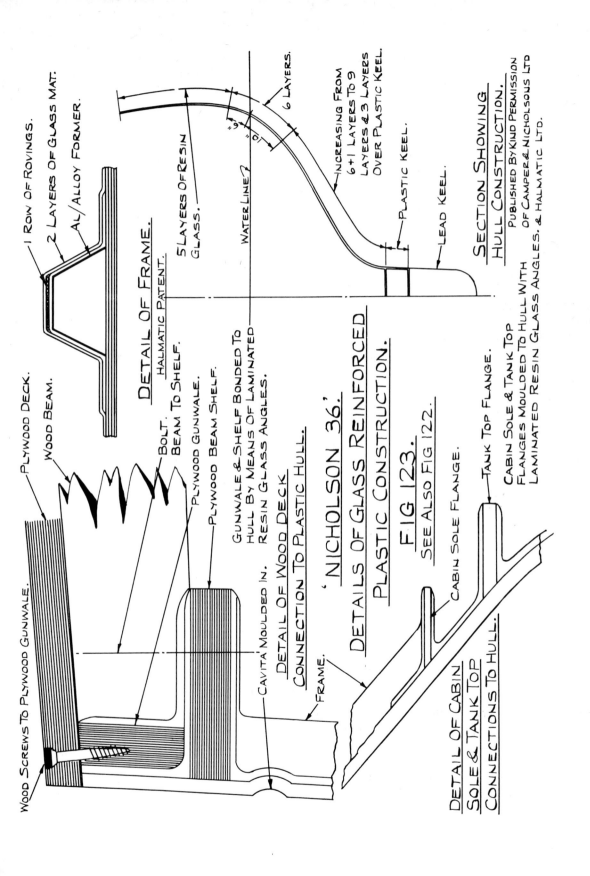

1 ROW OF ROVINGS.

2 LAYERS OF GLASS MAT.

AL/ALLOY FORMER.

DETAIL OF FRAME.
HALMATIC PATENT.

5 LAYERS OF RESIN GLASS.

WATER LINE

INCREASING FROM 6+1 LAYERS TO 9 LAYERS & 3 LAYERS OVER PLASTIC KEEL.

6 LAYERS.

"9"

"10"

PLASTIC KEEL.

LEAD KEEL.

SECTION SHOWING HULL CONSTRUCTION.

PUBLISHED BY KIND PERMISSION OF CAMPER & NICHOLSONS LTD & HALMATIC LTD.

PLYWOOD DECK.

WOOD BEAM.

BOLT.

BEAM TO SHELF.

PLYWOOD GUNWALE.

PLYWOOD BEAM SHELF.

GUNWALE & SHELF BONDED TO HULL BY MEANS OF LAMINATED RESIN GLASS ANGLES.

DETAIL OF WOOD DECK CONNECTION TO PLASTIC HULL.

'NICHOLSON 36'

DETAILS OF GLASS REINFORCED PLASTIC CONSTRUCTION.

FIG 123.

SEE ALSO FIG 122.

TANK TOP FLANGE.

CABIN SOLE FLANGE.

CABIN SOLE & TANK TOP FLANGES MOULDED TO HULL WITH LAMINATED RESIN GLASS ANGLES.

CAVITA MOULDED IN.

FRAME.

WOOD SCREWS TO PLYWOOD GUNWALE.

DETAIL OF CABIN SOLE & TANK TOP CONNECTIONS TO HULL.

size becomes reasonable and the shape is less severe than with smaller boats, making steel more easily worked.

Notes from Lloyd's Rules. In the rules for plastic yachts provision is made for inspection of works, including building, heating, insulation and ventilation, to ensure that both workshop and storage premises are up to an approved standard. 'The rules are based on the use of an unsaturated polyester resin system reinforced by glass fibres of the chopped strand mat type and moulded by a contact process.'

The hull thickness is given based on length L and is given in the form of ounces of glass mat per square foot of surface, in association with a basic stiffener spacing. For variations in stiffener spacing the weight of glass is modified to suit. The bottom thickness is carried up to 6 in. above the waterline to a thinner topside, which is increased locally to form a sheer strake. In sailing and auxiliary yachts the fin, tuck and keel are of increased thickness. Where changes of thickness of hull take place, the reduction to normal weight is to be at no greater rate than 2 oz. of reinforcement per $1\frac{1}{2}$ in. This is to prevent the formation of 'hard spots'.

The framing may be transverse, longitudinal or a combination of the two. With transverse framing the frame modulus is given, based on depth D and a basic stiffener spacing. If the spacing is different from this, the modulus is to be modified in direct proportion. Web frames or partial bulkheads are required not more than seven frame spaces apart. With longitudinal framing the modulus is given based on length L, a basic spacing and span. Web frames or partial bulkheads are required, not more than five frame spaces apart.

Section moduli of frames and longitudinals of top-hat section of given depth and face area, in association with a shell thickness of 14 oz. and 12 in. width, are given in chart form. This provides a convenient means of determining the frame size for the given modulus.

Floors are called for in some places, especially in way of ballast keels, engine seats, masts and at the fore end.

Bottom girders are required in full power yachts for supporting floors and frames.

Decks may be constructed similarly to the shell, by means of a plastic skin with transverse beams and fore and aft girders of top hat section.

Bulkheads, deckhouse sides and tops may be similarly constructed.

For the ocean racer type of boat, plywood structural bulkheads and decks combine well with the resin glass hull, as this requires a minimum of stiffening and these members may be formed from the flat sheets without the need to make use of the shape-forming qualities of resin glass. Tanks are a different proposition as resin glass will stand up to water and oil better than wood.

Oil fuel and water tank scantlings are given in the rules.

Rudder scantlings are given for steel only, although resin glass is highly suitable for forming the streamlined blades used on sailing boats.

Ballast keel bolts, rudder stocks and pintles, steering gears, anchors and cables are similar to those used in wood or steel construction. Ballast keel bolts may be dispensed with entirely by laying up the shell right around the keel and afterwards dropping in the pre-cast keel set in resin.

Connections and fastenings. Structural members are to be connected by angles

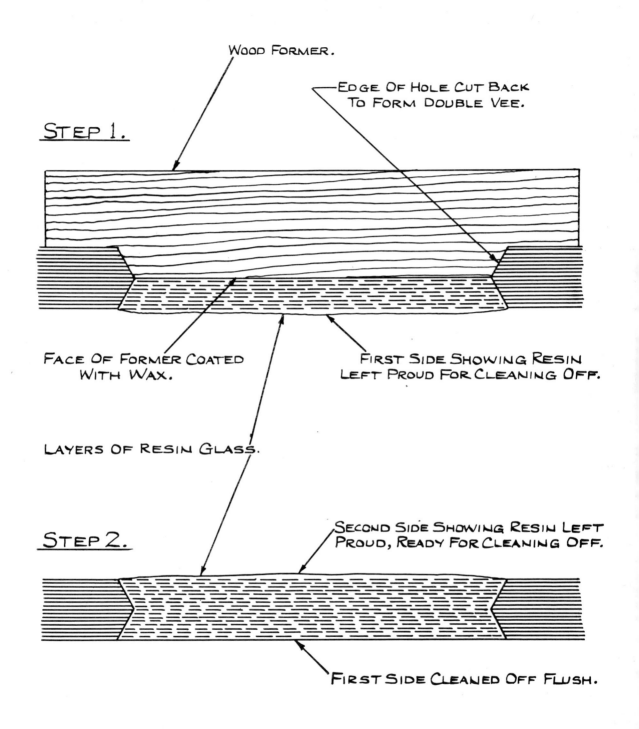

STEP 1.

WOOD FORMER.

EDGE OF HOLE CUT BACK TO FORM DOUBLE VEE.

FACE OF FORMER COATED WITH WAX.

FIRST SIDE SHOWING RESIN LEFT PROUD FOR CLEANING OFF.

LAYERS OF RESIN GLASS.

STEP 2.

SECOND SIDE SHOWING RESIN LEFT PROUD, READY FOR CLEANING OFF.

FIRST SIDE CLEANED OFF FLUSH.

FIG 124.
REPAIRS IN GLASS REINFORCED PLASTIC HULLS.

formed by layers of reinforcement rolled up *in situ* and bonded to the structure before the laminates are fully cured. The laminate is to be increased in weight in way of bolted and riveted joints, flanges and fittings. The edges of cuts and drilled holes are to be coated with resin to seal and bond the exposed ends of glass reinforcement. Where through fastenings are required for the attachment of fittings, washers must be used to prevent crushing of the laminate, of diameter at least 2.25 times diameter of fastenings. Heavy loads such as those produced in sailing boats by rigging, may be carried by perforated metal insert plates bonded into the laminate.

Repairs to resin glass structures may be carried out quite easily using repair kits which are available. Epoxide resin is probably best for this purpose, as ambient temperatures are not so important as with polyester resin and a more positive bond is obtainable. To repair a hole in the hull, the ragged edges are cut back and double veed to form a key, see Fig. 124. A former is required to hold the layers of glass and resin in place. The glass is kept below flush and the resin filled in to above flush, for final cleaning off with glass-paper to form the finished surface.

Chapter 8

Aluminium Alloy · Aluminium Alloys for Shipbuilding
Comparisons · Insulation of Alloy

Aluminium Alloy is an aluminium-magnesium-manganese alloy, lying in the medium-strength grade, but notable for its light weight, corrosion-resisting properties, and the ease with which it can be worked given suitable equipment. On the predominantly wooden cruisers and ocean racers being dealt with in this book it is highly suitable for masts and booms, coachroof and deck-house window frames, edge mouldings for bulkhead openings, steering wheels and steering pedestals, breasthooks, mast framing, cleats and bollards, davits, etc. The most universal use being for masts and booms which can show a weight and diameter reduction compared with wooden ones of the same strength.

It was first used for boatbuilding about 1930, and during the following years several small yachts were built of it, and quite a number of lifeboats, launches, dinghies and other small craft.

One of the earliest aluminium alloy yachts of fair size was *Diana II*, a motor yacht of 33 tons, built in 1931. The metal was not widely adopted, however, and with the outbreak of war in September 1939 normal development in yachts was postponed. Subsequently the sea water resistant alloys, not requiring heat treatment during fabrication, were developed. These are the B.S.S. 'N' grade. Aluminium alloy has certain advantages which make it well worthy of a place amongst shipbuilding materials, and provided it is used in the right place, and with discretion, observing the requirements as to painting, insulation, strength precautions, and other simple rules that have been found necessary by experience, there can be no objection to the use of aluminium alloy either ashore or afloat. A new generation of medium sized sailing yachts with hulls built entirely of aluminium alloy is now in being, *Pen Duick III* being a notable example.

It should be mentioned, however, that aluminium alloy costs about eight times as much as mild steel on basic price although this is difficult to ascertain accurately except in particular cases, owing to different cutting and quantity extras adopted by the two separate industries. By using aluminium alloy, however, 50 to 60 per cent can be saved on the weight, so that the cost difference is not so great as it seems at first sight.

Aluminium alloy is structurally very suitable for frames and beams if insulation is carefully carried out and fastenings of suitable material used; however, cost and the fact that most builders of these craft have no facilities for bending and bevelling angle frames, must be the reasons for the restriction of its use. For ships and large motor yachts aluminium alloy is much used for superstructures as there are here the two incentives of weight saving and improvement in stability for a given design.

Considerable use of alloy has been made in the superstructures of large ships and so far as is known with perfect success, both in weight saving, improved stability, increase of speed, or decrease of draught, according to the object aimed at, and we must remember that in some ships every ton saved on structure can be a ton added to the deadweight, which is the earning capacity of the ship.

The American liner, the *United States*, is reputed to have 2,000 tons of alloy in her upper works; her L/B ratio is about $9\frac{3}{4}$ against $8\frac{3}{4}$ in the *Queen Elizabeth*; and although the two vessels are about the same length, the *United States* is considerably less in displacement and draught.

If, on a given steel structure, a straightforward substitution of alloy was made for the steel, the reduction in weight would be over 60 per cent. But in strength members the difference in strength between the steel and the alloy demands larger scantlings for the latter, and this reduces the average weight saving. But for minor parts of no structural importance, such as short flying decks and bridges, small deckhouses and similar erections, alloy can replace steel without much variation in scantling. This weight saving in the upper works is of the highest importance from the point of view of stability, and in the case of power yachts, where new engines are constantly increasing in r.p.m. and b.h.p., and diminishing in weight, whilst the erections and boats show a tendency to go higher and become more extensive, it is a point which demands the closest attention.

Reverting to the 50 to 60 per cent weight saving previously mentioned, this means that one ton of weight is saved for every ton of alloy used. The author's firm has modified and refitted the superstructures and funnels, increasing their size, on several large motor yachts in aluminium alloy with great success. In fact, the fitting of larger superstructures on existing vessels is usually only possible by substituting aluminium alloy for steel.

Amongst the items on large yachts which can be obviously selected for construction in aluminium alloy are deckhouses, bridges, masts, funnels, accommodation ladders and shore gangways, etc. In small sailing yachts which, after all, are the subject-matter of this book, the practical uses for aluminium alloy are as previously stated.

Aluminium Alloys for Shipbuilding. The manufacturers publish a mass of information on aluminium alloys, but a few notes on the material suitable for shipbuilding may be useful. The term *sheet* applies to material under $\frac{1}{4}$ in. thick. This is cold rolled and is supplied in different tempers of O, $\frac{1}{4}$H, $\frac{1}{2}$H, $\frac{3}{4}$H and H.

O = annealed and H = hard.

In general the harder material has higher stress and lower elongation characteristics. A low temper or 'flanging quality' should be ordered for flanging. Lloyd's requirements refer only to material 0.18 in. thick and over. Below this thickness Lloyd's specify that the alloy shall be in accordance with a recognized specification and suitable for marine use. N.S. 4, N.S. 5, N.S. 6 and N.S. 8 are suitable for marine use. N stands for non-heat treatable material which does not require heat treatment to determine its properties, it may therefore be worked hot if required, without subsequent heat treatment to restore its characteristics. S = sheet and the figures 4, 5, 6, etc. denote its composition.

Plate is 3/16 in. thick and over and is hot rolled. There is some overlap between sheet (S) and plate (P) in thickness, between 3/16 in. and $\frac{1}{4}$ in. Lloyd's minimum requirements for plates are, 0.1 per cent proof stress 8 tons/sq. in., tensile breaking strength 17 tons/sq. in., elongation 12 per cent on 2 in. gauge length.

It is the general practice to specify a proof stress as a measure of the elastic limit. In Great Britain the 0.1 per cent proof stress is normally adopted, whilst in North America the 0.2 per cent proof stress is used.

NP5/6 and NP8 in the M (as manufactured) or O (annealed) condition are up to Lloyd's requirements. 'M' is normally used, but the 'O' condition is used if flanging or forming are required. This material is suitable for riveting or welding in both conditions.

Sections. The minimum mechanical properties are as required for plates. The British Standard notation for this is N.E.6 and N.E.8 in the 'M' condition. Alternatively H.E.30 in the fully heat treated (W.P.) condition satisfies Lloyd's requirements and is very suitable for riveted work, but is not recommended for welding. It is lower priced than N.E.6 and N.E.8.

H stands for heat-treatable material, which relies on the heat treatment to give its properties, must not be heated for working without subsequent heat treatment, or it will lose its properties.

Rivets. The aluminium alloy normally used is N.5 and this satisfies Lloyd's requirements. It must be supplied in the annealed condition. Aluminium alloy rivets are normally driven cold, but over $\frac{1}{2}$ in. dia. the operation is eased by heating for up to fifteen minutes at 400°C to 500°C. A specially designed portable furnace is needed.

Welding. The introduction of M.I.G. and T.I.G. welding equipment has allowed reliable welding for aluminium alloy to be produced. Care must be taken that welders learn the correct techniques and it is advisable that 'X'-ray tests are made on selected welds, which with expert interpretation will allow confidence to be justified.

Comparisons. Aluminium alloy, as compared to steel or wood construction, has its advantages and disadvantages. It can be rolled, drawn, forged, cast, stamped, pressed or extruded; it can be sheared, punched and drilled, riveted or welded; it is non-magnetic, easily worked, a great weight-saver, and fire-resisting. On the other hand, it is a metal lacking the stiffness of steel. The low modulus of aluminium alloy is a disadvantage, as it needs a larger moment of inertia when deflection equivalent to a steel member is required.

Aluminium alloy can be sawn or sheared, but should not be flame-cut like steel. Whenever hot working is required for plates, bars, rivets, or forging, temperatures must be carefully controlled at around 400°C. Strength of welds is about 10 tons per sq. in., a very low figure. The table below gives an interesting comparison of the principal properties of steel, alloy, and teak wood.

The melting-point of alloy is around 600°C, whereas that of steel is 1,300/1,400°C, so that alloy fire-resisting properties are somewhat restricted. Another disadvantage is that the alloy does not mix well with other metals, particularly copper and its various alloys, and in a lesser degree with steel. Therefore insulation of some sort is essential and bimetallic joints should be avoided wherever possible.

Insulation of Alloy. Although the alloy is practically non-corrosive, and is extremely durable in sea water and sea-going conditions, yet all aluminium alloys are anodic to copper, nickel and iron. Therefore, to prevent galvanic action, these metals and all

	Aluminium alloy	Mild steel	Teak
Specific gravity	2.7	7.86	.72
Weight per cu. ft.	169 lb.	490 lb.	45 lb.
Tensile strength, lb. per sq. in.	38,000	67,200	15,000
Yield point	Not sharply defined	50% tensile strength	—
Shear strength	60% tensile	75% tensile strength	About 10% tensile
Compressive strength, lb. per sq. in.	As tensile	As tensile strength	12,000
Low temperatures	Properties improve	Negligible	Negligible
High temperatures	Properties deteriorate		

their various alloys should be insulated from aluminium alloy by suitable methods. Zinc and cadmium can be safely brought into contact with alloy, so that galvanizing and cadmium plating are useful processes for insulating fastenings. But in general, bimetallic contacts should be avoided, and faying surfaces insulated by means of plastic marine glues, tufnol washers, zinc base paints, bituminous compounds, etc., to suit the nature and type of the contact. Timber in contact with alloy in exposed places should be protected by a coat of aluminium paint or bituminous paint, and a suitable jointing compound should be applied; the use of oak should be avoided.

Painting of alloy is important, all paints must be of the zinc oxide or zinc chromate base type. Alloy does not rust like steel; therefore a good adhesive surface for painting must be created by etch-priming after degreasing, which can be done by hand using suitable solvents. On exposed surfaces the zinc chromate primer should be followed by an undercoat, and a finishing coat of a type recommended by the undercoat suppliers. Synthetic resin paints are usually suitable.

Anti-fouling paints for the alloy should contain a high content of cuprous oxide, and should be applied over two coats of zinc oxide or primer to prevent corrosion. Anti-fouling paints based on organic poisons are suitable where frequent renewal is possible, but paints containing mercury, or mercury or copper salts, must never be used on the alloy.

TABLE I

TYPICAL DIMENSIONS OF MASTS.

OF HOLLOW SPRUCE CONSTRUCTION
& ELLIPTICAL IN CROSS SECTION
FOR A TYPICAL DRAWING OF A WOODEN MAST SEE FIG 69.

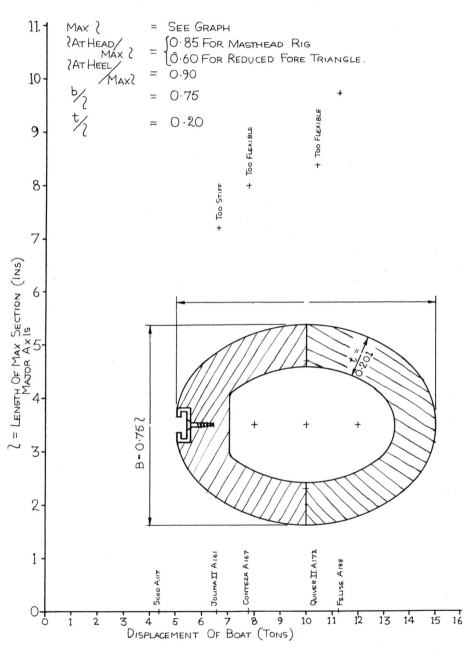

$$\text{MAX } l = \text{SEE GRAPH}$$

$$\frac{l \text{ AT HEAD}}{\text{MAX } l} = \begin{cases} 0.85 \text{ FOR MASTHEAD RIG} \\ 0.60 \text{ FOR REDUCED FORE TRIANGLE.} \end{cases}$$

$$\frac{l \text{ AT HEEL}}{\text{MAX } l} = 0.90$$

$$\frac{b}{l} = 0.75$$

$$\frac{t}{l} = 0.20$$

+ TOO STIFF

+ TOO FLEXIBLE

+ TOO FLEXIBLE

B = 0.75 l

$t = 0.20 l$

l = LENGTH OF MAX SECTION (INS)
MAJOR AXIS

SCOD A117

JOUMA II A161

CONTEZA A167

QUIVER II A172

FELISE A188

DISPLACEMENT OF BOAT (TONS)

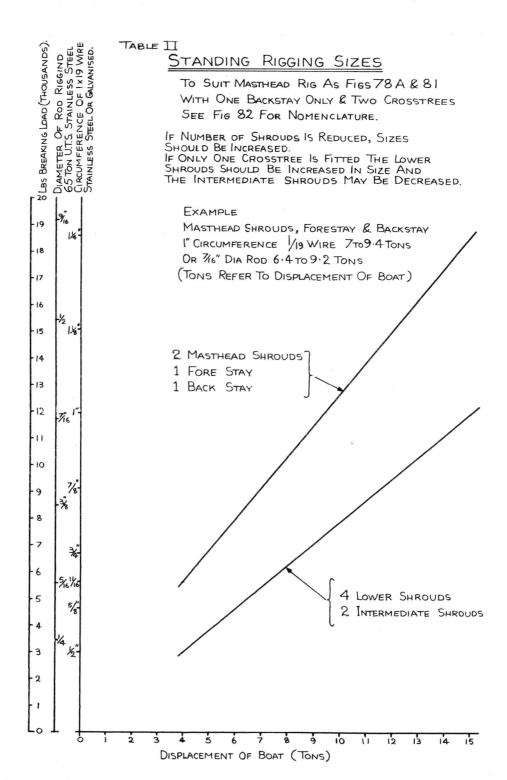

TABLE Ⅱ

STANDING RIGGING SIZES

To Suit Masthead Rig As Figs 78 A & 81
With One Backstay Only & Two Crosstrees
See Fig 82 For Nomenclature.

If Number of Shrouds Is Reduced, Sizes
Should Be Increased.
If Only One Crosstree Is Fitted The Lower
Shrouds Should Be Increased In Size And
The Intermediate Shrouds May Be Decreased.

Example
Masthead Shrouds, Forestay & Backstay
1" Circumference 1/19 Wire 7 to 9·4 Tons
Or 7/16" Dia Rod 6·4 to 9·2 Tons
(Tons Refer To Displacement Of Boat)

2 Masthead Shrouds
1 Fore Stay
1 Back Stay

4 Lower Shrouds
2 Intermediate Shrouds

Lbs Breaking Load (Thousands).
Diameter Of Rod Rigging 65 Ton U.T.S. Stainless Steel
Circumference Of 1×19 Wire Stainless Steel Or Galvanised.

Displacement Of Boat (Tons)

TABLE III

BLOCK AND RIGGING LIST FOR A 32-ft. W/L AUXILIARY SLOOP WITH MASTHEAD RIG

(Blocks are stainless steel bound, Tufnol cheeks and sheaves, except where otherwise marked)

No. of Blocks	*Size of sheave dia. × thickness*	*No. of Sheaves*	*Strop*	*Purpose*	*Rope*
1	$3\frac{1}{4}$ in. × 7/16 in. stainless steel	1	Swivel Eye	Spinnaker halyard	$\frac{3}{4}$ in. circ. 6/19 galvd. M.S. with red Terylene tail
1	$2\frac{1}{2}$ in. × $\frac{3}{8}$ in.	1	Shackle	Spinnaker staysail halyard	$\frac{1}{2}$ in. circ. 6/19 galvd. M.S. with white Terylene tail
1	$3\frac{1}{4}$ in. × 7/16 in.	1	Shackle	Main boom topping lift	$\frac{3}{4}$ in. circ. 6/19, ditto
1	$1\frac{3}{4}$ in. × $\frac{1}{2}$ in.	1	Upset swivel shackle	Spinnaker boom lift	$1\frac{1}{4}$ in. circ. red Terylene
1	2 in. × 9/16 in.	2	Oval eye and becket	Main sheet upper block	$1\frac{1}{2}$ in. circ. white Terylene
1	2 in. × 9/16 in.	2	Oval eye	Main sheet lower block	ditto
2	$3\frac{1}{4}$ in. × $\frac{3}{4}$ in.	1	Snatch with swivel snap shackle	Genoa sheet	2 in. circ. Braided blue Terylene
2	$3\frac{1}{4}$ in. × $\frac{3}{4}$ in.	1	ditto	Foresail sheet	ditto
2	$2\frac{1}{2}$ in. × $\frac{5}{8}$ in.	1	ditto	Spinnaker sheet	$1\frac{3}{4}$ in. circ. red Terylene
2	2 in. × 9/16 in.	1	ditto	Spinnaker boom fore guy	$1\frac{1}{2}$ in. circ. ditto
1	$3\frac{1}{2}$ in. × $\frac{5}{8}$ in.	1	—	Main halyard	$\frac{3}{4}$ in. circ. 6/19 galvd. M.S. with white Terylene tail
1	$3\frac{1}{2}$ in. × $\frac{5}{8}$ in.	1	—	Genoa halyard	$\frac{3}{4}$ in. circ. 6/19 galvd. M.S. with blue Terylene tail

Note.—Winches are supplied for the following: Main sheet, genoa sheet, spinnaker sheet, main halyard, genoa halyard and spinnaker halyard

Index

159

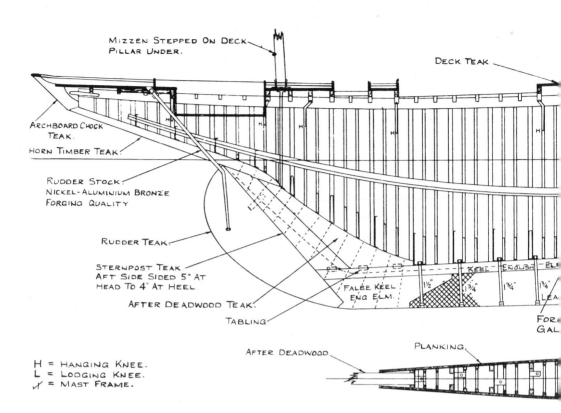

MIZZEN STEPPED ON DECK.
PILLAR UNDER.

DECK TEAK

ARCHBOARD CHOCK
TEAK.

HORN TIMBER TEAK.

RUDDER STOCK.
NICKEL-ALUMINIUM BRONZE
FORGING QUALITY

RUDDER TEAK.

STERNPOST TEAK
AFT SIDE SIDED 5" AT
HEAD TO 4" AT HEEL

AFTER DEADWOOD TEAK.

TABLING.

FALSE KEEL
ENG. ELM.

KEEL ENGLISH ELM

1½"   1¾"   1¾"   1¾"

FALSE KEEL
ENG. ELM.

LEA

FOR
GAL

H = HANGING KNEE.
L = LODGING KNEE.
⋎ = MAST FRAME.

AFTER DEADWOOD

PLANKING.

CHOCK FOR
RUDDER HEAD.

MIZZEN CHOCK.

COCKPIT

SKYLIGHT.

SKYLIGHT.

COMPANIONWAY.

BEAMS LARCH.

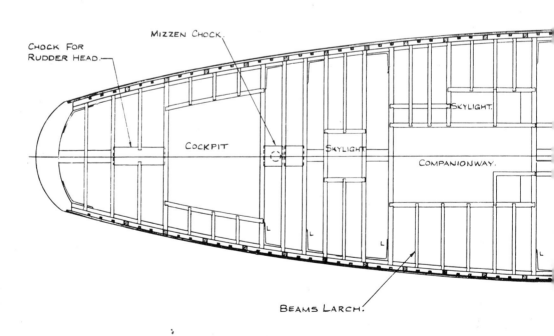